Creating
Gourmet
Gifts

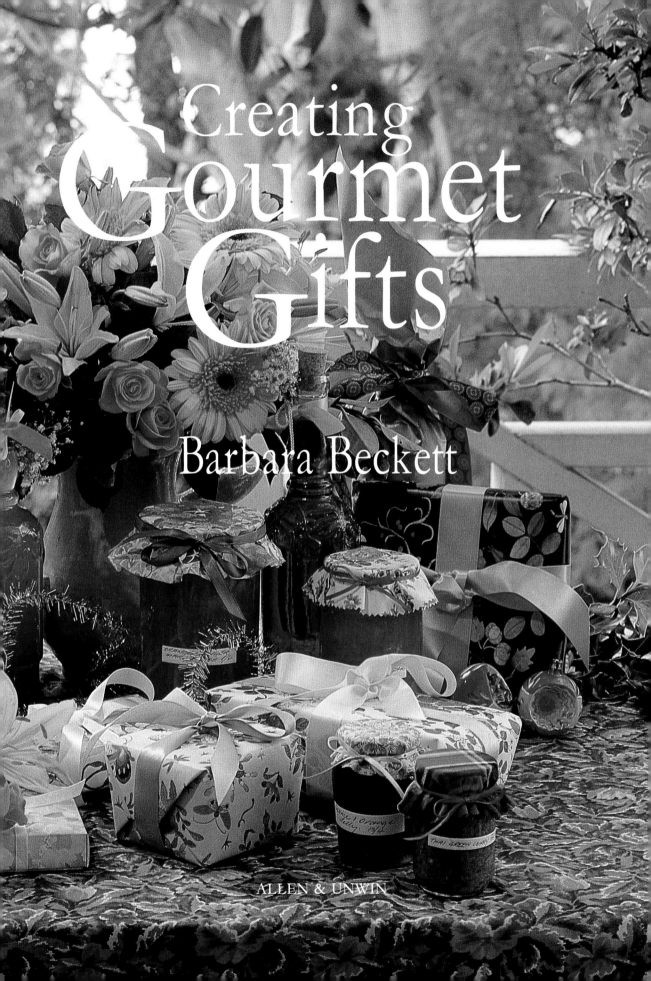

Creating Gourmet Gifts

Barbara Beckett

ALLEN & UNWIN

Pages 2 and 3
Christmas gifts waiting to be given away on a table in my living room. The gift boxes contain biscuits and sweets. I like to wrap boxes without using sticky tape—the ribbon will hold the paper in place. Somehow it seems more luxurious. Besides, the paper can be recycled, either ironed flat to wrap future presents or used to cover a box or as drawer liner.

First published in 1992.
Allen & Unwin Pty Ltd
8 Napier St, North Sydney, NSW 2059

Created and designed by
Barbara Beckett Publishing
14 Hargrave Street, Paddington,
Australia 2021

National Library of Australia
Cataloguing-in-publication entry:

Beckett, Barbara.
Creating gourmet gifts.

Includes index.
ISBN 1 86373 246 2.

1. Cookery.   2. Gifts.   I. Title.

641.5

Photographs by Ray Jarratt
Illustrated by Amanda McPaul
Typeset by Graphicraft Typesetters Ltd,
Hong Kong
Printed by South Wind Production,
Singapore

Measurements

Standard spoon and cup measurements are used in all the recipes. I recommend using a graduated nest of measuring cups: 1 cup, $\frac{1}{2}$ cup, $\frac{1}{3}$ cup and $\frac{1}{4}$ cup. The graduated nest of spoons comprises 1 tablespoon, 1 teaspoon, $\frac{1}{2}$ teaspoon and $\frac{1}{4}$ teaspoon. Use a standard litre or pint measuring jug, which also shows cup measurements, for liquids. Spoon and cup measurements are level. Metric and imperial equivalents given are not exact, so follow either one or the other system of measurements within the recipe.

Ingredients

Fresh fruit and vegetables should be used in the recipes unless otherwise stated. **Herb** quantities are for fresh herbs; if they are unavailable, use half the quantity of dried herbs. Use freshly ground black **pepper** whenever pepper is listed; use **salt** and pepper to individual taste. Use plain **flour** unless otherwise stated. Fresh **ginger** should be used throughout, unless ground ginger is called for. Use fresh **chillies**; if substituting dried chillies, halve the quantity. I use cold-pressed virgin olive **oil**, but any type may be used. I always use fermented wine **vinegar**. Cider and malt vinegar may be substituted if preferred. White granulated **sugar** is used unless stated otherwise. **Vanilla sugar** is made by inserting a vanilla pod in a screw-topped jar of sugar.

For my grandmother,
Tilly,
who taught me to read
and lay a fine table

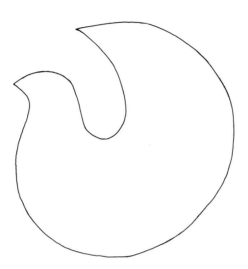

ACKNOWLEDGEMENTS

I WOULD LIKE to thank all my friends who have given me their recipes over the years, and for their dishes which have sparked off ideas for variations. In particular I would like to thank the Bay Tree, Say Cheese and John Williams Antiques for help with some of the props and equipment. Jean Hatfield kindly read the manuscript for me and offered invaluable advice, as did my husband, Bernd Benthaak. Thanks also to my artistic helpers: my sister, Rebecca Chapman, who decorated the jars and bottles; Amanda McPaul, who was responsible for the paper crafts and illustrations; her sister Louisa McPaul, who helped me with some of the cooking; and Ray Jarratt, who gave me his fine photographs. Lastly, I thank my father, Hugh Chapman, for his encouragement, and Peter Whetton, who suggested I write down my ideas about food in the first place.

Barbara Beckett

Contents

Introduction

8

1 Starters

*Nuts, olives, dips, cheese, eggs, potted meat
and fish and soups*

13

2 Preserving Fruit and Vegetables

*Jams, marmalades, jellies, conserves, fruit
pastes, chutneys and pickles*

28

3 Herbs and Spices

*Herb and fruit vinegars, oils, mustards,
sauces and spicy pastes*

73

4 Main Courses

*Food for festive occasions, pastry dishes,
pâtés and terrines, sausages, hams, jellied
meats, cold portable dishes*

86

5 Bread, Biscuits and Cakes

106

6 Desserts

Fruit flans, puddings and preserved fruit

130

7 Drinks

Fruit syrups, teas, fruit liqueurs and punches

143

8 Sweets

Toffee, nuts, honey, chocolate and fruit

156

Index

174

Introduction

The discovery of a new dish does more for the happiness
of mankind than the discovery of a new star.

—BRILLAT-SAVARIN

THE GIVING and sharing of food is an age-old custom. We do it to express joy at Christmas or on Easter Sunday, for birthday celebrations, to share an abundance of fruit and vegetables, or just out of *joie de vivre*. Jams, jellies, tapénade, mutton pies, peach sauce, Easter biscuits, cumquat brandy—whatever it may be, a homemade gift is something special. It requires time and thoughtfulness to prepare, which is what makes it much a treat.

Gourmet gifts are especially appreciated by friends and family who don't cook. They get the full goodness of home cooking—and nothing ever tastes as good as home cooking—without the bother of preparation. As well, they have the pleasure of knowing that someone has made this special terrine or walnut tart or fruit liqueur for their particular enjoyment. While edible gifts can be made without spending very much money (another thing in their favour), the expenditure of time and love is essential, and this is what is valued.

Even recipes themselves become gifts. Many recipes have been handed down from generation to generation or as presents to friends and families. Cookbooks as we know them have really only been in existence since the last century. It is interesting to consider your favourite everyday or party recipes. How many did you get from recipe books and how many were given to you?

For years now my friends and I have enjoyed feasting at communal lunches and dinners. We take it in turns to be host and hostess, and everyone brings a course and some wine. It is a most successful and enjoyable way to have a feast without having to do too much preparation or spend too much money. Some of the cooks are extremely competitive and vie with one another to make the most interesting dish; others are quietly brilliant and give us new dishes of excellence; those who don't cook concentrate on the drinks or buy an exquisite luxury such as a pot of beluga caviar.

So don't think only of Christmas, Easter and birthdays as the only times for celebrating. Any excuse will do. Eating is one of the great joys in life. Why not celebrate it and share it with friends and relations as often as your stomach and purse will allow?

There are recipes here for barbecues and picnics, buffet suppers, birthday parties; plenty of Christmas food and drink ideas; new ideas to celebrate Easter, Saint Valentine's Day, christenings, weddings, as well as dinners for lovers and hearty family get-together food. Whatever celebration you are planning, you will find plenty of ideas among the recipes. The index will help you plan a menu.

Good food begins with good shopping. Buy good-quality ingredients in the right condition for your recipe. For instance, when you make tomato jam the tomatoes should be firm and not quite ripe; but tomato sauce needs fully ripe, soft tomatoes. Go to the markets and buy large quantities when the prices are low so that it makes economic sense to preserve ten bottles of tomato sauce. A good green-grocer will get you cases of fruit and vegetables at a reasonable price if you don't have access to a market. And of course there are windfalls. If you have friends with fruit trees, don't be too shy to ask for some of their fruit. Once they have tasted what you've made from it they will be eager to help you harvest.

Fine cooking takes time, effort and a lot of thought. I find most cooking a very relaxing thing to do; but I lead a busy working life, so I tend to have a cook-up at the weekend to avoid having too much cooking to do during the week. That is how I came to collect these recipes. There are plenty of starters, desserts and drinks I can preserve so that when I'm having friends to dinner during the week the only thing I have to think about generally is a main course. I like to be relaxed about cooking and have time to talk to my friends—not be in the kitchen cooking up a storm. This is something I learnt from the French, who usually buy-in the first course and the dessert and concentrate on the main course.

I like to wake up on Sunday morning thinking: I'll make the mango chutney today and dry those apricots: I hope I have time to make that plum jam or I'll have to freeze the fruit. For me it is a great joy to share my preserves with other people. My only hassle is getting enough jars. I try to train friends to collect and return them to me, but most often to no avail. I think more warmly of those thoughtful friends who pop by with a box of empties. They know they'll get a full jar or two in return.

Cooking is never really precise. If you don't have some of the minor ingredients, leave them out or substitute. In the days before the wide-ranging distribution of foodstuffs, most of the time you could only cook with what was available in the limited area around you at that time of the year. There is never only one method or set of ingredients for a dish. The more cookbooks you read, the more you will realise just how much thought and experimenting continue to go into even the simplest recipe.

Some of the dishes made from recipes in this book will last for months or years; some have a limited life of two or three days. All are easily transportable in tins, boxes, bowls, vacuum flasks, small lidded pots, jars, bottles, cellophane and

paper bags and baskets. They can all be made to look very attractive as a homemade gift; after all, food is something to see and to smell as well as to taste.

I have included quite a few recipes to give to friends who are ill. There is nothing more appreciated by a family in bed with the flu than a visit by a Samaritan bearing chicken and barley soup and some orange syrup. Apart from a good book, what else do you want when you're confined to bed, but homely, healthy food and the thought that some one cared enough to make it. See the index for invalid and healing cooking. Many foods are believed to be healing. Whether they actually are or not, at the least they give you the hope that you are doing something positive to cure an illness. Hope is often a cure.

My recipes are for people of all ages—from party cakes for children to eggnogs for great-grandmothers. I have been collecting them since I started to cook when I was eight years old. They are mostly hearty family cooking recipes with a long history, and no doubt many changes have been made to them over the years. They incorporate old traditions of preserving food with sugar, salt, oil, vinegar, wine, alcohol and by drying and sterilising.

The recipes have been collected from cuisines around the world. It is fascinating to read how a recipe will evolve from one country to the next depending on availability of ingredients. For instance, mincemeat for mince pies had its genesis in Italy in Roman times and originally did contain meat. A version of halva was made in medieval times and has variations in India, all over the Middle East and Central Europe.

I have included ideas and instructions for decorating and wrapping gourmet gifts for special occasions; you will find these information segments scattered throughout the book. Many of the containers and decorations have been photographed so that you can see what they look like; the caption will direct you to the instructions. I have given techniques for making homemade wrapping paper and cards to match, all sorts of box shapes, bonbons, gingerbread men, cookie cutouts to decorate the Christmas tree, table centrepieces for Christmas and Easter, stencilled tablecloth and napkins and salt dough decorations—all crafts relating to the enjoyment and celebration of gourmet food.

I hope you enjoy reading and making these recipes as much as I have done. Most of them have served me well for many years. Remember that cooking is an expression of love: love of food and love for your friends.

PREVIOUS PAGES
A summer harvest display of preserved fruit and vegetables, kept in good condition by natural preservatives—sugar, alcohol, vinegar, salt, oil and spices.

1 Starters

Here is a collection of recipes for food gifts which serve as appetisers with drinks, snacks and more substantial dishes as a start to a meal. There are delicious dishes such as Potted Ham to give to your father-in-law, Omelette Cake to take to the office picnic, Spicy Black Olives for your best friend's luncheon, Cheese and Herbs in Oil for your cousin's birthday, Beef Tea for your favourite auntie in a nursing home, and Blueberry Soup for the first course of a golden wedding celebration. Some will last a few days, others for months. They are all easily transported and visually very attractive. Consider the appearance when deciding which pot or bowl to fill. Go lightly on the garnish. The colour of the wrapping paper should harmonise with the food. Don't forget the food itself is the star attraction; everything else should be supportive.

Make sure your kitchen and equipment is spotless when preparing long-lasting food. Sterilise the pots and jars by putting them into the oven heated to 100°C (200°F) for 20 minutes. They should not be touching each other or they might shatter.

Brined Green Olives

When olives are in season, it is an excellent opportunity to preserve welcome bottles of green olives for your friends. Green olives are very bitter, so they must be cured to make them milder before they are put in the brine. Olives can also be preserved in olive oil (see page 14).

1.5 kg (3 lb) green olives
1 cup salt
5 litres (9 pints) water
Rind of an orange
1 tablespoon oregano
2 tablespoons thyme
3 bay leaves
1 fennel stick
2 heads of garlic

Make sure all the olives are sound, and wash them. Squash them gently with a rolling pin so that the flesh cracks but the olive remains whole. Soak the olives in water a china bowl for eight days, changing the water every second day.

Drain the olives. Make the brine with the salt and water in a large jar and put in the olives. Add the orange peel and herbs. Bake the garlic for thirty minutes in the oven at 180°C (350°F) and add it, peeled, to the brine. Cover.

The olives are ready to eat in three weeks, though they will get milder the longer they remain in the brine. If they begin to ferment, change the brine.

Green Olives in Oil

A friend once presented me with an earthen-ware casserole dish filled with olives made from this recipe. I still think of it with pleasure everytime I use the dish. This is an excellent recipe to use if you cannot get fresh olives or you prefer not to keep your home-cured olives in brine. The oil and herbs made the olives more delicious to taste and they will last longer than preserved in brine. For a change you can add a chilli, a teaspoon of coriander seed and two sun-dried tomatoes to the marinade.

> 500 g (1 lb) brined green olives
> 2 cloves of garlic
> 3 sprigs of thyme
> Rind of an orange
> Olive oil to cover

Drain the olives and pack them into a sterilised jar with the garlic, thyme and orange rind. Cover them with the olive oil. Seal and label the jar and store in a cool place until ready to give away.

Brined Black Olives

Slightly underripe olives are best for pre-serving. Never throw away the left-over oil that the olives marinated in; it is wonderful for cooking casseroles and other earthy dishes.

> 2 kg (4 lb) black olives
> 1½ cups salt
> 1 tablespoon peppercorns
> 10 garlic cloves
> 6 bay leaves
> 2 tablespoons rosemary
> Olive oil to cover

Wash the olives and remove stalks and leaves. To make a brine, mix the salt and enough water to cover the olives in a china bowl. Add the olives, cover the bowl and leave for eight days. Change the brine if they look like fermenting.

Drain the olives and wash them. Pack into sterilised jars, add the peppercorns, garlic, bay leaves and rosemary and cover with the olive oil. Seal and store in a cool, dark cupboard.

Spicy Black Olives

A bowl of shiny black olives makes a very welcome gift. Include an attractive bowl as part of the gift.

> 500 g (1 lb) brined black olives
> 3 chillies, finely chopped
> 2 cloves of garlic, slivered
> 1 tablespoon oregano
> Rind of half a lemon
> Olive oil to cover

Drain the olives and place in sterilised jars along with all the spices and lemon. Cover well with the oil. Seal and label the jars and store in a cool cupboard.

Tapénade

Tapénade is a well-known caper-and-olive paste from Provence. The name comes from tapéna, *the Provençal word for capers. There are many ways to make this aromatic appe-tiser; some people add tuna, have fewer olives, add more capers or anchovy. It is fun to experi-ment. It will keep for weeks if you carefully pot and seal it with a thin layer of olive oil over the surface and refrigerate. A tasty contri-bution to any feast. Spread it on bread or biscuits to serve as an appetiser.*

> 500 g (1 lb) brined black olives,
>   stoned
> 125 g (4 oz) capers, washed and dried
> 60 g (2 oz) anchovies
> 2 tablespoons olive oil
> 3 tablespoons brandy
> 1 teaspoon strong mustard
> 1 teaspoon thyme
> ½ teaspoon ground pepper

Put all the ingredients into a food processor and blend to a smooth paste. Pot and seal.

RIGHT
It is always handy to have olives in the store cupboard for unexpected guests. The recipe for Green Olives in Oil is on this page. Tapénade is a delicious salty strong paste to spread on fresh bread or as sandwich fingers for a party.

Spiced Almonds

These spicy nuts are a welcome change as a snack with drinks. You can make a larger quantity and use half as a gift.

1 cup whole almonds
$\frac{1}{4}$ teaspoon cayenne pepper
$\frac{1}{2}$ teaspoon ground cumin
$\frac{1}{2}$ teaspoon ground coriander
$\frac{1}{2}$ teaspoon celery seeds
$\frac{1}{4}$ teaspoon salt

DROP the almonds in boiling water and let stand for 10 minutes. Remove the skins and dry. In a pan, dry roast the cayenne, cumin, coriander, celery seeds and salt for a few minutes, stirring occasionally so that the spices don't stick. Add the almonds and keep stirring for five minutes. Remove from the heat, and when they have cooled they are ready to serve or store in a clean jar. Label and decorate the lid with attractive paper.

Toasted Chickpeas

Chickpeas make a delicious, healthy snack before a meal. They have a rich, earthy flavour. Add cayenne or cumin for a change instead of salt. They would make a welcome gift at a barbecue presented in a small china bowl and wrapped in cellophane.

1 cup chickpeas
2 cups hot water
1 tablespoon olive oil
½ teaspoon salt
½ teaspoon cayenne, optional
1 teaspoon ground cumin, optional

Pour the hot water over the chickpeas and soak for two hours in a saucepan. Cook, covered, for about 40 to 60 minutes until they are tender but not mushy. Add more water if necessary.

Drain the chickpeas. To grill them, cover the grill pan with aluminium foil, spread out the peas and sprinkle the olive oil over them. Toast them under a very hot grill, stirring occasionally, until they have turned a golden colour. Remove from the heat and toss in a bowl with the salt or spices.

Hummus bi Tahina

The most popular dip from the Middle East. If you ever tasted it homemade you will know how infinitely superior it is to the bought dip. It will last to up to ten days in the refrigerator. Present it as a gift in a colourful plate.

250 g (8 oz) chickpeas
4 cloves of garlic
Salt
1 teaspoon ground cumin
½ teaspoon dried chilli
½ cup tahina paste
Juice of 3 lemons
Garnish
1 tablespoon olive oil
1 teaspoon paprika
1 tablespoon finely chopped parsley

Wash the chickpeas thoroughly and soak for at least three hours. Drain and cook in fresh water for an hour or until they are very soft. Drain the chickpeas and reserve some of the cooking liquid. Purée them with the garlic, salt and spices through a food processor, pouring in the lemon juice, tahina paste and a little of the cooking liquid until the purée is a creamy paste.

It is traditional to serve it on a shallow dish with a garnish of olive oil, paprika and parsley. Serve with pita bread.

Ajvar

A hot, spicy dip from Yugoslavia to serve with raw vegetables and bread. This dip will keep for weeks if bottled in sterilised jars and stored in the refrigerator.

1.5 kg (3 lb) capsicums (sweet peppers), seeded
750 g (1½ lb) eggplant (aubergines)
6 hot chillies, chopped
6 garlic cloves
1 teaspoon salt
1 teaspoon pepper
⅔ cup olive oil
⅓ cup wine vinegar

Put the washed capsicums and eggplant onto an oiled baking dish. Bake in a preheated oven 200°C (400°F) for 45 minutes or until soft. Dip them into cold water and then remove the skins.

Purée the vegetables in a food processor, adding the rest of the ingredients until the purée resembles a thick paste.

Ladle the dip into sterilised jars and pack well, dispelling any air bubbles. Pour a layer of olive oil on top to seal. Put the lid on, label and store.

Anchovy Paste

A delicious paste to use spread on freshly made bread, as a dip with crudité or a sauce with fresh fish. Store the paste in small earthenware pots with seals.

500 g (1 lb) salted anchovies or
   250 g (8 oz) tinned anchovies
1 cup milk
1 cup water
2 tablespoons wine vinegar
1 cup olive oil
1 teaspoon pepper

Soak the salted anchovies in the milk and water for an hour, then remove the bones and wash thoroughly. (If you have tinned anchovies, omit this step.)

Dry the anchovy fillets on kitchen paper and mash in a food processor. Gradually add the vinegar and oil while still beating. Add pepper to taste. Seal in small sterilised pots, leaving enough room for a layer of olive oil to seal the paste. Cover with waxed paper.

Caviar Cream

A luxurious dip for a very special friend. In fact a perfect start for a Saint Valentine's Day dinner. Present it in a fine porcelain bowl accompanied by a bottle of French champagne.

$\frac{2}{3}$ cup cream cheese
$\frac{1}{3}$ cup sour cream
1 tablespoon lemon juice
1 tablespoon chopped chives
Pepper
$\frac{1}{4}$ cup black caviar or any fish roe

Mix the cream cheese and sour cream, then gently fold in the lemon juice, chives and pepper. Take care folding in the caviar. Cover and refrigerate.

Potted Salmon

This is a very tasty recipe for potted salmon, the sardines adding an interesting depth of flavour.

$\frac{1}{2}$ cup chopped smoked salmon
$\frac{1}{2}$ cup chopped unsalted butter
2 canned sardines, chopped
1 tablespoon lemon juice
Pepper
A pinch of cayenne

Put the salmon, butter, sardines and lemon juice in a food processor and blend to a paste. Add pepper and cayenne to taste. Store in a small pot and seal. Keep refrigerated.

Brandade de Morue

Brandade de morue is a salt cod purée which can be used as a dip. Serve cold with black olives, toast and capers or with crudité of raw vegetables. Brandade was originally a feast dish in France and traditionally eaten at Easter. It makes an appropriate gift to take to the hostess of an Easter Sunday lunch. If you cannot get salt cod, substitute fresh cod or any white fish.

1 kg (2 lb) salt cod
3 bay leaves
8 peppercorns
2 cups olive oil
4 cloves of garlic, crushed
$1\frac{1}{2}$ cups milk
Ground black pepper

Soak the salt cod for 24 hours, changing the water six times. Drain and cut into large pieces and put into a pan with the bay leaves and peppercorns. Poach

gently for ten minutes. Drain and let the fish cool.

Remove the bones and skin. Heat the oil and garlic but do not boil. Heat the milk in a separate saucepan; again do not boil. Mince the fish in a food processor. Gradually add a little of the oil and milk alternately, just like making a mayonnaise. It is ready when it is a creamy thick purée. Season with pepper.

If the mixture curdles, keep beating and if it doesn't come good add a mashed potato.

Potted Ham

Potted ham will keep for up to ten days in the refrigerator. Serve with toast and pickled gherkins (page 66) or pickled onions (page 68). The gherkins or onions could be given as part of the gift.

250 g (8 oz) ham, shredded
3 tablespoons unsalted butter
Pepper

Put the ham and 2 tablespoons of the butter into a food processor and blend until it is a smooth paste. Press the mixture into sterilised small pots. Press down well so that there are no air bubbles.

Clarify the remaining butter (melt it gently and, when it is frothing, pour it into a bowl and skim). Now seal the potted ham by pouring a layer of butter over it. When it is cool, cover and store in the refrigerator.

Ajvar (page 16) and Brandade de Morue (page 17), ready to be presented as gifts. Both can be used as dips with bread or crudité. I made this brandade with fresh blue-eye cod. It isn't as strongly flavoured as salt cod, so it had a more delicate flavour.

Rillettes

This is a rich start to a winter's meal. It is usually served with toast or fresh crusty bread. Spicy Black Olives (page 14) or pickled onions (page 68) would be a very tasty addition to the meal or as an extra gift.

500 g (1 lb) shoulder of pork, diced
1½ cups diced pork fat
1 tablespoon salt
1 teaspoon pepper

Cook the pork and fat gently in a covered saucepan for 3 hours until the pork is tender. Pour off the fat through a sieve and reserve. Shred the meat with two forks when it gets cool enough to handle. Add salt and pepper to taste. Put the pork into sterilised bottles. Pour the reserved fat over the meat. When it is cool, seal the bottles and store in the refrigerator. They will last for months.

Fresh Cheese with Herbs (this page), ready to eat or be given away. A second batch made two jars of Cheese and Herbs in Oil (page 20).

Fresh Cheese with Herbs

A fresh cheese makes a thoughtful gift to take to an outdoor lunch in summer. Sprinkle herb flowers over it as well if you have some, to make it look extra special.

4 junket tablets (rennet)
8 cups milk
2 tablespoons thyme
2 tablespoons chives
2 tablespoons marjoram
1 teaspoon salt

Dissolve the junket tablets in a little cold water. Bring the milk to blood heat

(37°C; 98°F) in a saucepan, then remove from the heat. Stir in the rennet quickly and leave to set in a warm place. The curd should form in 30 to 60 minutes.

Wrap the curd in three layers of muslin and tie it up as a ball. Suspend it over a bowl to catch the drips of whey or put 3 layers of muslin over a small sieve and press the curd into it. This makes a nice mould, as well. Leave hanging overnight until all the whey has dripped from the curd, which now is soft cheese.

Chop the herbs finely and mix them along with the salt through the cheese. Turn onto a plate or dish and decorate with herb flowers. Stored in the refrigerator, it will become firmer. It will last a week refrigerated. If you want it to last longer, follow the next recipe.

Cheese and Herbs in Oil

Fresh cheese will last for months preserved in oil. It looks very attractive in a large bottle with twigs of thyme and red chillies.

> 250 g (8 oz) fresh cheese
>   (see previous recipe)
> 2 cloves of garlic
> 3 small red chillies
> A few sprigs of thyme
> ½ tablespoon pepper
> Olive oil to cover

Roll the cheese into small balls and place in a sterilised jar along with the garlic, chillies, thyme and pepper. Pour olive oil over until all the cheese is covered. Seal and keep in the refrigerator. Don't throw the oil away after you eat the cheese, as it will be good for cooking, or you may want to use it for another batch of cheese.

Bread Cheese

This is a baked cheese, a speciality from Finland. It is delicious with summer fruits, or it can be eaten like cake with fresh coffee.

Sprinkle with caster sugar for a sweeter cheese. Take it along to your next wine tasting, the flavour will not overpower the wine.

> 3 junket tablets (rennet)
> 9 cups milk
> 1 teaspoon salt

Dissolve the tablets in a little water. Bring the milk to blood heat (37°C; 98°F) in a saucepan, then remove from heat to a warm place. Stir in the rennet and salt and leave to set for about an hour. Return to the stove and heat gently until the curd separates. Lift the clots of curd out and drain in muslin for several hours over a bowl to catch the drips of the whey.

Put the curd into a round baking tin or dish and bake in a preheated oven at 180°C (360°F) for an hour or until it has turned golden brown.

Liptauer Cheese

This well-known cheese from Czechoslovakia makes a delicious appetiser with biscuits, homemade bread or vegetable crudité.

> ½ cup butter
> 1 cup cottage or fetta cheese
> ¼ cup cream
> 1 teaspoon caraway seeds
> 1 teaspoon paprika
> 1 tablespoon chopped chives

Beat the butter until it is soft, then combine with the cottage cheese and cream. Fold in the rest of the ingredients. Present as a round mould on a plate or in small white china dishes. Decorate with chopped chives or sprinkle with paprika. The china dishes can be part of your gourmet gift.

Herbed Cheese

Cheese is a very satisfying food to make yourself, and this is a surprisingly easy cheese to make. You can vary the herbs, add paprika, cover it with a thick layer of crushed pepper or decorate it with vine leaves. Make several and decorate them in different ways to take to a party. Lay them out on a breadboard and surround with some of the leaves and herbs.

500 g (1 lb) cottage cheese
1 cup sour cream
1 tablespoon chopped chives
1 tablespoon chopped parsley
1 tablespoon chopped thyme
3 garlic cloves, chopped
1 teaspoon salt
1 teaspoon pepper

PLACE a sieve over a bowl and press the cottage cheese and the sour cream through the sieve. Beat in the herbs and garlic and season with salt and pepper. Pack the cheese into a muslin-lined sieve suspended in a bowl with a weighted plate on top of the cheese, and refrigerate for 48 hours. Pack the cheese into small china dishes or one large dish. Keep in the moulds for transporting, and unmould for presentation. Sprinkle herbs and pepper over the cheese.

Cream Cheese with Celery

Here is a cheese for your friends on a diet or with cholesterol problems. Quark is made from reduced-fat milk, so use a reduced-fat yoghurt as well and you can happily relax knowing that this cheese is not only delicious to taste; it is actually good for you. Make sure the yoghurt is made with a live culture—yoghurts of this kind are much healthier than the thickened yoghurts, which also will not set.

2 cups yoghurt
500 g (1 lb) quark
Juice of two lemons
2 tablespoons olive oil
$\frac{1}{4}$ teaspoon cayenne
$1\frac{1}{2}$ cups finely chopped celery

HANG the yoghurt up in two layers of muslin cloth for four hours until the whey has dripped from it.

In a bowl stir together the quark, lemon juice and olive oil and mix until smooth. Fold in the yoghurt, cayenne and celery, and stir until smooth.

Put it in a pretty bowl and place a few celery leaves on the top. Refrigerate until ready to give it away. Wrap the bowl in plain cellophane and tie with a lemon satin ribbon.

Marbled Eggs

These beautiful marbled eggs make a lovely healthy gift as an Easter egg present or to take to an Easter lunch. Dyed hard-boiled eggs were traditionally given at Easter as symbols of fertility and new life. Carry them in a basket lined with leaves and flowers. They will last in the refrigerator for five days. The tea gives the eggs a lovely delicate flavour as well as marbling the egg.

12 eggs
3 tablespoons black tea
1 tablespoon lemon grass
2 spring onions
1 tablespoon thinly sliced ginger
$\frac{1}{2}$ tablespoon salt
2 tablespoons soy sauce

PUT all the ingredients into a saucepan and bring to the boil. Lower the heat and gently cook for 10 minutes. Remove the eggs and reserve the liquid. Crack the shells gently all over when they are cool enough to handle. Put the eggs back into the saucepan and strain the liquid back in. Simmer for another 35 minutes. Turn off the heat and let the eggs soak in the liquid until cold. Drain and refrigerate.

When the eggs are carefully peeled they have a marbled surface where the dark brown liquid penetrated the cracked shell.

Spicy Chicken Omelette

A spicy cold omelette cake—a perfect addition to a celebration picnic lunch.

6 cups chicken stock
2 cups tagliatelle
8 eggs
1½ cups cooked and flaked chicken
3 cardamom pods, cracked
½ teaspoon ground coriander
½ teaspoon salt
½ teaspoon dried chilli
½ tablespoon oil
2 tablespoons parsley

BRING the chicken stock to the boil in a pan and add the tagliatelle until *al dente*. Drain. Beat the eggs in a bowl and add the chicken, tagliatelle, cardamom pods, coriander, salt and chilli. Mix well. Heat the oil in a large frying pan. Add the mixture and cook slowly until almost set. Brown the top under a hot griller. Take out of the pan and keep refrigerated. It looks rather like a cake.

Decorate with parsley and black olives.

RIGHT
Spicy Chicken Omelette (this page), wrapped in clear cellophane and tied with a ribbon to present as a gift for a luncheon party.

Baskets of Gourmet Gifts

Baskets filled with homemade food are welcomed by everyone. Here are some suggestions to make from this book.

BEST FRIEND'S BASKET

Line the basket with a hand-stencilled tea-towel.
Jar of tapénade in a brightly coloured bowl
Nectarine jam
Mango chutney
Pickled grapes
Blueberry vinegar
Box of shortbread shapes
3 mincemeat pies wrapped in a fine linen hankerchief
Lemon liqueur
Chocolate truffles

IN-LAWS' BASKET

Line the basket with a coloured tissue paper that harmonises with the gifts.
Potted salmon in a porcelain pot
Orange whisky marmalade
Barbecue sauce
Small Christmas cake
Blackberry liqueur
Quince jellies

LOVER'S BASKET

Line a picnic hamper with a tablecloth stencilled with deep pink hearts.
Rose petal preserve
Honey spread
Pickled cherries
Pâté de campagne
Heart-shaped gingerbread
Rich chocolate cake
Raspberry ratafia

Spinach Omelette Cake

An easily transported dish for an outdoor lunch. Lay some vine or fig leaves on a round of heavy cardboard and place the omelette on top. Wrap it up with clear cellophane. It is a classic southern European omelette to eat cold like a cake. Cut it in wedges to serve.

1 tablespoon olive oil
⅓ cup chopped bacon
1 tablespoon finely chopped spring
   onions
6 eggs
1½ cups chopped cooked spinach
Juice of half a lemon
½ cup grated parmesan cheese
1½ cups chopped parsley
½ teaspoon grated nutmeg
½ teaspoon salt and pepper

Heat the oil in a pan and sauté the bacon and spring onions for a few minutes until the onion is soft. Meanwhile, mix the remaining ingredients in a bowl. Pour the egg mixture into the pan and cook on a low heat until the omelette is almost set. Either turn it over and cook the other side or put it under a hot grill to brown.

This omelette has many variations. For example, substitute ⅔ cup of puréed black olives, or 1½ cups of spicy tomato sauce (page 77), for the spinach. If it is a large party, cook all three versions separately and pile them on top of one another. The slices of green, black and red cake look wonderful together.

Duck Broth

This is a flavoursome soup from Scotland for an outdoor lunch in the colder months. Take it to a picnic hot in a large vacuum flask and serve in tin mugs. A dash of sherry in the broth when serving is an extra luxury.

1 tablespoon butter
½ cup chopped bacon
½ cup chopped onion
½ cup diced carrot
½ cup diced turnip
1 tablespoon flour
1 tablespoon tomato paste
7 cups duck stock
⅓ cup pearl barley
A bouquet garni
Salt and pepper
1 cup cooked duck meat, flaked

Melt the butter in a saucepan and stir in the bacon and onion. Cook until the onion softens. Add the carrot and turnip for another minute, then stir in the flour and tomato paste. Stir for a minute, then pour in the stock, barley and bouquet garni, and season with salt and pepper. Simmer, covered, for an hour or until the barley is tender. Add the duck meat for the last five minutes.

To continue the Scottish tradition you could serve it with some homemade scones (page 112).

Iced Blueberry Soup

*Served icy cold with a garnish of yoghurt and lemon rind, this soup is a lovely spicy start to a summer lunch. To make **vanilla sugar**, keep one vanilla pod in a screw-top jar of sugar; the flavour quickly penetrates the sugar. If you keep the sugar topped up, you will always have some on hand. It can be made with caster sugar as well.*

4 cups blueberries, washed
3 cups water
2 cloves
1 teaspoon grated ginger
1 cinnamon stick
½ cup vanilla sugar
Juice of an orange
3 tablespoons crème de cassis
   (blackcurrant liqueur [page 151])
1 tablespoon blueberry vinegar
   (page 77)
Plain non-fat yoghurt
1 tablespoon grated lemon rind

Into a saucepan put the blueberries, water, cloves, ginger, cinnamon, sugar and orange juice. Bring to the boil and simmer for 20 minutes or until the berries are tender. Blend the soup in a food processor. Stir in the crème de cassis and vinegar. When cold keep the soup refrigerated. Serve with a dob of yoghurt and a sprinkle of lemon rind.

Bean Soup

A very nutritious vegetarian soup to serve to those who have lost their appetite.

2 cups white dried beans
8 cups water
1 teaspoon salt
1 teaspoon pepper
2 tablespoons olive oil
3 tablespoons chopped parsley
1 lemon

Soak the beans for 12 hours, or pour boiling water over them and let them stand for 3 hours. Drain and put them in a saucepan with the 8 cups of water. Bring to the boil and simmer until the beans are soft. Purée the beans and water in a food processor. Season with salt and pepper and stir in the oil.

Bring the soup to the boil, add more water if necessary, and simmer for a few minutes before serving. Garnish with chopped fresh parsley and a wedge of lemon. If you are taking the soup to a sick friend, bring it to the boil and transfer it to a warmed vacuum flask.

Beef Tea

A perfect gift for a friend convalescing. It is very soothing. Serve with Melba toast.

1 kg (2 lb) gravy beef
3 cups water
Salt (optional)

Mince the beef and pack it into the top of a double saucepan. (If you don't have a double saucepan, a saucepan set over another one half-filled with water will do just as well.) Pour the 3 cups of water over the minced beef so that the water just covers the meat. Add salt to taste if that's in order. Cover and cook slowly for 4 to 5 hours or until the juice is really concentrated. Strain off the beef tea and heat it up again when serving.

Cherry Soup

Fruit soups make excellent soothing foods for people not in the best of health. They can drink a soup like this any time of the day. It is better than fruit juice because you are not removing the fibre. Fill a vacuum flask; the patient can keep it by the bed. Omit the sugar if preferred. Mind you, drinking this in the first place may prevent you from ever getting ill at all. Freeze cherries when cheap to use later in the year.

1 kg (2 lb) cherries, stoned
2 tablespoons sugar
$\frac{1}{2}$ teaspoon ground cinnamon
1 teaspoon ground allspice
3 cups water
2 tablespoons sour cream or plain yoghurt

Wash the cherries and put them into a saucepan with the sugar, spices and water. Bring to the boil and simmer until the cherries are cooked and tender. Purée the soup in a food processor. When it has cooled, stir in the sour cream or yoghurt. Chill in the refrigerator.

Consommé

A clear soup, strongly flavoured with beef or chicken, consommé is a classic soup to tempt the palate at the start of a feast. It is also an ideal gift for an invalid to drink instead of coffee or tea. Garnish with parsley, chervil or tarragon. A teaspoon of tomato paste per serve makes an interesting change.

For chicken consommé, substitute a boiling fowl for the lean beef.

500 g (1 lb) veal bones
500 g (1 lb) beef bones
500 g (1 lb) lean beef
1 tablespoon olive oil
2 onions
3 carrots
2 sticks of celery, including leaves
2 bay leaves
6 sprigs of thyme
3 sprigs of parsley
1 teaspoon peppercorns
1 teaspoon salt
3 litres (5 pints) water

Gᴇᴛ the butcher to chop the bones into small pieces. Cube the beef. Heat the oil

The fresh ingredients for preparing Chicken and Barley Soup (opposite page), a hearty meal on its own.

in a saucepan and brown the bones and meat. Remove the bones and meat and brown the vegetables. Put the browned meat and bones back into the pan, add the herbs, spices and water, bring to the boil slowly. Simmer for $2\frac{1}{2}$ to 3 hours with the lid three-quarters on. Strain off the liquid and, when cool, refrigerate.

The fat will be solid on the top the next day. Carefully remove it all to leave a splendid clear consommé.

Chicken and Barley Soup

The soup to cure all ills. When all medicine fails, chicken soup will revive the poor in spirit and make most patients rally. Sometimes known affectionately as Jewish penicillin.

2 onions
3 carrots
2 turnips
2 sticks of celery
1½ tablespoons butter
8 cups chicken stock
½ cup pearl barley, soaked overnight
2 chicken breasts
1 teaspoon salt
1 teaspoon pepper
2 tablespoons finely chopped parsley

WASH and cut up the vegetables into bite-size pieces; cut the onions into eight segments. Melt the butter in a saucepan and put in the onions. When they begin to turn translucent, add the rest of the vegetables. Stir for 5 minutes to sweat, then pour in the stock and barley. Cover and cook slowly for 20 minutes. Add the chicken meat, cut into bite-size pieces, and season with salt and pepper. Cover and simmer for 10 to 15 minutes or until vegetables and chicken are cooked.

Garnish with the parsley.

Herb and Garlic Soup

A soup full of healing herbs and garlic. The friend who gave this to me when I was recuperating some years ago told me that it is known as soup that will save your life. How true!

1 tablespoon olive oil
20 garlic cloves, crushed
Rind of half an orange
3 bay leaves
1 teaspoon fresh sage
2 large sprigs of rosemary
5 cups water
½ cup vermicelli
1 teaspoon salt
1 teaspoon pepper
Chopped chervil

HEAT the oil in a saucepan. Put the garlic cloves in and cook for a few minutes. Tie together the orange rind, bay leaves, sage and rosemary and put in the pan. Stir and quickly add the water. Add the vermicelli, salt and pepper. When it comes to the boil, cook for 5 minutes and it is ready. Garnish with chervil.

Wine Broth

An old French recipe guaranteed as a pick-me-up. This is just like Jewish chicken soup— it makes you begin to feel better just thinking about it.

1 cinnamon stick
2 cloves
4 cups white wine
1 cup water
½ nutmeg, grated
5 egg yolks
1 tablespoon sugar

TIE up the cinnamon and cloves in a muslin bag. Put the wine, water and all the spices into a saucepan and bring to the boil. Simmer for a few minutes and then remove the muslin bag. (If you intend giving the broth to a sick friend, put the spiced wine in a vacuum flask at this stage and take it to your friend's place with the remaining ingredients.)

Beat up the egg yolks with the sugar and then slowly add to the wine, constantly whisking. A thick foam will form on the top. Serve in cups accompanied by thin slices of toast.

2 Preserving Fruit
and Vegetables

PRESERVING fruit and vegetables with sugar, vinegar and spices is a very old tradition that we are happily still carrying on, especially in our home kitchens. The better the quality of fruit you use, the better the result will be, which is not something you can trust commercial companies to care about these days. Jams, marmalades, jellies, fruit conserves and pastes, relishes, chutney and pickles—how wonderful it is to be able to open up a store cupboard and take out some of these jewels to give to a dear friend. Giving food is a way of showing love.

Don't think of jam and chutney as just something to spread on bread or eat with curries. Many of them are excellent accompaniments to many varieties of meats and cheese. Some jams are delicious eaten with a spoon while having a cup of coffee or spread as a topping over a cake.

I have also included some methods for drying fruit and tomatoes. It's fun to do, and even though they don't look as good without preservatives, they taste great and they are much healthier.

Chutneys and pickles are easy to make; jams, jellies and marmalades require more skill. If you are new to jam making, don't let this put you off. If you follow my instructions carefully you won't have a failure. It only takes a few successes for you to begin to feel confident. When making conserves and fruit pastes, read the instructions for jam first.

To Make Jam

A good jam should be clear and bright and near to the colour of the original fruit. It should be set but not too stiff, and should keep well.

Jam pan. Never use copper or iron pans. The ideal is a large, deep, heavy-based saucepan coated with enamel. It should be large enough so that the jam with all the ingredients added only comes halfway up. Aluminium or stainless steel is all right but will never be as successful as a heavy-based enamel. Use only a wooden spoon for stirring.

Fruit. Scrub and wash the fruit to remove pesticides and wax. The fruit, first of all, should be fresh and slightly underripe. That is when it contains the most pectin, which is what is going to make the jam set. Acid is also necessary as it helps to extract the pectin and brighten the colour and prevents the sugar from crystalising. Different kinds of fruit have varying amounts of pectin and acid, which also vary according to ripeness of the fruit.

Fruits high in pectin, and therefore having a good setting quality, are apples, blackcurrants and redcurrants, gooseberries and plums. Fruits of medium setting quality are blackberries, raspberries, loganberries and apricots. Other fruits low in pectin and acid can have them added to make an excellent jam.

The fruit needs to be cooked gently for some time in order to break down the cell walls of the fruit and extract the pectin. Water is sometimes added.

Acid and pectin. If the fruit is low in acid, lemon juice or citric acid can be added. If the fruit is low in pectin—for example, raspberry—it can be mixed with a fruit high in pectin, such as apple. Fruit juices high in acid and pectin are excellent to add. I prefer not to use commercial pectins.

Sugar. The other essential ingredient is sugar. This is the preservative. It is important to have the right amount. Too much and the jam will crystalise; too little and it will ferment. I use white refined sugar. Caster sugar is just as good, but raw sugar will darken the jam. When the fruit needs to be cooked for only a short time, the sugar is warmed in the oven before adding to the fruit so that it will dissolve faster.

The fruit is first cooked slowly, then the sugar is added and the jam cooked very quickly in order to get to the setting point, which occurs five to twenty minutes after the sugar has dissolved. If the sugar and fruit boil too long together, the colour and flavour are spoilt.

Setting point. There are a few ways to tell when setting point is reached. One way is to test the temperature. Setting point is reached when the jam is boiled to 110°C (220°F). To get a true reading, first put the thermometer into hot water, then stir the jam and put the thermometer in to take the temperature.

Another way is to dip a wooden spoon into the jam and turn it sideways. If the jam partly sets on the spoon and the drops break off in a clear way, then setting point is reached.

You can also drop half a teaspoon of jam on a plate taken straight from the freezer. The jam should set and crinkle when pushed with your finger. Turn the plate upside down; if the jam doesn't fall, setting point is reached.

Finishing off. When the jam reaches setting point, remove it from the heat. Take off any scum that is on the surface. Pour the jam into warm sterilised jars. (To sterilise the jars, put them in the oven at 100°C (200°F) for twenty minutes. Don't let them touch.) Fill the jars right to the top, as the jam will shrink a bit. To prevent fruit rising in the jar, allow the jam to cool in the pan for up to half an hour, stir once and

29

then bottle. Press the jam down firmly and dispel any air bubbles. Either seal immediately or cover with a clean tea-towel and seal when cool.

Jams keep best covered with cellophane or parchment paper. Screw-top jars are fine, but never use an unlined metal lid. A seal of paraffin wax can be used to give an extra precaution against the jam going mouldy. Buy wax discs or melt paraffin wax over a low heat and pour on just enough to seal the fruit. Never forget to label the jam. The right storage is important; a cool, dark, airy place is perfect.

To Make Marmalade

Fruit marmalades are made with any type of citrus fruit—oranges bitter and sweet, lemons, limes, grapefruit and cumquats—or quince and many combinations. The principle of cooking is the same as for jam, so read that section before attacking a marmalade recipe. The big difference is that the thick peel takes longer to cook, so the fruit has to cook for up to two hours before the sugar is added. And it needs water for the longer cooking time.

Pectin. The pectin is found in the pips and the pith. Generally you don't want to eat these, so they are tied in a muslin bag and cooked with the fruit. The bag is removed when the fruit is cooked. Squeeze it as hard as you can between two plates to extract all the pectin and let the pectin drop back into the pan.

If you like chunky marmalade and the pith isn't too thick, you need only put the pips into a muslin bag. For jelly marmalade, only the skin is used; it is taken off with a vegetable peeler. You can have fine or thick peel according to your preference; but whichever you decide on, cut uniform-size pieces so that they are all cooked at the same time.

Sugar. The sugar should not be added until the peel is soft. If you think there is too much water in the pan at the end, boil it off. After the sugar is dissolved, boil rapidly until setting point is reached.

Finishing. When the marmalade has reached setting point, skim the top immediately or the jam will discolour. To prevent the peel rising in the jars, allow the marmalade to cool in the pan until a thin skin begins to form, then stir once, gently, and pour into jars. Cover and store the same as for jams.

To Make Jellies

A fruit jelly should be clear and bright, set but a little wobbly, and should taste of the fruit. The correct balance of pectin, acid and sugar is required, the same as for jam.

Fruit. The most suitable fruits are apples, crab-apples, gooseberries, quinces, currants and loganberries. Blackberries are excellent if they are mixed with apple to give the required pectin and acid. The fruit must be fresh but not too ripe.

*Fresh summer fruits preserved for future joy and pleasure. I often include
the recipe with the food gift—to friends who love cooking, of course.*

The fruit should always be washed thoroughly. It is not necessary always to peel or take stalks off, because the fruit pulp will be strained. The fruit is simmered in water, the amount of which varies according to cooking time. To get a jelly, the fruit has to break down so that the acid and pectin may dissolve in the water.

Jelly bag. The fruit is strained through a jelly bag into a bowl for several hours. If you don't have a jelly bag, line a colander with three layers of muslin. Be sure to scald the equipment before using. Never squeeze the jelly bag or try to force the juice through the muslin. It will cloud the jelly.

Sugar. When the fruit pulp has been strained, measure the juice by the cupful as you put it back into the pan. You will need one cup of sugar for every cup of fruit juice. Bring the juice slowly to the boil and add the sugar. Boil rapidly after the sugar has dissolved. Test for setting point the same way as for jam.

Finishing. Finish off the way you would jam, but tilt the jar when pouring in the jelly to prevent air bubbles forming. Bottle when still hot, and do not move the jar until the jelly is set. Only use small containers, as you will have trouble with the setting in a large jar. Store as jam.

To Make Chutney

Chutneys are easy to make. Once you have a little experience it is fun to experiment with different combinations of fruits and spices, white or brown sugar or even flavours of vinegars. There is plenty of opportunity for the imagination. A good chutney should be smooth and have a mellow flavour. Most will keep for up to two years, maturing all the time. I find it is best to keep them for at least one or two months before opening. The difference is amazing; the harsh vinegar taste has mellowed and the flavours have all enhanced one another. Read the instructions for jam before proceeding.

Ingredients. Fruits used most are apples, mangoes, plums and green and red tomatoes. The fruit should be firm and slightly underripe. Other ingredients most often used are onions, chillies, garlic, fresh ginger, raisins or sultanas, dates, salt, sugar and spices and, of course, vinegar. Sugar, salt, spice and vinegar are the preservatives. I mostly use a fermented white wine vinegar. Brown sugar and malt vinegar will darken the chutney, if that is what you prefer. If you want a light chutney, use white sugar and white vinegar and add the sugar after the basic ingredients are soft. Ground spices or whole spices can be used. Some people like to put the whole spices into a muslin bag and remove it before bottling.

Use only a heavy-based enamel pan, the same type as for jam making. Use a wooden spoon for stirring.

Setting. Chutneys usually cook slowly for up to two hours to allow the fruit to absorb the vinegar. You can tell when chutney is ready by drawing a wooden spoon across the bottom of the pan; if there is no free liquid left it is ready. As chutney becomes very thick, it should be carefully watched towards the end of the cooking time and frequently stirred.

Bottling. Bottle chutney in warm sterilised jars while it is still not. Pack it down firmly to dispel any air bubbles. Plastic covers or *lined* metal covers are fine to use. Chutneys need a firm seal or else they will shrink, because the vinegar evaporates. A wax disc or a paraffin wax seal is an excellent precaution. Label and seal the same as for jam.

To Make Pickles

To avoid getting yourself in a pickle, read up the jam and chutney information before embarking on a pickling morning. Fruit and vegetables are preserved, or pickled, by the salt, vinegar and sugar. Like chutney, pickles are easy to make and to experiment with. Different combinations of herbs and spices can make fascinating variations.

The fruit and vegetables should be just ripe and without blemishes. Almost any sort of fruit or vegetable can be pickled. When bottling, cover to within 2.5 cm (1 in) of the top. Make sure the brine covers the contents. Carefully dispel air bubbles. Bottle and store the same way as jam.

Apple Jam

One of my neighbours gave me this homely jam recipe. Apple jam can be served as a sauce for hot roast lamb and pork or spread on slices of tea bread or toast.

    1.5 kg (3 lb) cooking apples
    Juice and zest of 2 lemons
    2 cups water
    1.5 kg (3 lb) sugar

WASH, peel and core the apples and chop into cubes. Put them in a heavy-based pan with the lemon and water. Cook slowly until the apple is soft. Add the sugar and stir until it has dissolved. Turn up the heat and bring to a rolling boil. Cook rapidly until setting point is reached.

Remove from the heat and ladle into sterilised jars, seal and label.

Apple and Passionfruit Jam

A delicious combination of flavours guaranteed to please the most jaded of palates.

    1.5 kg (3 lb) cooking apples
    Juice and zest of 2 oranges
    2 cups water
    20 passionfruit
    1.5 kg (3 lb) sugar

PEEL, core and chop the apples roughly. Put them into a pan with the orange juice and zest, water and the pulp of the passionfruit. Bring gently to the boil and simmer until the fruit is soft and tender. Add the sugar; stir until it has dissolved. Bring the jam to a rolling boil and continue until setting point is reached.

Leave the fruit to settle for 30 minutes, then ladle the jam into sterilised jars, seal and label. Store in a dark, cool cupboard.

Apricot Jam

Apricot jam will always be appreciated as a gift. There are savoury as well as sweet ways to eat this classic jam. I serve it as a sauce with pork and lamb roasts and also as a filling for poached peach halves, served warm and sprinkled with slivered almonds.

    1 kg (2 lb) apricots
    Juice, peel and pith of 1½ lemons
    1 cup water
    1 kg (2 lb) sugar
    1 tablespoon blanched almonds

WASH and stone the apricots. Put them into a heavy pan with the lemon juice and water. Put the lemon peel and pith into a muslin bag and add to the fruit. Bring slowly to the boil and simmer until the fruit is tender. Remove the muslin bag and squeeze the juice into the jam. Then add the sugar, stirring until it is dissolved. Turn up the heat to a rolling boil. Keep stirring until setting point is reached. Stir in the almonds. Let the jam stand for 15 minutes after removing from the heat. Spoon into sterilised jars, label and seal.

Blackcurrant Jam

Blackcurrants are rich in pectin, which makes this jam easy to make. Blackcurrant tea can be prepared from it as a remedy for colds: dissolve one tablespoon in a glass of hot water; to make it more effective, add a tablespoon of brandy.

1 kg (2 lb) backcurrants
3 cups water
1.5 kg (3 lb) sugar

REMOVE the stems of the blackcurrants; wash the fruit and put it into a heavy-based pan with the water. Simmer gently until the fruit is soft and the liquid reduced considerably. Add the sugar and stir until it is dissolved. Bring to boiling point and keep at a rolling boil until the setting point is reached, in about 15 to 20 minutes. Rest for 15 minutes, then spoon into sterilised jars, seal and label.

Blueberry Jam

This jam is a splendid bluey purple and well worth a trip to the markets to buy blueberries when the prices come down in the summer. I love to eat it in winter as a reminder of the past summer.

1 kg (2 lb) blueberries
Juice, zest and pith of 2 lemons
1 kg (2 lb) sugar

WASH the blueberries and put them into a heavy-based pan with the lemon juice and zest. Wrap the pith in a muslin bag and put it in with the fruit. Bring the fruit very slowly to the boil and cook until tender. Stir continually

throughout the cooking in case the fruit sticks. Remove the muslin bag and squeeze the juice into the jam. Add the sugar; when it is dissolved, turn the heat up high and bring to a rolling boil. Continue for about 15 to 20 minutes until setting point is reached. Let it stand for 15 minutes off the heat, then spoon it into sterilised jars. Seal, label and store in a dark, cool place.

Cherry and Redcurrant Jam

The lemon and the redcurrant juice add the necessary pectin to cherry jam. Serve it also as a dessert with thick cream. Put serving suggestions on the label when giving the jam to someone.

1 kg (2 lb) cherries
Juice, peel and pith of 2 lemons
2 cups redcurrant juice
1 kg (2 lb) sugar

STONE the cherries and wash them. Put the stones into a muslin bag with the peel and pith of the lemons. Into a heavy pan put the cherries, lemon juice, muslin bag and redcurrant juice. Bring slowly to the boil and simmer until the cherries are tender. Remove the muslin bag and squeeze the juice into the jam. Add the sugar, stirring until it dissolves. Bring to a rapid boil, stirring, and boil until setting point is reached.

Remove from the heat and let it settle for 15 minutes, then ladle into sterilised jars, seal and label. Store in a dark, cool place.

Fig and Orange Jam

A rich jam, this can be used as a dessert with vanilla ice-cream or frozen yoghurt as well as spread on bread and cakes. Make suggestions for serving on the gift label.

1 kg (2 lb) green or purple figs
Juice, peel and pith of 2 oranges
Juice, peel and pith of 1 lemon
1 tablespoon grated ginger
750 g (1½ lb) sugar

Wᴀsʜ and quarter the figs and remove their skins. Put them into a heavy pan with the orange and lemon juice. Tie the peel and pith up in a muslin bag and put in with the figs. Cook slowly until the figs are very soft. Remove the muslin bag and squeeze the juice into the jam. Stir in the sugar; when it has dissolved, turn up the heat and bring to a rapid boil. Keep stirring. It should reach setting point in 10 to 20 minutes.

Remove from heat and let it stand for 15 minutes before spooning into sterilised jars. Cover, label, and store in a dark, cool cupboard.

Fig and Tomato Jam

Figs and tomatoes may seem an unusual combination, but the jam has a beautiful, delicate flavour. The green tomatoes go pale pink in the cooking. Pink and green make an attractive looking jam. Delicious with crusty bread for lunch or a snack.

500 g (1 lb) green figs
500 g (1 lb) green tomatoes
Juice, pith and peel of 2 lemons
1 kg (2 lb) sugar

Wᴀsʜ and quarter the figs and tomatoes and remove the skins. (If they are large tomatoes, cut each quarter again.) Put them into a heavy pan with the lemon juice. Tie the pith and peel up in a muslin bag and put it in with the fruit. Cook gently until the fruit is soft. Remove the muslin bag and squeeze the juice into the fruit. Stir in the sugar; keep stirring until it is dissolved. Now turn the heat up and bring it to a rapid boil. Keep stirring so the jam does not stick. It should reach setting point in 15 to 20 minutes.

Remove from heat, let it stand for 15 minutes, and then ladle into sterilised jars. Seal, label and store in a dark, cool place.

Gooseberry and Orange Jam

Gooseberries are another fruit laden with pectin, which makes this an almost foolproof jam to make. It tastes wonderful with cold meats.

1 kg (2 lb) gooseberries
2 oranges
1 cup raisins
1 kg (2 lb) sugar
1 teaspoon ground ginger

Wᴀsʜ the gooseberries and cut and tail them with a pair of scissors. Take the rind off the oranges with a vegetable peeler and cut into julienne strips. Remove the pith from the oranges and finely chop the flesh. Put the gooseberries and the orange rind and pulp in a heavy pan together with the raisins and slowly cook. When the fruit is tender, add the sugar and ginger. Stir while it comes to the boil. Turn up the heat and cook fast until setting point is reached—in 10 to 20 minutes. Pack into hot sterilised jars, seal and label.

Harmony Jam

I am sure this was named after the harmonious blend of the three fruits. A good jam to make for church and school fêtes.

500 g (1 lb) apples
500 g (1 lb) pears
250 g (½ lb) plums
1 cup water
1 kg (2 lb) sugar
1 tablespoon grated ginger

Pᴇᴇʟ and core the apples and chop roughly. Tie the cores and peel up in a

muslin bag. Peel, core and dice the pears and stone the plums. Put all the fruits into a heavy pan along with the water and the muslin bag. Cook slowly until the fruit is cooked. Remove the muslin bag and squeeze the juice into the jam. Add the sugar and the ginger, stirring until it is dissolved. Bring to a rapid boil and continue for 10 to 20 minutes until setting point is reached.

Let the jam settle for 15 to 20 minutes, then ladle into sterilised jars, seal and label.

Kiwi Fruit and Melon Jam

This is a delicious pale green jam with a subtle, delicate flavour. Perfect with afternoon tea for your favourite aunt.

500 g (1 lb) kiwi fruit
1 kg (2 lb) honeydew melon
Juice, pith and zest of 2 lemons
1 teaspoon ground ginger
1.5 kg (3 lb) sugar

PEEL the fruit and remove the melon seeds, chop and put into a heavy pan. Add the lemon juice, zest and ginger. Tie the lemon pith up in a muslin bag and put in the pan. Slowly cook the fruit until it is tender. Remove the muslin bag and squeeze the juice into the jam. Add the sugar; stir until it is dissolved. Turn up the heat and bring to a rolling boil. After 15 to 20 minutes, setting point should be reached. Test and remove from heat. Let the jam settle for 15 minutes before ladling into sterilised jars. Seal, label and store in a cool, dark place.

LEFT
On the shelf in the larder, dressed ready for presentation, are jars of Nectarine Jam (this page), Apple and Ginger Jelly (page 46) and Quince and Orange Jelly (page 47).

Mulberry Jam

A friend in the country with a large fruit garden gives me a jar of this jam every year. The dark red colour looks wonderful on pale breads and cakes. Be careful handling the mulberries, as the juice stains can be hard to wash out of clothes.

1 kg (2 lb) mulberries
500 g (1 lb) cooking apples
Juice, pith and peel of 2 lemons
1.5 kg (3 lb) sugar

WASH the mulberries and place them in a heavy-based pan. Peel, core and chop the apples and put them into the pan with the lemon juice and all the pith and peel in a muslin bag. Bring slowly to the boil. When the fruit is tender, remove the muslin bag, squeezing the juice into the jam. Add the sugar; stir while it dissolves. Boil rapidly now for about 15 minutes or until setting point is reached.

Let it stand for 15 minutes and remove any foam off the surface. Spoon into sterilised jars, seal and label.

Nectarine Jam

A simply delicious jam that my friends can't get enough of. It is a lovely way to capture this splendid summer fruit.

1.5 kg (3 lb) nectarines
Juice, zest and pith of 2 oranges
Juice, zest and pith of 2 lemons
1 kg (2 lb) sugar
$\frac{1}{2}$ cup blanched almonds, chopped
$\frac{1}{2}$ cup brandy (optional)

WASH and stone the nectarines. Put them into a heavy-based pan with the juice and zest of the oranges and lemons. Put the pith and pips into a muslin bag and cook with the fruit. Bring the fruit to the boil slowly and simmer until tender. Remove the muslin bag, squeezing the juice into the jam. Add the sugar and the almonds; stir until the sugar has dissolved. Turn up the heat and continue at a fast boil until the jam has reached setting point. Remove from the heat. Stir the brandy through the jam if liked. Leave the jam for 15 minutes, then ladle into sterilised jars, seal, label and store.

Brandied Peach Jam

The brandy, spices and almonds give this peach jam a rich flavour. It is pleasant to eat as a dessert with a brioche. I buy a case of peaches at the market each summer to make sure there is enough jam to go round.

  1 kg (2 lb) peaches
  Juice, zest and pith of 2 lemons
  1 teaspoon ground cinnamon
  1 tablespoon grated ginger
  1 kg (2 lb) sugar
  2 tablespoons slivered almonds
  3 tablespoons brandy

REMOVE the skin and kernels from the peaches and chop the flesh, taking care to save the juice. Put the flesh and juice into a heavy pan along with the lemon juice and zest. Tie the lemon pith up in a muslin bag and put it in the pan with the cinnamon and ginger. Bring slowly to the boil and keep cooking until the peaches are soft. Remove the muslin bag, squeezing the juice into the jam. Add the sugar and almonds and stir until the sugar is dissolved, then turn up the heat and bring to a rolling boil, constantly stirring. Setting point should be reached in 15 to 20 minutes.

Remove from heat and let the jam rest for 15 minutes before gently stirring in the brandy. Ladle into sterilised jars, seal and label.

Pear and Vanilla Jam

A thoughtful gift for a person who has everything—you could never buy a jam with a taste as subtle as this.

  2 kg (4 lb) underripe pears, peeled and chopped
  Zest and juice of 2 lemons
  3 cups water
  1 vanilla bean, split
  2 kg (4 lb) sugar

PUT the pears, lemon, water and vanilla bean into a saucepan. Simmer until the fruit is tender. Remove the vanilla bean and add the sugar; stir until the sugar is dissolved. Bring to the boil and boil hard until setting point is reached—test with a sugar thermometer (110°C; 220°F) or until a drop sets on a chilled plate and does not run.

Take off the heat and let the jam rest for 15 minutes. Ladle into sterilised jars, seal and label. Store in a cool, dark place.

Plum and Raisin Jam

Plum jam can be made from windfall plums at the beginning of summer. The flavour varies according to the type of plum used.

  1 kg (2 lb) plums, stoned
  1 cup raisins
  1 cup water
  1 kg (2 lb) sugar
  1 tablespoon grated ginger

PUT the plums and raisins into a heavy-based pan with the water. Gently bring to the boil and simmer until the fruit is cooked. Add the sugar and ginger, stirring until the sugar is dissolved. Turn up the heat and bring to a rolling boil. Continue to cook fast for 10 to 20 minutes until setting point is reached.

Take from the heat and ladle into sterilised jars. Seal, label and store in a dark, cool place.

Pumpkin and Carrot Jam

This is a good jam to give friends in the depth of winter. It makes a delicious, hearty jam to eat for breakfast on a cold morning.

1 kg (2 lb) pumpkin
2 lemons
1 cup diced carrot
1 tablespoon grated ginger
3 cups water
1 kg (2 lb) sugar
$\frac{1}{2}$ cup white rum

PEEL, seed and cube the pumpkin. Cut the lemons in half and slice thinly. Into a heavy-based pot put the pumpkin, lemon, carrot, ginger and water. Bring slowly to the boil and cook until the pumpkin, lemon and carrot are soft. Add the sugar and stir until it dissolves. Bring to a rolling boil and continue stirring until setting point is reached.

Remove from the heat and stir in the rum. Let the jam settle for 15 minutes, then ladle into sterilised jars, seal and label.

Rhubarb and Apple Jam

I have always liked rhubarb, although I don't quite know why that astringent flavour with added sweetness is so satisfying. This jam is a favourite with my elderly friends.

1.5 kg (3 lb) rhubarb
3 apples
Juice and zest of 1 lemon
2 oranges, finely sliced
$\frac{1}{2}$ cup water
1.5 kg (3 lb) sugar

CUT up the rhubarb into small pieces. Peel, core and slice the apples. Put the rhubarb and apples into a heavy pan along with the lemon juice and zest, the oranges and the water. Bring to the boil slowly and simmer until all the fruit is soft. Add the sugar and stir until it is dissolved. Now turn the heat up and bring to a rolling boil. Continue stirring until setting point is reached, in about 10 to 20 minutes.

Remove from heat and let it stand for 30 minutes for the fruit to settle. Ladle into sterilised jars, seal and label.

Strawberry and Lemon Jam

I have arrived at this recipe by trial and error—I particularly like it because the strawberries remain whole. Choose only slightly underripe, firm strawberries for making jam. The lemon adds the pectin.

1 kg (2 lb) sugar
Juice and zest of 2 lemons
1 cup water
1 kg (2 lb) strawberries, hulled

PUT the sugar, lemon and water in a heavy pan. Heat and stir to dissolve the sugar, then bring to a rolling boil. Skim if necessary. Put the strawberries in and remove from the heat for 10 minutes. Then return to the heat and cook the strawberries for another 10 minutes, removing any scum that appears. Remove the strawberries with a slotted spoon and drain them. Continue to cook the syrup rapidly until setting point is reached.

Remove from the heat and fill the sterilised jars with syrup and strawberries slowly, so that the strawberries don't rise to the top. Close the lids, label and store in a cool place.

Sultana Grape Jam

Grape jam makes a wonderful dessert. Serve it with slices of rockmelon and frozen yoghurt. Add serving suggestions to the label of the jam when giving it away.

  1 kg (2 lb) green sultana grapes
  Juice and zest of 1 lemon
  1 cup water
  1 kg (2 lb) sugar
  1 tablespoon grated ginger

Wash the grapes thoroughly and remove the stalks. Place the grapes in a heavy-based pan with the lemon and water. Slowly bring to the boil and simmer until the grapes are soft. Add the sugar and the ginger and stir until the sugar is dissolved. Turn up the heat and bring to a rolling boil. Continue stirring until setting point is reached, in approximately 10 to 20 minutes.

Remove from the heat, let the jam stand for 30 minutes and then spoon into sterilised jars, seal and label.

Green Tomato Jam

This jam is very popular in my house—I have to hide it away so that I have some jars to give to friends. The apples and lemons add the necessary pectin, as tomatoes are low in pectin. Try making the same recipe with red tomatoes. Or leave out the apples—I like experimenting.

  1.5 kg (3 lb) green tomatoes
  500 g (1 lb) apples
  Juice, zest and pith of 2 lemons
  2 kg (4 lb) sugar
  2 tablespoons dark rum (optional)

Remove the skin and core of the tomatoes and chop. Peel, core and chop the apples. Put all the tomatoes and apples in a heavy-based pan along with the juice and zest of the lemons. Add the pith in a muslin bag. Bring the fruit slowly to the boil and cook until it is tender. Remove the muslin bag, squeezing the juice into the jam. Add the sugar; stir while it dissolves. Boil rapidly now for 15 to 20 minutes or until setting point is reached.

Remove from the heat and stir in the rum. (Or drink it after all that hard work!) Leave the jam for 15 minutes, then spoon it into sterilised jars, seal and label. Store in a cool, dark place.

Watermelon Jam

Make this lovely pink jam when watermelons are cheap in summer.

  2 kg (4 lb) watermelon
  2 oranges
  2 lemons
  1 teaspoon cinnamon
  2 kg (4 lb) sugar
  2 tablespoons white rum

Remove the skin and the seeds from the watermelon and cut it into dice. Thinly slice the oranges and lemons. Put the pips into muslin bag. Put all the fruit, cinnamon and muslin bag into a heavy pan. Cook over a low heat until the fruit is tender. Remove the muslin bag, squeezing the juice into the jam. Add the sugar and stir until it is dissolved. Bring the jam to a rolling boil and boil until setting point is reached. Remove from heat and stir in the rum.

Spoon into sterilised jars after 15 minutes. Seal, label and store.

Amber Marmalade

This marmalade is a beautiful colour and not too sweet. It is interesting to experiment with different combinations of citrus fruits, depending on what is in season, and you can do so with this recipe provided the total weight of the fruit is 1.5 kg (3 lb).

  2 grapefruit
  4 lemons
  2 sweet oranges
  11 cups water
  3 kg (6 lb) sugar

WASH and scrub the fruit. Cut each piece of fruit into very fine slices. Keep the seeds and put them into a muslin bag. Put the fruit and bag in a pan with the water and bring slowly to the boil. Simmer for up to two hours or until the fruit is tender. Remove the muslin bag, squeezing the juice into the marmalade. Pour the sugar in and stir until it is dissolved. Turn up the heat and bring to a rolling boil. Continue until setting point is reached.

Remove from heat, skim and let stand for an hour. Stir gently once, then ladle into warm sterilised jars. Place wax circles on when cold. Cover and label.

Pumpkin and Carrot Jam (page 39), is very tasty served with leg ham and salad. I save scraps of fabric to be used for jam covers.

Cumquat Brandy Marmalade

Marmalade with an air of festivity. I always associate cumquats with Christmas. Encourage friends who don't cook to give you their cumquats in exchange for a bottle of marmalade.

1.5 kg (3 lb) cumquats
Juice of 2 lemons (save skins)
12 cups water
3 kg (6 lb) sugar
2 tablespoons brandy or Armagnac

SCRUB the fruit and slice very finely, removing any seeds. Put the seeds and lemon skins in a muslin bag. Into a heavy-based pan put the cumquats, lemon juice, muslin bag and water. Bring slowly to the boil. Simmer for $1\frac{1}{2}$ hours or until the fruit is tender.

Remove the muslin bag, squeezing it well. Pour in the sugar and stir until it dissolves. Turn up the heat and bring to a rolling boil. Continue until setting point is reached.

Remove from heat, stir in the brandy and leave until a skin begins to form on the surface. Stir gently and ladle into warm sterilised jars. Place a wax disc over the surface when cold. Cover, label and store.

dissolved, then add the shreds and boil rapidly until setting point is reached.

Remove from the heat and let the marmalade stand until a skin begins to form. Stir gently and ladle into warm sterilised jars. Do not move the bottles until you are sure the jelly has set firmly. Seal, label and store in a dark, cool place.

Grapefruit Jelly Marmalade

This jelly marmalade shines like a jewel when held to the light. It's more complicated than most to make but well worth the effort. If you don't have a jelly bag, strain the fruit through two layers of muslin in a sieve. The combined weight of the fruit should be 1 kg (2 lb). You can make this same recipe replacing the grapefruit with 2–3 Seville oranges.

    2 grapefruit
    2 lemons
    1 orange
    9 cups water
    Sugar to measure

SCRUB the fruit and remove the rinds with a vegetable peeler. Shred the rinds finely. Cut up the rest of the fruit and pith coarsely.

Put all of the fruit apart from the shredded rind into a pan with 6 cups of water. Cover and cook for two hours. In the meantime, cook the shredded peel in 3 cups of water for $1\frac{1}{2}$ hours. Drain the liquid from the shreds and add it to the pulp in the pan. Strain the bulk of the fruit and juice through a jelly bag and allow to drip into a bowl for an hour. Measure the juice into a pan and for every cup of juice set aside one cup of sugar. Bring the juice slowly to the boil, add the sugar and stir until it is

Lime and Ginger Marmalade

I look forward to autumn when the limes become cheap enough to buy in large enough quantities to make marmalade. This is my husband's favourite. I have to smuggle it out of the house to give to friends. If you can't obtain limes, substitute oranges; orange and ginger marmalade is very good.

    1.5 kg (3 lb) limes
    Juice and zest of 1 lemon
      (save pith and seeds)
    12 cups water
    3 kg (6 lb) sugar
    1 cup grated ginger

SCRUB the limes and slice them very thinly, removing any seeds. Lime seeds are not used for pectin; use the pith and seeds of the lemon in a muslin bag. Put the limes, lemon juice and zest, muslin bag and water into a pan and bring slowly to the boil. Cook for $1\frac{1}{2}$ hours or until the fruit is tender. Remove the muslin bag and squeeze the pectin into the pan. Add the ginger and pour in the sugar, stirring until it is dissolved. Turn up the heat and bring to a rolling boil. Continue until setting point is reached.

Remove from the heat and let the marmalade stand until a skin begins to form. Stir gently, then pour into warm sterilised jars. When cold, seal with wax discs, cover and label.

Orange and Apple Marmalade

This is a chunky marmalade which is delicious on thick toast for a hearty breakfast eater. My father always insists that the marmalade I give him must be very chunky. I think he believes that jam is good for him.

1.5 kg (3 lb) oranges
4 cups unsweetened apple juice
7 cups water
3 kg (6 lb) sugar

SCRUB the oranges and cut them in halves. Squeeze out the juice and save the pips. Cut the peel into chunky pieces of approximately equal size. Place the pips in a muslin bag. Put the orange peel and juice, the apple juice and water into a pan. Bring to the boil and cook gently for 2 hours or until the fruit is tender. Remove the muslin bag, squeezing the pectin back into the jam. Add the sugar and stir until it is dissolved. Boil rapidly until setting point is reached.

Remove from the heat, skim off any scum and let it stand until a skin begins to form. Stir gently once, then ladle into warm sterilised jars. Place wax circles on when cold. Cover, label and store.

Orange Whisky Marmalade

Make this jam extra special by lacing it with a dash of a good malt whisky. It is such a delicious marmalade that your friends will be begging for more. Try not to drink all the whisky while waiting for the fruit to cook.

1.5 kg (3 lb) oranges
Juice of 2 lemons
10 cups water
3 kg (6 lb) sugar
3 tablespoons malt whisky

SCRUB the fruit well and cut into halves. Squeeze out the juice and reserve all the pips. Remove the pith from the rind if it is thick. Slice the peel, making sure the slices are the same thickness, either thick or thin, as liked. Wrap the pips and pith in muslin and put it and all the fruit, juice and water in a heavy-based pan. Bring to the boil and cook gently for 2 hours or until the peel is quite soft. Remove the muslin bag, squeezing it well. Add the sugar and stir until it is dissolved. Turn up the heat and continue a rolling boil until setting point is reached.

Remove from the heat, skim off any scum and let it stand until a skin begins to form. Stir gently. Ladle into warm sterilised jars and pour wax circles on when cold. Cover, label and store in a dark, cool place.

Quince and Lemon Marmalade

1.5 kg (3 lb) quinces
Juice and zest of 2 lemons
10 cups water
3 kg (6 lb) sugar

PEEL and core the quinces and cut them up into chunky pieces. Put the peel and cores into a muslin bag and put it in a pan with the quince chunks, the lemon juice and zest and the water. Bring slowly to the boil and cook gently for up to 2 hours or until the fruit is tender. Remove the muslin bag, squeezing the juice hard back into the jam. Add the sugar; when it has dissolved, bring the mixture to the boil fast. Continue boiling until setting point is reached.

Remove the pan from the heat, skim and let it rest for an hour. Stir gently once, then ladle into warm sterilised jars. Place a wax disc on when cold, cover and label.

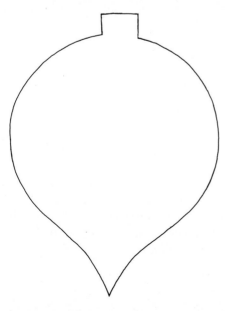

Orange and Ginger Marmalade (page 42) and Amber Marmalade (page 40). Oranges can be used not only in marmalades but to make sweets and desserts, to flavour liqueurs and even as pomanders to decorate a table or hang in cupboards to sweeten the air. The instructions for making pomanders are on the opposite page.

RIGHT
These oranges are underripe—note the green tinge—and in perfect condition for making Orange Whisky Marmalade (page 43). Seville Marmalade (page 46) is the most popular of all the marmalades with its bitter-sweet flavour.

Pomanders

The fragrance in these pomanders will last for years. When you have taken down the Christmas decorations, hang the pomanders in your wardrobe or as a deodorant in the bathroom. Spicy pomanders can be made with apples as well as oranges.

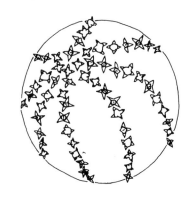

Oranges or apples
Whole cloves
1 cup ground cloves
1 cup ground cinnamon
1 cup ground nutmeg
1 cup ground orrisroot

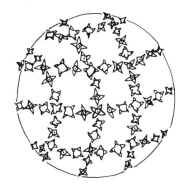

Stud the fruit with the whole cloves, all over if you wish, or make some patterned ones as in the illustrations. Combine all the ground spices in a bowl and roll the fruit in the powder until well covered. Leave the fruit to dry out in individual paper bags. When the pomanders have dried hard, dust off the powder and either hang them up with ribbon or arrange them in a bowl.

Seville Marmalade

Seville oranges originally came from Seville in Spain. Nowadays any bitter oranges are called Seville oranges. They only come into the markets for a short season, so freeze them if you don't have time to make marmalade immediately. It is well worth the effort. The bitterness of the oranges combines with the sugar to give the marmalade a great depth of flavour.

  1.5 kg (3 lb) Seville oranges
  Juice of 2 lemons (save pips and pith)
  11 cups water
  3 kg (6 lb) sugar

SCRUB the oranges well and cut them into halves. Squeeze out the juice and reserve it and the pips. If the pith is thick, remove it. Slice the peel thinly and evenly. Wrap the pips and pith of the oranges and lemons in a muslin bag. Put the peel, orange juice, lemon juice, muslin bag and water into a pan. Bring to the boil and simmer for 2 hours or until tender. Take out the muslin bag, squeezing the juice back into the pan. Add the sugar and dissolve, stirring constantly. Continue to boil fast until setting point is reached.

Remove from the heat and let the marmalade rest until a skin begins to form. Stir once, then ladle into warm sterilised jars. When cold, place on wax discs, cover and label.

Apple and Ginger Jelly

Jellies are a welcome gift at any time. Their translucent and subtle colour are reminiscent of precious jewels. No need to use the best-quality fruit to make them, as only the juice is needed. Windfall apples are the most economical and often the tastiest. Crab-apples can be substituted for the apples.

  2 kg (4 lb) apples or crab-apples
  9 cups water
  1 tablespoon sliced ginger
  Peel of 1 lemon
  Sugar to measure

WASH and cut up the fruit, removing any bad parts. Put into a saucepan with the water, ginger and lemon to just cover the fruit. Simmer for an hour or until the fruit is tender. Strain the fruit through a jelly bag or a colander lined with three layers of clean muslin. Do not squeeze the fruit or the jelly will become cloudy. After two hours the juice should be extracted.

Now measure the juice and for every cup of juice measure out one cup of sugar. Bring the juice slowly to the boil and add the sugar. After it is dissolved, boil rapidly until setting point is reached. To test: the jelly should remain firm on a chilled plate and not run. Skim the jelly. Ladle into small sterilised jars and seal and label. A perfect jelly should be firm but slightly wobbly.

Herb Jellies

Fresh herbs added to apple jelly make aromatic jellies to enhance the rather dull taste of the apple. Replace the ginger in the previous recipe with a bunch of herbs instead.

Mint jelly. Add one bunch of mint to the fruit while it is cooking. Look at the colour after the juice is strained and add a few drops of green colouring if it is not as colourful as you'd like it.

Rosemary jelly. Add several sprigs to the fruit while it is cooking. Add green colouring if you fancy it, and a sprig of rosemary in the jars before pouring the jelly over.

Redcurrant and Raspberry Jelly

Jellies make great gifts because many people believe they are terribly hard to make. We know better! This jelly is delicious to eat with all kinds of meat as well as with bread and cake.

1.5 kg (3 lb) redcurrants
500 g (1 lb) raspberries
1½ cups water
Sugar

JUST wash the currants and raspberries and place them in a pan with the water. Bring slowly to the boil and simmer for about 45 minutes or until the fruit is tender.

Mash the fruit and then strain through a jelly bag for up to two hours. Measure the juice into a pan and for every cup of juice reserve one cup of sugar. Bring the juice slowly to the boil and add the sugar. When it has dissolved, boil rapidly until setting point is reached. Skim the jelly and pour into warm sterilised jars. Seal and label when cold and a firm set.

Blueberry and Apple Jelly

This jelly is delicious with meats as well as on scones and cake.

1 kg (2 lb) blueberries
1 kg (2 lb) apples
1 cup lemon juice
5 cups water
Sugar

WASH the blueberries and apples and cut the apples into small pieces. Put the fruit into a pan with the lemon juice and water. Bring slowly to the boil and simmer for about an hour until the fruit is tender.

Mash the fruit and then strain it through a jelly bag for up to 2 hours. Measure the juice into a saucepan and for every cup of juice set aside one cup of sugar. Bring the juice slowly to the boil and add the sugar. When the sugar has dissolved, boil fast until setting point is reached. Skim the jelly and pour into warm sterilised jars. Seal and label when cold and firmly set. Store in a cool place.

Quince and Orange Jelly

Quinces are very rich in pectin, so they are an ideal fruit to make into jelly. This one is coloured a beautiful deep pink fading to orange.

2 kg (4 lb) quinces
3 cups orange juice
½ cup lemon juice
5 cups water
Sugar

WASH the quinces and cut them up. Put them in a pan with the orange and lemon juice and the water. Bring to the boil and simmer for an hour or until the fruit is tender. Strain through a jelly bag for one or two hours until it stops dripping.

Discard the pulp and measure the strained liquid into a pan. For every cup of juice you need one cup of sugar. Bring the juice slowly to the boil, add the sugar, and when the sugar has dissolved boil hard until setting point is reached, in about 15 minutes. Skim the jelly and ladle it into sterilised jars. Seal and label when cold and firmly set. Store in a dark, cool place.

Bitter Orange Jelly

I got the inspiration for this jelly from an old recipe from Carême, the famous French chef. It is delicious with pickled meats and tongue.

2 kg (4 lb) bitter oranges
2 lemons
9 cups water
Sugar

WASH and dry the oranges and lemons and grate the rinds. Reserve the grated rinds. Cut the pith off the fruit and discard. Chop the fruit roughly into small pieces and put it into a pan with the water. Bring to the boil and simmer for about an hour or until the fruit is tender. Strain through a jelly bag for one or two hours.

Measure the juice into a pan and for every cup of juice measure out one cup of sugar. Add the grated orange and lemon rind to the juice. Bring slowly to the boil. Add the sugar, stirring while the sugar dissolves, then boil until setting point is reached. Skim the jelly and ladle into sterilised jars. Seal and label when cold and firmly set. Store in a cool and dry cupboard.

Blackberry Jelly

A rich, dark jelly to make after a morning picking blackberries. The beauty of making jellies is that you don't have to worry about hulling the fruit. As long as the fruit is washed well, just throw it in the pan, leaves and all.

1.5 kg (3 lb) blackberries
½ cup lemon juice
1 cup water
Sugar

Wash the fruit and put it in a pan with the lemon juice and water. Bring to the boil and simmer for about 45 minutes or until the fruit is tender. Mash the fruit and then strain through a jelly bag for two hours.

Measure the juice into a pan; for every cup of fruit juice measure out one cup of sugar. Bring the juice slowly to the boil, add the sugar, and when the sugar has dissolved continue at a rolling boil until setting point is reached.

Skim the jelly and pour into warm sterilised jars. Seal and label when cold and firmly set. Store in a cool place.

Plum and Apple Jelly

Plums and apples harmonise wonderfully together. I added some spices to liven up the jelly a bit. Make it with windfalls and you will have lots of jars to give away as gifts without spending much money—just time and love of good food.

1 kg (2 lb) plums
1 kg (2 lb) apples
3 cloves
1 tablespoon grated ginger
9 cups water
Sugar

Wash and cut the fruit up, removing any bad parts. Put into a pan with the cloves and water. Bring to the boil and simmer for one hour or until the fruit is tender. Strain the fruit through a jelly bag for two hours.

Measure the juice into a pan and for every cup of juice set aside one cup of sugar. Bring the juice slowly to the boil and add the sugar, stirring constantly till it dissolves. Bring to a rolling boil and continue until setting point is reached.

Skim the surface of the jelly and pour into warm sterilised jars. Seal and label when cold and firm. Store in a dark, cool place.

Pineapple and Mint Jelly

I think this jelly sounds delicious as well as tasting so. My god-daughter loves it, and I try to give her a bottle among her presents every Christmas. Children love jellies.

2 kg (4 lb) pineapple, skinned
3 apples
Juice and zest of 2 lemons
A large bunch of mint
Sugar

Chop up the pineapple and wash and chop the apples. Put the fruit into a pan with the lemon juice, mint and water. Bring to the boil and simmer until the fruit is soft, about one hour. Strain through a jelly bag for two hours.

Measure the juice into a pan; for every cup of juice you will need one cup of sugar. Add the lemon zest to the juice and bring slowly to the boil. Add the sugar; when it has dissolved, continue to boil rapidly until setting point is reached. Skim the jelly and pour into warm sterilised jars. Seal and label when cold and firmly set. Store in a dark, cool place.

Apricot Preserve

I think apricots taste much better preserved than fresh—the preserving intensifies their flavour.

> 2 kg (4 lb) apricots
> 2 kg (4 lb) sugar
> 1 vanilla pod
> 1 cup brandy

Wash the apricots, cut them into halves and remove the stones. Put the sugar, vanilla and lemon juice into a pan and simmer until the sugar is dissolved. Bring to the boil and cook until the syrup has thickened. Add the fruit for two minutes. Remove from the heat and add the brandy. Pack the apricots into sterilised jars. Pour the syrup over the apricots while hot. Seal, label and store in a cool, dark place.

Black Jam (Confiture Noire)

A well-loved preserve made in the south of France from summer fruits. All your Francophile friends will welcome you with open arms, a well-known syndrome diagnosed as cupboard love.

> 500 g (1 lb) fresh figs
> 500 g (1 lb) pears
> 500 g (1 lb) quinces
> 500 g (1 lb) watermelon
> 1.5 kg (3 lb) sugar
> Rind and juice of 2 lemons
> $\frac{1}{2}$ cup chopped walnuts

Wash the fruits. Keep the figs whole, peel and quarter the pears and quinces, and slice the watermelon. Put the fruit into a large bowl with the sugar and let

stand for several hours. Transfer the mixture to a heavy pan and cook slowly until the sugar has dissolved. Add the lemon rind and juice and walnuts and bring to the boil. Keep boiling rapidly until the syrup thickens and reaches setting point. When cool, spoon into warm sterilised jars, seal and label.

Preserved Oranges

This preserve is a very attractive translucent orange, which makes it a most appealing gift in a jar with a pretty cloth top. The oranges are delicious to eat as a dessert or served in a sherry glass with coffee.

> 10 oranges
> 2 cups water
> 1.25 kg (2$\frac{1}{2}$ lb) sugar
> Juice of 1 lemon
> $\frac{1}{2}$ cup silvered almonds

Pare the oranges and discard the peel. Cut each orange into 8 pieces by quartering and then halving the quarters. Put the oranges and water into a pan and bring to the boil. Simmer for 1$\frac{1}{2}$ hours or until they are soft.

Remove the fruit from the water and reserve. Add the sugar and lemon juice to the pan. Dissolve the sugar and bring to the boil for 15 minutes. Pour the syrup over the oranges and leave to stand overnight. The next day put the syrup and the oranges back into the pan and bring to the boil. Keep at a rolling boil for half an hour or until the syrup thickens. Remove from the heat and add the almonds.

When cool, ladle into sterilised jars, seal and store in a dark place.

Plum Conserve

A Polish friend gave me this wonderful recipe for my book. This particular plum conserve is a classic blend of fruit flavours. The fruit will remain suspended in the syrup.

1 kg (2 lb) plums
1 orange
1 lemon
1 cup sultanas
2 cups sugar
1 teaspoon ground cinnamon
1 teaspoon ground ginger
1 cup chopped almonds

PIT the plums. Roughly chop the orange and lemon, skin and all.

Put the plums, citrus fruit, sultanas, sugar and spices into a large bowl and let it stand, covered, for several hours.

Transfer the mixture to a pan and slowly bring to the boil. Stir constantly until setting point is reached. It may take up to 40 minutes. Stir in the almonds and remove from heat.

Ladle into warm sterilised jars, seal and label.

Raspberry Conserve

A gift for those friends with a sweet tooth. Raspberry conserve can be used as a spread on bread and scones or as a sauce on ice-creams and puddings.

1 kg (2 lb) sugar
1 kg (2 lb) raspberries
Zest and juice of one lemon

WARM the sugar in a baking dish in the oven. Wash the raspberries and crush them with a wooden spoon. Put them in a pan and set it over a low heat. Stir until they are nearly boiled. Add the warmed sugar, stirring until it is dissolved. Bring to the boil and remove from the heat.

Ladle the raspberries immediately into warm sterilised jars and seal. Label and store in a dark place. It may look too liquid, but it will thicken with time.

Rose Petal Preserve

A romantic preserve to make with the roses your friend or friends have given you. You can

give back some of the pleasure they gave you. A perfect gift for Saint Valentine's Day. To dry the roses, sprinkle the petals on brown paper and leave them in the sun. They will take about three days to dry. The fragrant dark red ones are usually the best.*

500 g (1 lb) rose petals
1 kg (2 lb) sugar
2 cups water
Juice of 1 lemon

WASH the petals and clip off the white or yellow heels, as they have a bitter flavour. Put the petals into a pan with a cup of the sugar and a cup of water. Cover and bring to the boil. Remove the lid and add the rest of the sugar and water. Dissolve the sugar, stirring all the time, then bring to the boil. Add the lemon juice. Simmer for an hour or until the syrup thickens. Remove from the heat and skim.

When cool, spoon it into sterilised jars, cover and label.

Watermelon Conserve

A very popular sweet preserve from the Balkans. It is served in a dish with small spoons. You eat a spoonful of conserve with alternate sips of water and Turkish coffee. Add some Turkish coffee to the present.

1 kg (2 lb) watermelon
1 kg (2 lb) sugar
1 vanilla pod
Zest and juice of 2 lemons
1 teaspoon cinnamon

REMOVE the outer rind of the watermelon and cut the flesh into 2 cm (1 in) cubes. Put in a pan with water to cover and boil for 10 minutes. Drain, add fresh water to cover and boil again until the fruit is nearly soft. Drain and reserve the fruit.

Put the sugar, vanilla pod and 3 cups of water into a pan. Heat slowly, stirring until the sugar is dissolved. Bring to the boil, add the lemon and cinnamon, and cook until the syrup thickens. Gently put in the watermelon, cook for 5 minutes, then remove the pan from the heat. When the conserve is cool, remove the vanilla pod and ladle the conserve into warm sterilised jars, seal and label.

Apple Butter

Present this spicy spread in small earthenware pots sealed with waxed paper covers. Apple butter is delicious on roast pork or grilled pork chops.

2 kg (4 lb) cooking apples
1 cup water
Zest and juice of 2 lemons
1 cup cider
2 kg (4 lb) brown sugar
1 teaspoon ground cinnamon
1 teaspoon ground cardamom
3 cloves

Wash, peel, core and quarter the apples. Put them in a pan with the water, lemon zest and juice and cider and cook until soft. Purée them in a food processor.

Into the pan put the apple purée, sugar and spices. Cook slowly until the mixture is thick and brown. Ladle it into warm sterilised pots or jars. Seal and label.

Mango Butter

A delicious way to preserve mangoes when they are cheap at the markets. Butters will keep about three months stored in a cool place.

1 kg (2 lb) mangoes
1 kg (2 lb) sugar
1 cup lemon juice
$\frac{1}{2}$ teaspoon ground cinnamon
$\frac{1}{4}$ teasppon ground cloves

Peel and seed the mangoes and chop the flesh. Put the fruit into a pan along with the rest of the ingredients. Cook slowly and stir until the sugar dissolves.

Bring to the boil and, still stirring, simmer for about 45 minutes or until the syrup has thickened.

Put the mixture into a food processor and purée. Ladle the mango butter into small sterilized pots or jars. Seal and label.

Orange Curd

This recipe is better known made with lemons. For lemon curd, just reverse the number of oranges and lemons. The curd will last for two months at least in the refrigerator.

4 oranges
2 lemons
4 whole eggs
4 egg yolks
1 teaspoon ground cinnamon
2 cups sugar
1 cup butter

Wash the oranges and lemons. Grate the zest, then squeeze the juice. A double boiler is needed for the next step; if you don't have one, put a saucepan inside a larger one of simmering water. Break the eggs into the saucepan, add the four extra yolks and cinnamon and beat well. Then gradually add the sugar, whisking all the while, until the mixture thickens.

Now slowly pour in the juice, zest and butter, stirring continuously the mixture thickens. Ladle the orange curd into sterilised jars and pots and seal.

Quince Paste

It is such a joy to see quinces becoming readily available in fruit markets. This quince paste puts the bought variety to shame. Eat it as a dessert or serve it with the cheese course.

1 kg (2 lb) quinces
Juice of 1 lemon
3 cloves
Sugar to measure

WASH the quinces, then peel and core them. Cut them up roughly and put them into a pan with the lemon juice, cloves and just enough water to cover them. Bring to the boil and simmer until the quince is soft and the water has evaporated.

Remove the cloves and put the pulp through a food processor. Measure the fruit in cupfuls as you put it back into a pan. Add one cup of sugar for every cup of fruit. Stirring constantly, bring the mixture to the boil and stir until very thick.

Pour the paste into a shallow gratin dish so that it is about 2.5 cm (1 in) thick. Dry it in the sun or put it in the oven for an hour at 150°C (300°F). Cut the paste into squares, as needed, roll the squares in caster sugar and wrap them up in waxed paper to give away as a gift. Tie with satin ribbon.

Dried Apricots and Apples

A foolproof and tasty method of drying fruit when there is a glut. String them as garlands to present as a gift. Dried chillies, bay leaves and tomatoes can be added to brighten up the garland. The fruits darken as they dry, so they are not as attractive in colour as the commercial product, but they are so much more delicious. And when they are dried this way you know you aren't eating chemical preservatives. They will cost half the price, too, if you buy wisely.

1 tablespoon salt
$\frac{1}{2}$ cup lemon juice
3 kg (7 lb) apples or apricots

MAKE a brine of the salt and lemon juice in a large bowl. When using apples, peel and core them and cut them into rings 7 mm ($\frac{1}{4}$ in) thick. Put the rings into the brine as you slice them, to prevent discoloration. When using apricots, cut them in half, remove

the stone and place the fruit in the brine.

After the fruit has soaked for 15 minutes, remove the pieces from the brine with a slotted spoon and allow them to drain on kitchen paper. Pat them dry.

If the weather is warm and dry, arrange the fruit on bamboo trays or wire racks and leave to dry in the sun for several days or until no liquid is released when the fruit is squeezed. Even if the weather is perfect for drying, you may have problems with insects; if so, dry the fruit in the oven, as you would do in cold or overcast weather.

Put the fruit on racks in the oven set at 120°C (240°F). After 3 hours, turn off the heat and let the drying fruit remain in the oven overnight. They should be dry and pliable in the morning. Store in a box or paper bags.

Sun-Dried Tomatoes in Oil

The traditional method of preserving tomatoes is to hang them up in bunches still attached to stems in a sunny place outside until the skin has dried, then transfer them inside to hang in a cool, airy place. (Tomatoes already detached from stems can be dried on bamboo trays or wire racks.) If, like me, you have trouble with every fruit fly in the neighbourhood feasting on your picturesque garlands of tomatoes hanging on the terrace, dry them in the oven. Prick them with a skewer, then put them in the oven at 120°C (240°F) for up to 6 hours to dry. They'll be ready when they have flattened a bit and you can hardly feel any juice inside. They smell delicious while they are drying.

Dried tomatoes normally last for a year, but they can also be preserved in oil once they have hung outside to dry. Use good oil so that it can be used as salad oil when the tomatoes have been eaten.

Sun-Dried Tomatoes in Oil (this page) and Preserved Limes (page 54). Give serving suggestions on the gift tag; both of these preserves are lovely in salads or as an accompaniment to cold meats.

3 cups dried Tom Thumb or cherry
  tomatoes
3 teaspoons salt
6 cloves of garlic
3 teaspoons chopped oregano
Cold-pressed virgin olive oil

WASH and destalk the dried tomatoes and pack them into small three sterilised jars along with 1 teaspoon each of salt and oregano and 2 garlic cloves in each jar. Pour olive oil over to cover. Seal and label the jars.

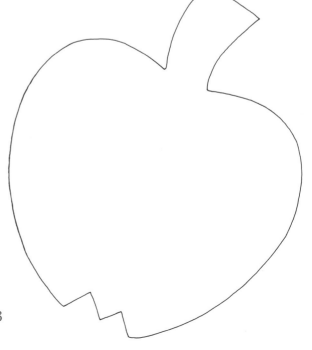

Lemons Preserved in Salt

These lemons look stunning packed down in glass jars. Add cooking ideas to the label when presenting them as a gift. They are salted this way in Moroccan cooking. The lemons are used to add piquancy to stews and curries, salads, fish and chicken kebabs. The pulp, the rind and the salty juices can all be used. Limes are just as delicious.

1 kg (2 lb) lemons or limes
½ cup sea salt

WASH the lemons well and cut them lengthwise into quarters to within about 1 cm (½ in) of the stem end so that the segments are not completely separated. If you are using limes, cut them into halves, similarly attached. Sprinkle salt inside the fruit. Use a wide-necked, sterilised jar and fill it with the fruit. Press the lemons down hard with a weight. The juice is gradually released by the salt and it will preserve the skins. Add water if you don't get enough to cover. They will be ready in a month.

Preserved Limes

A spicy way to preserve limes or lemons. Pack them into an attractive, wide-necked preserving jar so that the bottle is part of the present. Tie a large bow on the wire holding the lid down and you have a most attractive gift. Delicious to eat with cold fish and chicken or as a sandwich spread with cold lamb.

1 kg (2 lb) limes
10 red chillies
1 tablespoon grated ginger
2 tablespoons black mustard seeds
1 tablespoon coriander seeds
6 bay leaves
½ cup sugar
½ cup salt

CUT half the limes into quarters. Squeeze the juice from the rest of the

limes and reserve. Put the lime quarters into a wide-necked sterilised jar, layering with all the spices and herbs, sugar and salt. Pour the lime juice over. If it doesn't cover, add more lime juice or vinegar.

Stand in a warm place, ideally out in the hot sun, for 5 days with a cloth over the jar. Seal and store for one month before testing to see if the fruit is soft and mellow.

Apple and Mango Chutney

2 cups white wine vinegar
750 g (1½ lb) cooking apples, peeled and sliced
1 cup raisins, chopped
1 cup chopped mangoes
1 cup brown sugar
12 chillies, finely cut
1 cup preserved lemon peel, chopped
1 cup ginger, chopped
2 garlic cloves, chopped
1 teaspoon salt
2 tablespoons mustard seeds
1 tablespoon ground ginger

BRING the vinegar to the boil and put the apples into it. Simmer until the apples are cooked. Add the rest of the ingredients and cook until the mixture has thickened. Spoon into warm sterilised jars, seal, label and store.

Apricot Chutney

A luxurious chutney to make as a gift. If you are canny you will have dried the apricots yourself when there was a glut at the markets (see recipe, page 52).

500 g (1 lb) dried apricots
1 cup sultanas
½ cup preserved or fresh lemon peel, chopped
1 cup white wine vinegar

½ cup sugar
10 garlic cloves
6 chillies
1 teaspoon cumin powder
1 teaspoon ground cardamom
2 teaspoons caraway seeds
1 teaspoon ground cinnamon
1 tablespoon salt
1 cup water

COVER the apricots with water and soak for an hour. Drain and put into a pan with the sultanas, lemon peel and vinegar. Bring slowly to the boil and simmer gently until the fruit is tender.

Stir in the rest of the ingredients and simmer until the chutney has thickened. Pour into warm sterilised jars, cover and label.

Banana Chutney

Small sugar bananas, slightly green, are best to use if you can get them. This chutney will make a most suitable gift for a curry lover.

1 kg (2 lb) bananas
500 g (1 lb) onions, chopped
1½ cup dates, chopped
4 garlic cloves, chopped
2 cups white wine vinegar
3 cups sugar
1½ cup raisins
3 tablespoons chopped ginger
½ cup lemon juice
½ cup orange juice
1 tablespoon yellow mustard seeds
3 cloves
1 tablespoon ground cinnamon
1 tablespoon salt
3 chillies

PEEL and chop the bananas and put them into a pan with the onions, dates, garlic and vinegar. Cook slowly for about half an hour or until the bananas are soft. Add the remaining ingredients. Stir until the sugar has dissolved, then simmer until the mixture has reached a smooth, thick consistency. Ladle into warm sterilised jars, seal and label.

Beetroot and Apple
Relish

A great stand-by as a sandwich filler with cheese and meat.

500 g (1 lb) beetroot, peeled and
　roughly chopped
500 g (1 lb) apples, peeled, cored and
　roughly chopped
1½ cups roughly chopped onions
2 cups white wine vinegar
1 cup sugar
3 garlic cloves
3 chillies
1 tablespoon grated ginger
1 teaspoon ground cinnamon
3 cloves

PUT the beetroot, apple and onion into a food processor and mince. Then put them into a pan with the vinegar and simmer until tender. Add the rest of the ingredients and continue cooking slowly until the chutney is smooth and thick. Spoon into warm sterilised jars and seal.

Chilli Chutney

This is a good gift for a reluctant cook. It is a fiery chutney that will add piquancy to the dullest dish. I even like it just spread on wholemeal or pita bread for a snack.

½ cup dried red chillies
½ cup unsalted peanuts
2 teaspoons grated ginger
3 garlic cloves
½ cup lemon juice
1 teaspoon salt

PUT all the ingredients into a food processor and blend. Adjust the seasonings if you prefer less of one or more of another. Seal in a sterilised jar and keep refrigerated. It will last for at least two months.

Date Chutney

500 g (1 lb) dried dates
2 oranges
1 tablespoon grated ginger
½ cup raisins
1 teaspoon ground cinnamon
3 cloves
1 cup brown sugar
1 cup white vinegar

Pit and chop the dates. Peel the oranges and chop the flesh. Place all the ingredients into a pan and stir until the sugar is dissolved. Simmer until the mixture is smooth and thick. Pour into warm sterilised jars, seal and label.

Fiery Eggplant (Aubergine) Chutney

1 kg (2 lb) eggplant
⅓ cup salt
2 cups white wine vinegar
1 cup sultanas
2 tomatoes, skinned and chopped
1½ cups brown sugar
1 cup finely chopped onions
10 chillies, chopped
6 garlic cloves, chopped
1 tablespoon chopped ginger
1 tablespoon ground coriander
1 teaspoon ground cumin

Wash and slice the eggplant. Sprinkle with salt and leave for an hour to expel the bitter juice. Wash and dry. Put in the pan with the vinegar and sultanas. Cook slowly until the eggplant is tender, then add the rest of the ingredients and mix well. Simmer until the mixture is thick and smooth. Spoon into warm sterilised jars, seal and label.

Mango and Date Chutney (page 58) and Banana Chutney (page 55), ready to serve with spicy yoghurt kebabs. Homemade chutney is always a popular gift, because it is impossible to buy a chutney of such fine quality.

Kashmir Chutney

A friend who was stationed in India during the war gave me my first jar of this tasty chutney. It is a chutney direct from nineteenth-century India in the days of the British raj. Peaches can be used instead of apples for a more luxurious flavour. It is a rich brown colour darkened by the malt vinegar and brown sugar.

1 kg (2 lb) cooking apples
500 g (1 lb) pitted dates
500 g (1 lb) sultanas
3 tablespoons grated ginger
5 garlic cloves
4 cups malt vinegar
3 cups brown sugar
1 tablespoon salt
½ teaspoon cayenne
1 teaspoon ground allspice
1 teaspoon celery seeds

Wash, core and quarter the apples and chop the dates. Put the apples, dates, sultanas, ginger and garlic into a large pan with the vinegar and simmer until the apples are soft. Add the sugar, salt and spices and stir until the sugar is dissolved. Continue to cook until it is thick and smooth. Bottle the chutney into warm sterilised jars and seal. Label and store in a cool, dark place.

Lime and Fig Chutney

An absolute favourite chutney in our home. Lime is transformed by the chutney preserving. Keep for at least two months before eating.

12 limes
500 g (1 lb) dried figs
2 tablespoons grated ginger
8 garlic cloves, chopped
1 cup vinegar
1 cup water
1½ cups sugar
2 teaspoons ground cumin
2 teaspoons chilli powder
2 teaspoons ground coriander

PUT the limes, figs, ginger and garlic into a pan with the vinegar and water. Cook slowly until the fruit is soft. Add the sugar and spices, stirring until the sugar is dissolved. Keep cooking gently until the mixture is smooth and thick. Ladle into warm sterilised jars, cover and label.

Mango and Tomato Chutney

Test this chutney on your friends and see if you get the kind of response I did. I put a very large bowl of it on the table to serve with a lamb curry and was amazed when the bowl was wiped clean in next to no time, with demands for more.

1 kg (2 lb) tomatoes, peeled and chopped
1 kg (2 lb) mangoes, peeled, stoned and chopped
1 cup peeled, cored and chopped apples
1 cup chopped onions
1 tablespoon chopped ginger
3 garlic cloves
2 cups white wine vinegar
3 cups sugar
1 tablespoon salt
3 cloves
3 chillies
1 teaspoon mustard seeds
1 teaspoon ground coriander

PUT the tomatoes, mangoes, apples, onions, ginger and garlic into a pan with the vinegar. Cook slowly until the fruit is tender, then add the sugar, salt and spices. Stir until the sugar has dissolved. Keep simmering until the mixture has reached a thick consistency. Spoon into warm sterilised jars and seal. Label and store in a cool, dark place.

Mango and Date Chutney

Mangoes reach an affordable price in the markets in midsummer, a good time to lay down mango chutneys even though it is hot.

500 g (1 lb) mangoes, peeled and chopped
500 g (1 lb) dates, stoned and chopped
3 tablespoons chopped ginger
3 garlic cloves, chopped
2 cups white wine vinegar
2 cups sugar
2 cups raisins
2 tablespoons chopped almonds
2 teaspoons salt
1 teaspoon pepper
3 chillies
1 teaspoon ground allspice
4 cloves
1 cinnamon stick
1 teaspoon ground cardamom

PUT the mangoes, dates, ginger, garlic and vinegar into a pan and simmer until the fruit is soft. Add the sugar, raisins, almonds, salt and spices and stir until the sugar has dissolved. Continue to cook until the mixture has thickened to a smooth consistency. Spoon into warm sterilised jars and seal. Label and store in a dark place.

Nine-Jewelled Chutney

A tropical mixture of fruits to serve with Indian curries. It is also delicious with cold lamb in a sandwich and a filling for pita bread with a sliced banana.

> 1 cup peeled and sliced banana
> 1 cup peeled, cored and chopped apple
> 1 cup peeled, stoned and chopped mango
> 1 cup peeled, cored and chopped pineapple
> ½ cup dates
> 2 tablespoons raisins
> 1 tablespoon grated ginger
> 1 cup raw sugar
> 4 chillies
> 1 cup malt vinegar
> 1 teaspoon salt
> ½ teaspoon cumin seed
> ½ teaspoon coriander seed
> ½ teaspoon fennel seed
> 2 tablespoons slivered almonds

Put all the fruits, ginger, sugar, chilli, vinegar and salt into a pan. Simmer until all the fruit is soft. In the meantime, dry roast the cumin, coriander, fennel and almonds and grind coarsely. Add to the fruit, mix and continue to cook until the chutney is thick. Ladle into warm sterilised jars, cover and label.

Onion Chutney

If you have never eaten onion chutney before, you and your friends are in for a real treat. It will harmonise with all meats, hot or cold.

> 750 g (1½ lb) onions, sliced
> 1 tablespoon ghee or olive oil
> 3 garlic cloves, chopped
> 1 teaspoon ground ginger
> 1 teaspoon pepper
> 1 teaspoon salt
> ⅔ cup sugar
> 2 cups white wine vinegar
> 1 cup red wine

Put the onions into a pan with the ghee or olive oil. Cook, stirring constantly, until the onions are approaching golden brown. Stir in the spices and sugar. Cover and cook gently for 15 minutes, stirring several times. Uncover and add the vinegar and wine. Cook, stirring occasionally, until it is thick. Spoon into sterilised jars, cover and label.

Pawpaw Chutney

Save this chutney to give to a curry lover. Its tropical flavour and perfume make it something special to eat with a festive spicy meal.

> 500 g (1 lb) peeled, sliced and seeded pawpaw
> ½ cup stoned dates
> 2 cups white wine vinegar
> 1 cup sultanas
> 1 onion, chopped
> 3 garlic cloves, chopped
> 2 tablespoons chopped ginger
> 2 chillies
> Ground cinnamon
> 2 tablespoons mustard seeds
> 2 cups brown sugar

Put the pawpaw and dates into a pan along with the vinegar. Simmer until the fruit is tender. Add the rest of the ingredients and simmer until the chutney has thickened. Ladle into warm sterilised jars, cover and label.

Pineapple and Orange Relish

Relishes always taste better when they're homemade. These condiments are generally minced finer than chutneys, so they don't have to cook so long, which results in a fresher taste.

2 cups roughly chopped pineapple
4 green chillies
1 cup chopped onions
1 cup orange juice
1½ cups vinegar
1 teaspoon nutmeg
1 tablespoon chopped ginger
1 tablespoon mustard seeds
3 cloves
1 cup raw sugar
1 teaspoon salt

Mince the pineapple, chillies and onions in a food processor. Put them in a pan with the orange juice and vinegar. Simmer until the pineapple is tender, then mix in all the other ingredients. Cook slowly until the relish has reached a thick consistency. Spoon into warm sterilised jars, label and seal.

Plum and Apple Chutney

Many jars of chutney can be made out of windfall plums in summer. I make an annual pilgrimage to my sister's two heavily laden plum trees every summer to pick the fruit for my chutneys, jams and liqueur.

1 kg (2 lb) underripe plums
1 kg (2 lb) cooking apples
500 g (1 lb) onions, chopped
4 cloves of garlic, chopped
2 tablespoons chopped ginger
2 red chillies
1 tablespoon mustard seeds
3 cloves
1 teaspoon salt
2 cups white wine vinegar
2 cups white sugar

Wash and pit the plums. Peel, core and chop the apples roughly.

Combine all the ingredients and cook slowly for an hour or more until the chutney has thickened and the vinegar has been absorbed. You should be able to draw a wooden spoon across the bottom of the pan without there being

any free liquid. Watch the pan carefully in the last stages of thickening in case the chutney begins to stick.

Ladle the chutney into warm sterilised jars, seal and label. Store in a cool, dark place to mature for at least two months before opening it.

Rhubarb Chutney

Rhubarb chutney tastes great with pork, ham and lamb. I find my older friends and relatives particularly appreciate this old-fashioned chutney. Many a fascinating tale has unfolded after a taste or two of it.

1 kg (2 lb) rhubarb
2 lemons
10 garlic cloves
500 g (1 lb) sultanas
4 cups sugar
1 teaspoon salt
1 tablespoon grated ginger
2 cups vinegar

Wash the rhubarb and chop it up finely. Peel the lemons and slice them finely, removing the pips. Crush and slice the garlic. Put all the ingredients into a pan and simmer until the mixture is thick and smooth. Ladle into warm sterilised jars, seal and label.

Sweet Corn and Celery Relish

Another old-fashioned relish for sandwich fillers and cold meats.

2 tablespoons butter
1 cup finely chopped onions
1 green capsicum (sweet pepper), finely diced
1 red capsicum (sweet pepper), finely diced
2 cups finely diced celery
3 cups sweet corn kernels
2 garlic cloves, finely chopped

1½ cups sugar
1 teaspoon salt
1 teaspoon celery seeds
2 cups white wine vinegar

Melt the butter in a pan and add the onions, capsicum and celery. Cook slowly until they are soft, add the rest of the ingredients and simmer until the mixture is thick and smooth. Spoon into warm sterilised jars, cover and label.

Sweet Tomato Chutney

This chutney is not one to keep; it lasts only four to six weeks in the refrigerator. It is a good one to make if you want to cut down on sugar. Serve it hot or cold.

1 tablespoon oil
1 cinnamon stick
1 bay leaf
3 cloves

2 teaspoons mustard seeds
3 chillies
10 garlic cloves
½ teaspoon turmeric
⅓ cup sugar
500 g (1 lb) tomatoes, skinned and
    chopped
2 tablespoons sultanas
½ teaspoon salt

Heat the oil and put in the cinnamon stick, bay leaf and cloves. After a minute, add the mustard seeds. When they begin to pop, add the chillies, garlic, turmeric and sugar. Mix well, then add the tomatoes, sultanas and salt. Simmer for about 10 minutes. If the chutney gets too thick, add a little water. Ladle into warm sterilised jars and seal.

Onion Chutney (page 59) and Plum and Apple Chutney (opposite page), dressed with handcrocheted doilies.

Tamarind Chutney

A recipe for a connoisseur of Indian chutneys. This is not a long-lasting chutney; keep it refrigerated and it will last a month.

500 g (1 lb) tamarind pulp
1½ cups sugar
1 teaspoon salt
4 chillies, finely chopped
2 cloves
1 teaspoon cumin seeds, roasted and ground
1 teaspoon coriander seeds, roasted and ground

SOAK the tamarind pulp in half a cup of boiling water for half an hour. Squeeze the soft pulp to remove the juice and strain through a sieve. Repeat this process three times to extract the soft pulp.

Add the rest of the ingredients to the strained tamarind pulp. Mix and spoon into a sterilised jar, seal, label and refrigerate.

Spiced Apples

These spiced apples are delicious eaten with pork and ham. Crab-apples are also very successful prepared in this way.

1 kg (2 lb) small apples
Juice of 1 lemon
1½ cups sugar
2 cups vinegar
1 teaspoon cloves
1 teaspoon ground cinnamon
1 teaspoon grated nutmeg
2 chillies

WASH and core the apples and cut them into halves. Put them into a bowl with the lemon juice and water to cover so that they do not discolour. Make a spiced vinegar by putting the remaining ingredients into a pan and bringing them to the boil, dissolving the sugar. Add the drained apples and simmer until they are almost tender.

Remove the apples with a slotted spoon and carefully pack them in warm sterilised jars. Pour the spiced vinegar over the fruit. Seal and label.

Baby Beetroots in Raspberry Vinegar

This beetroot pickle is always appreciated. If you can't get those darling little beetroots, buy larger ones and cut them into wedges.

1.5 kg (3 lb) beetroot
1 cup raspberry vinegar (page 79)
2 cups wine vinegar
2 teaspoons salt
½ cup sugar
8 juniper berries
1 teaspoon mustard seeds
1 teaspoon whole peppercorns

WASH the beets and cut the stalks to 1 cm (½ in) long. Cook the beets in a pan of boiling salted water until tender. Let them cool, then peel them.

In the meantime, put the vinegars, salt, sugar and spices into a pan and bring them to the boil, dissolving the sugar. Remove the pan from the heat and let it stand for 10 minutes. Place the beets into warm sterilised jars and cover with the vinegar. Seal and store at least 10 days before eating.

Pickled Chinese Cabbage

1 kg (2 lb) Chinese cabbage
1 tablespoon salt
1 tablespoon Szechuan peppercorns
1 leek, chopped
2 garlic cloves, crushed
6 chillies
1 tablespoon grated ginger
½ cup soy sauce
2 cups white wine vinegar
½ teaspoon sesame oil

WASH and chop the cabbage coarsely. Press it hard to remove excess juices. Place the cabbage in a large bowl along with all the other ingredients. Stir well and then spoon the combination into large sterilised jars. Seal, label and store. The pickled cabbage will be ready to eat in a week.

Pickled Cauliflower

I use this pickle as part of an antipasto, or starter to a meal.

1.5 kg (3 lb) cauliflower
5 cups white wine vinegar
1 tablespoon salt
1 tablespoon sugar
6 chillies
1 teaspoon ground cinnamon
3 cloves
1 teaspoon mustard seeds

WASH the cauliflower and cut it into florets. Blanch them in boiling water for 5 minutes and drain.

Put the vinegar, salt, sugar and spices into a pan and bring to the boil, letting it simmer for 5 minutes.

Pack the cauliflower florets into sterilised jars and pour the spiced vinegar over them. Seal, label and store for at least two weeks before eating.

Sweet and Sour Cherries

1 kg (2 lb) cherries
1 cup brown sugar
3 cups wine vinegar
5 peppercorns
2 cloves
1 cinnamon stick
1 bay leaf

WASH the cherries and cut the stalks off to within 5 mm ($\frac{1}{4}$ in) of the fruit. Put the cherries into a dish and cover them with the sugar. Put the dish in a low oven (100°C; 200°F) and leave it there until the cherries begin to soften. Remove the dish from the oven and when the cherries are cooled, spoon them into warm sterilised jars.

At the same time, make a marinade by putting the vinegar, spices and bay leaf into a pan and bringing to the boil. Allow the marinade to cool, and pour it over the cherries to cover. Seal the jars well, label and keep the cherries for a fortnight before eating.

Damson Pickle

2 cups vinegar
1 cinnamon stick
1 teaspoon ground allspice
1 teaspoon grated nutmeg
1.5 kg (3 lb) damsons
$1\frac{1}{2}$ cups sugar

PUT the vinegar and spices into a saucepan and bring to the boil. Wash the damsons, remove the stalks and prick the fruit with a needle to prevent the skins from bursting. Pour the spiced vinegar over them and let them stand for 24 hours. Strain the vinegar off and put it into the pan with the sugar. Dissolve the sugar and bring to the boil. Pack the plums into warm sterilised jars and pour the syrup over to cover. Seal, label and store in a cool, dark place. They are ready to eat in 6 to 8 weeks.

Eggplant (Aubergine) Pickle

An excellent stand-by for snacks or lunches with cold meats, salads or bread. It also makes a great party dip.

1.5 kg (3 lb) eggplants
6 chillies, chopped
6 garlic cloves, crushed
1 tablespoon chopped ginger

Eggplant Pickle (this page) is very easy to make. When eggplants are cheap, put down a large quantity to last the year.

2 tablespoons mustard seeds
1 tablespoon ground coriander
1 teaspoon turmeric
2 teaspoons garam masala (page 85)
$\frac{1}{2}$ cup olive oil
1 teaspoon salt
$\frac{1}{2}$ cup sugar
1 cup wine vinegar

WASH the eggplants and cut them into halves lengthwise. Place them skin-down on an oven rack in a preheated oven at 200°C (400°F) for 45 minutes. Meanwhile, blend the chillies, garlic, ginger, mustard seeds, coriander, turmeric and garam masala in a food processor and set aside.

Peel the skins off the eggplants and purée them in the food processor. Put the oil, salt, sugar and vinegar into a saucepan and bring to the boil. Add the blended spices. Pour this liquid over the eggplant and mix well. Spoon the mixture into warm sterilised jars, seal and label.

Gift Tags

MAKE tags or labels to match your paper in a shape according to the theme of your gift, such as hearts for a wedding anniversary, an egg for Easter, a tree for Christmas or the initial of your friend's name. Cut them into these shapes or draw, stencil or paint the design on. Punch a hole to give a clean look when the tag is to be attached with silk cord, ribbon or string. Use any sort of paper or card that takes your fancy. There are usually scraps left over when wrapping presents so they can be utilised as labels. Keep all the scraps in a basket so that you always have some ready to use. See also the directions for making pressed flower cards on page 162 and printing papers on page 122.

Labels for Jars and Bottles

MAKE up your own label design, and write the name of the chutney or jam on it and the date. Cut it out and glue it on the cleaned jar with rubber solution. Vary the shapes: cut an outline of an apple for apple and mint jelly, a pumpkin for pumpkin jam. Trace my designs if you can't come up with any of your own. Look at the designs throughout my book to see if they are suitable for the jar in question.

Japanese Ginger Slices

Decorate the lid of the preserving bottle with a Japanese chopstick holder, and sit the bottle in a Japanese serving dish for the ginger to be served in. Substitute dry sherry for the rice vinegar if you cannot buy rice vinegar.

2 cups water
2 cups sliced ginger
1 cup rice vinegar
½ cup honey

BRING the water to the boil. Put the ginger in a bowl and pour the water over it. Let it stand for one minute, then drain. Put the vinegar and honey into a saucepan and cook until the honey has dissolved. Put the ginger into warm sterilised jars and pour the vinegar over it to cover. Seal and label. It will be ready to eat in three days.

Pickled Grapes

Pickled grapes go well with chicken and fish dishes.

3 cups seedless grapes.
2 tablespoons sugar
1 teaspoon salt
2 cups vinegar
1 tablespoon peppercorns
1 tablespoon allspice berries

WASH and destalk the grapes. Place the rest of the ingredients into a saucepan and bring to the boil. Remove from the heat and cool. Pack the grapes into sterilised jars and pour the spiced vinegar over them to cover. Seal and label.

Pickled Gherkins

Gherkins, or pickling cucumbers, are gathered green and small for preserving in vinegar. Watch out for them in the shops, as they are only marketed for a month or two.

1 kg (2 lb) gherkins
1 cup salt
1 cup small pickling onions
2 sprigs of tarragon
2 sprigs of thyme
3 chillies
1 tablespoon peppercorns
3 cups white wine vinegar

WASH the gherkins and put them into a bowl, sprinkling the salt over each layer. Leave them for 24 hours for the salt to draw the water out.

Drain and wash the gherkins. Pack them into sterilised jars along with the onions, tarragon, thyme, chillies and peppercorns. Cover with the vinegar, seal and label. They will be ready in 4 to 5 weeks.

Pickled Gherkins
with Fennel

1 kg (2 lb) gherkins (small pickling cucumbers)
1 cup salt
½ cup fennel sprigs
1 tablespoon horseradish shavings
1 teaspoon mustard seeds
1 tablespoon peppercorns
3 cups white wine vinegar

WASH and trim the gherkins. Place them in a bowl with the salt and leave to stand overnight.

Drain and wash the gherkins and pack them into sterilised jars, layering with the sprigs of fennel and horseradish shavings. Put the mustard seeds, peppercorns and vinegar into a saucepan and bring to the boil. Pour over the gherkins to cover. Seal and label the jars and store for about 4 weeks before eating.

RIGHT
These Spiced Pears (page 68) were made with tiny European pears. I made a huge jar of Spiced Apples (page 62) for a friend who gave me a case of apples from her tree.

Dressing Jars

Aттractive cloth or paper tops on the lids of jars with a pleasant label give a homemade gift an additional appeal. Trace circles around saucers or plates onto your fabric and cut out with scissors. Put a thin layer of rubber solution on the lid and centre of the fabric and stick it down. Now screw the lid on the jar and tie a ribbon or string around the edge of the lid. This way you can take the lid off and the decoration remains intact.

Pickled Onions

Red wine vinegar makes an interesting change to a perennial favourite. It also makes the picked onions look especially attractive, which is an important point when giving homemade gifts.

1 kg (2 lb) small onions
2 tablespoons salt
4 cups red wine vinegar
4 dried chillies
4 garlic cloves
½ cup mint leaves

BLANCH the onions in boiling water for several minutes, then drain them. This will make them easier to peel. Put the peeled onions in a large bowl and sprinkle the salt over them. Let them stand for several hours. Rinse the salt off, drain, and pat dry.

Put the vinegar into a pan with the chillies, garlic and mint leaves and bring to the boil. Simmer for 10 minutes. Pack the onions into warm sterilised jars and pour the vinegar over. Put a chilli and a clove of garlic into each jar. Seal, label and store for at least 5 weeks before eating.

Spiced Pears

These pears look very beautiful in an attractive bottle with a brown paper cover tied with string. They can be eaten as a dessert or with meats. If you can find the small European pears, keep them whole with the skin on. Prick each one eight times with a skewer through to the core.

1.5 kg (3 lb) firm pears
2 cups sugar
6 cinnamon sticks
1 teaspoon whole cloves
1 tablespoon chopped ginger
2 cups water
2 cups white wine vinegar

PEEL and thickly slice the pears. Put the remaining ingredients in a large saucepan and bring to the boil. Put in the pears and simmer until they begin to get tender. Take out the fruit and put into warm sterilised jars. Strain the pickling vinegar and pour over the pears. Seal and label and store in a cool, dark cupboard.

Piccalilli

The homeliest of the pickles, this was most likely the first pickle you ever ate, in a cold lamb sandwich. It is still delicious. I think the nicest way to serve it is with rare roast beef and freshly made wholemeal bread. Everyone loves getting a jar, so make plenty. Green beans and cucumbers are often added to the ingredients.

500 g (1 lb) small zucchini
   (courgettes)
125 g (4 oz) green tomatoes
3 cups cauliflower florets
500 g (1 lb) tiny onions, peeled
250 g (8 oz) cooking apples, peeled,
   cored and chopped
½ cup salt
5 chillies, chopped
3 cloves
6 cups vinegar
1 tablespoon chopped ginger
½ cup sugar
2 tablespoons English mustard
   powder
1 tablespoon turmeric
3 tablespoons cornflour

WASH and dry the vegetables and cut into bite-size pieces. Place in a large bowl, sprinkling with the salt, layer by layer. Leave for 24 hours.

Wash and drain the vegetables. Put the chillies and cloves into a muslin bag. Put it in a saucepan with 4 cups of the vinegar, the ginger and the sugar and bring to the boil. Add the vegetables and simmer for 10 minutes. Remove the vegetables and pack them into warm sterilised jars. Remove the muslin bag.

Mix the mustard, turmeric and cornflour to a smooth paste with the remaining vinegar. Add it to the saucepan, stirring gently, and bring back to the boil. Stir until the mixture has thickened. Pour it over the vegetables, seal and store.

Spiced Pineapple

A welcome gift, this spicy pineapple makes a perfect accompaniment to cold chicken or ham.

¾ cup water
4 tablespoons white wine vinegar
2 cinnamon sticks
10 peppercorns
2 cloves
1 tablespoon chopped ginger
1 cup sugar
500 g (1 lb) pineapple chunks

Put the water, vinegar, spices and sugar into a saucepan, heat and slowly dissolve the sugar. Add the pineapple and cook for about 15 minutes or until tender. Remove the pineapple and ladle it into a sterilised jar. Reduce the syrup by boiling it hard for a further 10 minutes, then strain it and pour it over the fruit, making sure the pineapple is completely covered. Seal and label. It can be eaten immediately chilled, or it will keep for weeks.

Sauerkraut

Your European friends will be delighted with a jar of homemade sauerkraut. It is far superior to the tinned variety. There are many different recipes, but I find this one is excellent. It enables me to change the flavour in different ways when I cook it. The only drawback to making your own is that it has a strong smell when it is fermenting. Make it in winter only, as it should be kept in a cool place.

2 kg (4 lb) cabbage
2 cups salt
2 tablespoons juniper berries

Remove the outer leaves and the stem of the cabbage. Slice it up finely, wash and drain. Sterilise an earthenware crock and line it with cabbage leaves or vine leaves. Lay down the sliced cabbage in layers. Sprinkling each layer with the salt and juniper berries.

Cover the surface with a clean tea-towel and put on top a wooden cover which is slightly smaller than the top of the crock. Keep this lid pressed down with a weight.

The next day liquid will have risen above the lid. Make sure this occurs. If it doesn't, add water to cover the lid. Keep the crock in an airy place. In about three weeks, when no more froth appears on top of the cabbage, the sauerkraut is ready. Replace the liquid with fresh water.

Always keep the sauerkraut covered with the cloth, wooden top and weight. After you have taken out some sauerkraut, add fresh water. Alternatively, you can keep it for a month in the refrigerator after transferring it into warm sterilised jars.

When giving jars of sauerkraut away as a gift, you could include the cooking instructions.

Cooking sauerkraut. To prepare sauerkraut for eating or cooking, rinse it, squash it thoroughly, and soak it in fresh water for 20 minutes. You can eat it uncooked or cook it in boiling water slowly for 2 hours; add a teaspoon of caraway seeds, a bay leaf and some black pepper. My husband's family from Hamburg cook it in champagne for festive occasions. Sliced apple or pineapple is a pleasant addition to sauerkraut. Serve it with frankfurts, sausages, ham or pork and boiled waxy potatoes.

Shallots in Vinegar

Shallots, or eschalots (not to be confused with spring onions, or scallions, which are often called shallots), can be difficult to find in the

markets all the year round, so it makes sense to put down a plentiful supply of shallots in vinegar. Their subtle flavour enlivens many a sauce to accompany meat and fish dishes. I think they make an even better pickle than onions.

1 kg (2 lb) shallots
6 bay leaves
A bunch of thyme
10 peppercorns
4 cups white wine vinegar

P EEL the shallots and wash them. Put them into sterilised jars with the bay leaves, sprigs of thyme and peppercorns. Bring the vinegar to the boil and then pour it over the shallots until it is almost to the top of the jars. Seal and label. They will be ready in three weeks, though they will last for months.

Green Tomato Pickle

2 kg (4 lb) green tomatoes
¼ cup salt
4 cups wine vinegar
2 tablespoons sugar
1 tablespoon mustard seeds
1 tablespoon garam masala (page 85)
6 chillies
2 cups thinly sliced onions

W ASH the tomatoes and slice thinly. Sprinkle with the salt and let stand overnight.

Put the vinegar, sugar, mustard seeds, garam masala and chillies into a saucepan and bring to the boil. Add the tomatoes and onions and simmer for 5 minutes. Remove from the heat and pack into warm sterilised jars, seal and label.

Piccalilli (page 68), Pickled Onions (page 68), Chinese Vegetable Pickles (this page) and Pickled Cauliflower (page 63). I often make large jars of pickles and ladle them into smaller jars when I want to give some away. It saves time on the pickling day, and there are often times when I have run out of small jars.

Chinese Vegetable Pickles

Pickled vegetables are an important preserve in Chinese cuisine. The Chinese even make special porcelain urns, like vases, to marinate their pickles in. This pickle makes enough to fill a gallon (4.5-litre) jar, if you have one. When giving the pickles away, simply ladle some vegetables and brine into a sterilised jar. You can replace them with more vegetables if you like. Just add a little salt and gin to strengthen the brine. The brine will last for three months, but the vegetables should not be kept for more than three weeks in the brine, as they loose their crispness.

2 cups green cabbage
1 cup carrot
2 cups white turnips
1 cup green beans
2 cups cucumber
2 cups broccoli
Brine
4 tablespoons salt
2 tablespoons Szechuan peppercorns
4 chillies
8 cups water
1 tablespoon sliced ginger
2 tablespoons gin

W ASH and dry the vegetables and cut them into large bite-size pieces. Put all the brine ingredients except the gin into a saucepan and bring to the boil. Remove from the heat, cool and add the gin. Pack all the vegetables into the sterilised jar, making sure they are all covered with the brine. Seal and keep refrigerated. They will be ready to eat in five to seven days.

Vegetable and Fruit Pickle

A very special pickle to make at the beginning of summer. This recipe will provide you with enough to fill plenty of jars to give away.

71

1 cup asparagus tips
1 cup baby carrots
1 cup radishes
1 cup quartered turnips
1 cup cubed celariac
1 cup cauliflower florets
1 tablespoon blanched almonds
1 cup cumquats
1 cup quartered small apples
1 cup mushrooms
½ cup salt
6 cups water
Marinade
6 cups wine vinegar
1 tablespoon coriander seeds
2 tablespoons grated ginger
2 tablespoons peppercorns
2 tablespoons mustard seeds
2 teaspoons chilli seeds
½ teaspoon saffron
1 tablespoon salt
2 cups olive oil

Wash all the vegetables and fruits and cut to similar sizes. Add the salt to the water and bring to the boil. Blanch the vegetables for one minute in the salted water, drain and place in a bowl.

To make the marinade, put the vinegar and all the spices into a large saucepan and bring to the boil. Let it stand for 10 minutes, then strain it onto the vegetables and fruit. Add the olive oil. When cool, spoon the vegetables and fruit into warm sterilised jars and cover with the marinade. Seal firmly and label. Let the jars stand in the sun for a fortnight, then store in a cool, dark place.

Torshi (Mixed Pickles)

In brine made with salt, water and vinegar, Torshi lasts up to two months refrigerated.

3 kg (7 lb) vegetables, made up of
  pickling cucumbers, carrots,
  cauliflower, capsicum (sweet
  pepper), small turnips, beetroots
  and green beans.

6 garlic cloves
6 chillies
3 teaspoons celery seeds
6 cups water
2 cups wine vinegar
½ cup salt

Wash and trim the vegetables and cut into bite-size pieces. Pack them into sterilised jars with the garlic, chillies and celery seeds.

Make the brine by bringing the water, vinegar and salt to the boil in a saucepan. Pour hot over the vegetables to cover. Seal the jars and store them in a warm place. The pickle should be ready in about two weeks.

Watermelon Chow
Chow

6 cups watermelon rind
2 green capsicums (sweet peppers),
  diced
1½ cups diced cucumber
2 tablespoons salt
2 cups sugar
3 cups white wine vinegar
1 teaspoon allspice
1 teaspoon mustard seeds
3 bay leaves

Cut the green skin off the rind of the watermelon. Cut the white rind into bite-size pieces and put them into a large bowl, sprinkling with salt as you layer. Put the capsicum and cucumber into another bowl, sprinkle with salt and pour water over to cover. Let all stand for 24 hours.

Strain the melon rind and vegetables and wash the salt off with several changes of fresh water. Drain. Put the sugar, vinegar and spices into a saucepan and bring to the boil. Add the melon rind and vegetables and simmer until the rind is tender (in 30 to 40 minutes). Remove from the heat and pack into warm sterilised jars, seal and label.

3 Herbs and Spices

For generations the art of creating flavour was, on the whole, forgotten or neglected. Recipes called for 'a pinch of cinnamon', ' garlic if liked', 'sprinkle with a teaspoon of dried parsley' or 'half a teaspoon of dried mixed herbs'. Even onions were suspect. Our rather bland English food was gradually transformed through the influence of Italian, French, Greek and Lebanese immigrants, bringing with them a tradition of European and Middle Eastern styles of food and flavourings—those herbs and spices which originally came from India and China. More recently we have begun another love affair with Thai, Vietnamese, Japanese and Malayan cuisines, and we are learning yet new ways to use those now familiar herbs and spices.

It is a very exciting development: so many new cuisines and methods of cooking basically the same raw ingredients with different combinations of herbs and spices! An example of this is a recipe for Thai green curry paste (page 85), which includes a method for cooking curry with it, using coconut milk. On the same page is a recipe for an Indian red curry paste, with the same cooking method but a different spice preparation and cooked in yoghurt instead of coconut milk.

In this chapter there are gift ideas for herbed and fruit vinegars, herbed and spiced oils, mustards, fruit and spicy sauces and spicy pastes—plenty of condiments to make everyday cooking life easier. A teaspoon of garam masala sprinkled on pumpkin soup gives it a greater depth of flavour and stimulates the appetite; all you have to do is take the jar from the fridge. Barbecue and plum sauces liven up the sausages and chops at a family get-together barbecue without your having to lift a finger. You suddenly realise it is your best friend's birthday! Not to worry: out comes some basil and chilli oil and some raspberry vinegar, already packed in attractive bottles; just tie a satin ribbon around the necks. The next-door neighbour saves your little moggy from a roaming tomcat—a pot of your honey spread will make a welcome thank-you present. I hope you will find lots of ideas in this tasty chapter.

Sauces are basically cooked the same way as chutneys, so a browse through the introduction to chapter 2, 'Preserving Fruit and Vegetables', will remind you of the basic principles: just ripe and unblemished fruit, sterilised jars and bottles, etc. Remember when preparing food for long storage, everything in the kitchen must be spotlessly clean.

Barbecue Sauce

There is always a warm welcome for this popular sauce, a perfect gift to take to a barbecue. It goes well with fish or meats.

3 tablespoons olive oil
3 onions, chopped
1 tablespoon tomato paste
1 cup cider vinegar
1 cup Worcestershire sauce
1 tablespoon chopped thyme
3 cloves garlic, chopped
3 tablespoons honey
2 tablespoons Dijon mustard
1 teaspoon salt
1 teaspoon pepper
$\frac{1}{4}$ teaspoon cayenne

PUT the oil in a saucepan and cook the onion until it is translucent. Add the tomato paste and vinegar, stirring all the time.

Cook for several minutes and add the remaining ingredients. Keep simmering until the sauce is smooth and thick. Spoon into sterilised bottles, seal and label. Store in the refrigerator.

Chilli Sauce

1 cup washed and finely chopped
  chillies
1 cup finely sliced onions
1 cup peeled, cored and sliced apples
Zest of half a lemon
2 teaspoons mustard seeds
1 teaspoon pepper
1 teaspoon salt
1 cup white wine vinegar

WHEN preparing the chillies, take care not to touch your eyes, and wash your hands afterwards. Put all the ingredients into a saucepan and cook until the sauce is soft and mushy. Blend in a food processor. If the sauce is a bit watery, put it back into the pan and boil, stirring until it has thickened. Pour into warm sterilised bottles, seal and label.

Garlic and Basil Sauce

This sauce will keep for several weeks refrigerated. It goes well with roast veal and lamb. Mix in half a cup of grated parmesan cheese just before serving to turn it into a pesto sauce for pasta.

4 cups basil leaves, washed
5 garlic cloves
2 tablespoons pine nuts
Salt and pepper
Olive oil

IN a food processor blend together the basil, garlic and pine nuts and season with salt and pepper. Gradually add olive oil until the sauce is smooth and thick. Spoon into a sterilised jar and pour a thin layer of olive oil over the surface to seal.

Mushroom Ketchup

The large open mushrooms, if you can get them, are the best for this ketchup. Don't wash the mushrooms, just wipe them with a damp cloth and trim off the ends of the stalks.

3 tablespoons salt
1 teaspoon pepper
1 teaspoon ground cinnamon
1 teaspoon ground cloves
1 kg (2 lb) mushrooms
1 tablespoon chopped ginger
1 tablespoon thyme
1 tablespoon marjoram
2 tablespoons tomato paste
1 cup vinegar

MIX the salt, pepper, cinnamon and cloves. Slice the mushrooms and layer them in a large open-mouthed bottle, sprinkling with the spiced salt. Let stand for 3 days in a cool place, covered.

Put the mushrooms into a saucepan with the rest of the ingredients. Bring to the boil and cook until the mushrooms are tender. Blend the sauce in a food processor and pour into sterilised bottles. Seal and label.

Spicy Plum Sauce (page 76) and Spicy Tomato Sauce (page 77) make popular presents to take to a barbecue. Both have a fresh tang that is an infinitely superior flavour to that of any commercial sauce.

Onion Sauce

A hearty sauce with all cold meats and cheese. It looks very attractive as a gift in small earthenware pots with lids. Pour over paraffin wax to seal.

1 kg (2 lb) onions
2 tablespoons olive oil
⅔ cup sugar
1½ cups malt vinegar
3 cloves
2 chillies, chopped
1 teaspoon thyme leaves
1 teaspoon pepper
1 teaspoon salt
2 tablespoons tomato purée

Peel and finely slice the onions. Put them in a saucepan with the olive oil and cook them until they become translucent. Add all the other ingredients and simmer until the sauce has thickened and become like a jam. Spoon it into warm sterilised bottles or pots, seal and label.

Orange Sauce

I created this sauce when I went to make a Cumberland sauce for a roast duck and discovered that I didn't have any redcurrant jelly. I had homemade marmalades on the shelf, so I substituted orange marmalade. It was delicious and harmonised well with the rich flavour of the duck.

1 lemon
2 shallots, finely sliced
1 cup orange marmalade
1 tablespoon Dijon mustard
1½ tablespoons red wine
½ cup port
Salt and pepper

PEEL the skin off the lemon with a vegetable peeler and cut the peel into julienne strips. Put the peel and the shallots into a saucepan, cover with water and bring to the boil. Simmer for 5 minutes and drain.

Melt the marmalade in a heavy-based saucepan. Stir in the mustard, red wine, port, shallots and lemon. Season with salt and pepper. Simmer for about 20 minutes or until the sauce begins to thicken. It is ready to serve immediately or can be stored in a sterilised jar and sealed. It will last for months stored in a cool, dark cupboard.

Peach Sauce

A wonderful rich sauce to serve with poultry and game or spooned over ice-cream.

1 kg (2 lb) peaches
Juice and zest of 2 lemons
10 basil leaves, tied together

Half a vanilla pod
500 g (1 lb) sugar
½ cup slivered almonds
2 tablespoons brandy

POUR boiling water over the peaches and leave them for a few minutes to make them easier to peel. Skin, stone and slice the peaches and put them into a saucepan with the lemon juice and zest, basil leaves and the vanilla pod. Cook gently until the peaches are tender.

Add the sugar and almonds and stir until the sugar has dissolved. Then boil rapidly for about 15 minutes or until setting point (see page 29) is reached. Remove the basil leaves. Stir in the brandy and ladle the sauce into warm sterilised bottles. Seal and label.

Spicy Plum Sauce

Another sauce that will last for years. This will make many gifts. But have you enough bottles to give away? Train your non-cooking friends and relations to save their empty bottles for you. After all, they will be rewarded.

3 kg (7 lb) plums
3 cups white wine vinegar
3 cups sugar
1 teaspoon salt
1 teaspoon pepper
1 teaspoon cayenne
1 tablespoon ground cloves
½ cup grated ginger

WASH the plums and remove the stalks. Put all the ingredients into a saucepan and simmer until the fruit is soft and tender and the stones have come away. Stir occasionally to prevent the fruit sticking. Strain the sauce through a coarse sieve, then spoon it into warm sterilised bottles, seal and label.

Spicy Tomato Sauce

It is worth while making a large quantity of this tomato sauce, as it lasts almost indefinitely. Buy a case of ripe tomatoes at the market. To make tomatoes easier to peel, pour boiling water over them and let them stand for five minutes.

5 kg (11 lb) tomatoes, peeled and
    chopped
4 cooking apples, peeled, cored and
    chopped
750 g (1½ lb) onions, finely sliced
15 garlic cloves, crushed
1 cup chopped ginger
2 tablespoons salt
2 cups sugar
5 cups white wine vinegar
2 bay leaves
5 chillies
1 teaspoon cayenne
1 tablespoon celery seeds
1 tablespoon mustard seeds
1 tablespoon pepper
2 cinnamon sticks

Put the tomatoes, apples, onions, garlic and ginger into a large saucepan and simmer for 3 hours. Leave overnight.

Blend the mixture through a food processor, then put it back in the saucepan along with the salt, sugar and vinegar and the bay leaves and spices tied up in a muslin bag. Bring to the boil and simmer for about an hour until the sauce is thick and smooth. Remove the muslin bag. Ladle the sauce into warm sterilised bottles, seal with paraffin wax and label. Allow the sauce to mature for four weeks before eating it. Refrigerate after opening a bottle.

Walnut and Garlic Sauce

This sauce can be used as a dip with crudité or a sauce with poultry and fish. It can also be turned into a pasta sauce by adding half a cup of ricotta cheese and a quarter of a cup of grated parmesan cheese to half a cup of the sauce. Add the cheeses just before serving.

1½ cups walnuts
4 garlic cloves
3 tablespoons chopped marjoram
1 teaspoon salt
1 teaspoon pepper
½ cup oil

Put the walnuts, garlic, marjoram, salt and pepper into a food processor and blend to a smooth paste. Gradually add in the oil and blend to a creamy sauce. Spoon into sterilised jars or pots, seal and label.

Blueberry Vinegar

An interesting new flavour to add to salads or sauces. Fruit vinegars are also excellent as a remedy for sore throats and colds. Add one tablespoon of vinegar and one tablespoon of sugar to a mug of hot water. A bit of brandy added may cure you even faster.

3 cups blueberries
9 cups white wine vinegar

Wash and mash the blueberries in a colander over a bowl and put the fruit and juice into a large jar. Pour the vinegar over and macerate for 8 days, stirring every day. Strain and bottle into sterilised bottles, seal and label.

Carnation Vinegar

Carnation vinegar is believed to relieve headaches. Sprinkle some on a handkerchief or a pillow and inhale. It is very refreshing to inhale, so sprinkle some around the bedroom of a sick friend.

2 tablespoons carnation petals
2 cups white wine vinegar

Infuse the petals and vinegar in a jar for a fortnight. Strain and filter into small bottles.

Vinegars are fun to make. It is interesting to watch the white wine vinegar gradually change colour. Blueberry Vinegar (page 77) makes a lovely cordial as well. Save and dry rose petals for making Red Rose Vinegar (this page) and Spicy Potpourri, (opposite page). An easy and attractive way to present this potpourri is to wrap it in balls made from two layers of different coloured tissue paper and tie with ribbons.

Red Rose Vinegar

A thoughtful Saint Valentine's Day gift. Use red or white wine vinegar depending on how colourful you want your vinegar to be.

1 cup red rose petals
8 cups wine vinegar

Wash the dried rose petals and dry. Macerate in the vinegar for 10 days. Stir each day. Strain into sterilised bottles, label and store.

Garlic Vinegar

Use in marinades and for flavouring potato salad.

24 garlic cloves, peeled and crushed
4 cups white wine vinegar

Put the garlic in a bottle and pour the vinegar over. Leave the bottle in a sunny spot for a month. Shake it every day. Strain the vinegar and pour it into a sterilised bottle, seal and label.

Herb Vinegar

A lovely vinegar to have with school prawns or fresh oysters, even with fish and chips.

8 cups white wine vinegar
4 shallots, finely chopped
2 garlic cloves, crushed
2 bay leaves
4 sprigs of thyme
2 sprigs of tarragon
10 black peppercorns, crushed
$\frac{1}{2}$ teaspoon salt

Put the vinegar into a saucepan and boil rapidly until it has reduced by half. Into a bowl mix all the other ingredients. Pour the vinegar into the bowl to cover the mixture and leave it to macerate for 4 hours. Strain the herbed vinegar into sterilised bottles. Decorate the bottles with fresh sprigs of herbs.

Orange Mint Vinegar

This makes a sweet change to mint sauce.

1 cup mint leaves
1 tablespoon sugar
1 teaspoon redcurrant jelly
Zest and juice of 1 orange
3 cups white wine vinegar

Put all the ingredients into a saucepan and bring to the boil. Remove from the heat and leave to macerate for 4 hours. Strain and pour into sterilised bottles, seal and label.

Raspberry Vinegar

I have included some fruit vinegars with the herbed vinegars, as they make a pleasant change. Raspberry vinegar has many uses as a vinegar as well as a syrup to add to sweet sauces and cool drinks. For a refreshing drink, add one tablespoon of raspberry vinegar to a cup of iced water.

1.5 kg (3 lb) fresh raspberries
4 cups white wine vinegar
Sugar as required

Wash the raspberries and place them in a large jar. Cover with the vinegar and allow to stand, covered, for 8 days. Stir gently every day.

Spicy Potpourri

This spicy potpourri is ready as soon as it is made. For giving away as a present, put it into a beautiful bowl and include the bowl as part of the gift. Or wrap in cellophane bags and tie with a ribbon. Make a box (instructions, page 159) and line it with tissue paper and store the potpourri in it.

20 cardamom pods
20 whole cloves
15 whole star anise
20 juniper berries
6 cinnamon sticks
8 whole nutmegs
$\frac{1}{2}$ cup dried orange and lemon peel
15 bay leaves
15 eucalyptus leaves
2 cups rose petals
1 cup chamomile
1 stick of lemon grass, cut into small pieces

Mix all the ingredients thoroughly with your hands and store.

Strain through a jelly bag. Measure the strained liquid by the cupful into a saucepan and for every 3 cups of liquid add 1 cup of sugar. Bring to the boil, stirring until the sugar has dissolved, and simmer for 10 minutes. Skim if necessary, then pour the raspberry vinegar into warm sterilised bottles.

Salad Vinegar

Chervil and salad burnet are sometimes hard to find, so when you come across them, make this vinegar so that you have the peppery flavours with you for the rest of the year and can share them with your friends.

1 cup tarragon
½ cup watercress
1 cup chervil
⅓ cup salad burnet
3 garlic cloves, crushed
1 chilli
1 teaspoon peppercorns
8 cups white wine vinegar

Put all the herbs and spices into a large wide-necked jar. Pour the vinegar over and allow to stand, covered, for 8 days in a sunny place. Strain and pour into sterilised bottles. Add a sprig of tarragon and salad burnet as a decoration, if you like. Seal and label.

Spiced Vinegar

Spiced vinegar can be used as a short cut in making chutneys and pickles. You only have to add the sugar and salt to the fruit and vegetables.

2 tablespoons peppercorns
1 tablespoon celery seeds
1 tablespoon mustard seeds
2 tablespoons chopped ginger
1 cinnamon stick
1 teaspoon nutmeg
4 chillies
3 garlic cloves
8 cups white wine vinegar

Tie the spices up in a muslin bag and put the bag into a saucepan with the vinegar. Bring to the boil and simmer for 15 minutes. Cool and store in a large jar for 4 weeks.

Remove the spice bag and pour into sterilised bottles, seal and label.

Tarragon Vinegar

Use this vinegar to add flavour to sauces, gravies and salad dressing. It is excellent for dipping fresh baby prawns into and to sprinkle over oysters, with just a twist of the pepper mill.

1 cup tarragon
3 cups red wine vinegar

Put the tarragon into a wide-mouthed jar and pour the vinegar over. Cover and allow it to stand in a sunny place for 3 weeks. Strain and pour into sterilised bottles. Add a fresh sprig of tarragon to each bottle as a decoration. Seal and label.

Thyme Vinegar

Thyme is an aromatic herb which is believed to help cleanse the blood. Thyme vinegar, besides being used in sauces and salad dressings, can be used as a disinfectant and, like smelling salts, as a cure for headaches.

1 cup thyme
4 cups white wine vinegar

Put the thyme into a wide-mouthed jar and pour the vinegar over. Cover and set in a sunny position for a month. Strain into sterilised bottles, seal and label.

RIGHT
In the large jar, Basil and Chilli Oil (page 82) is macerating until it is ready to be strained into smaller bottles. Spicy Herb Oil (page 82) makes a most attractive gift. I am always looking for unusual jars and bottles.

Basil and Chilli Oil

A thoughtful gift to bestow when basil is out of season. Sprinkle this oil on salads with lemon juice and serve with spicy dishes.

4 cups cold-pressed olive oil
1 cup basil leaves
1 tablespoon black pepper
10 chillies

PUT all the ingredients into a jar, cover and leave it in a cool, dark place for 30 days. Strain into sterilised bottles, seal and label. Decorate with a few chillies.

Spicy Herb Oil

A useful gift for a chilli addict. Sprinkle this oil over salads, pizzas or steamed vegetables.

1 tablespoon peppercorns
1 tablespoon coriander seeds
4 bay leaves
4 sprigs of rosemary
6 red chillies
1 teaspoon fennel seeds
4 cups cold-pressed olive oil

PUT all the spices and herbs into one or two sterilised bottles and pour the oil over them. Store in a cool, dark place. It is ready in 4 weeks.

Hazelnut Honey

A simple recipe for a honey spread for bread or toast. Buy a good-quality honey and label your honey accordingly—'Hazelnut and Clover Honey', 'Hazelnut and Ironbark Honey' or whatever. I fold it lightly through vanilla ice-cream and freeze again until serving.

1 cup hazelnuts
500 g (1 lb) honey
1 teaspoon ground cinnamon

CHOP the hazelnuts up in a food processor and mix them in with the honey and cinnamon. Pour into small sterilised jars or pots and cover.

Rose and Honey Syrup

This will make a thoughtful Saint Valentine's gift. The rose is the symbol of love and peace. Rose and honey syrup is also excellent for sore throats and colds as a gargle or a comforting, soothing drink: put one tablespoonful of the syrup in a mug and top it up with boiling water and a nobbler of gin. So if your lover has a cold on St Valentine's Day, save the champagne and try this syrup.

$\frac{1}{2}$ cup dried rosebuds
$\frac{1}{2}$ cup distilled water
1 kg (2 lb) honey

PUT the roses into a bowl and pour the boiling distilled water over them. Let the rose tea infuse for 5 hours. Strain the liquor off into a saucepan, then stir in the honey. Bring slowly to the boil and simmer until it is a thick syrup. Pour into sterilised bottles, seal and label.

French Mustard

$1\frac{1}{2}$ cups black mustard seeds
1 cup white wine vinegar
1 tablespoon chopped tarragon
1 tablespoon chopped thyme
1 cup olive oil
2 tablespoons honey
1 teaspoon salt
1 tablespoon grated ginger

GRIND the mustard seeds in a food mill or clean coffee grinder. Combine all the ingredients in a food processor and blend to a smooth paste. Pack the mustard into sterilised small jars or porcelain pots. Seal with cellophane as you do for jam. Label. Open in 2 weeks.

Grainy Mustard

The yellow mustard seeds are much stronger than the black, so this recipe is sharper than the previous one. As mustards need to mature and thicken, open two weeks after making.

½ cup yellow mustard seeds
½ cup black mustard seeds
1 tablespoon black peppercorns
1 cup olive oil
1 cup white wine vinegar
2 teaspoons chopped tarragon

GRIND the mustard seeds in a food mill or clean coffee grinder. Combine with all the other ingredients in a food processor and blend to a smooth paste. Spoon the mustard into sterilised jars or pots, cover and label.

Spicy Basil Sauce

A great addition to outdoor cooking. Basil sauce can be used as a dipping sauce or as a marinade for a barbecue. It goes especially well with fish, shellfish and chicken.

1 cup basil leaves, chopped
10 garlic cloves, chopped
2 tablespoons grated ginger
2 tablespoons chopped chillies
1 teaspoon salt
1 teaspoon pepper
1 teaspoon white wine vinegar
1 teaspoon sesame oil
1½ tablespoons oil
1½ tablespoons lemon juice

COMBINE all the ingredients in a food processor and blend to a smooth paste. Store in sterilised jars in the refrigerator with a layer of oil on the surface of the paste to seal it.

Chilli Sambal

½ cup chopped chillies
10 garlic cloves, crushed
1 tablespoon chopped ginger
1 onion, chopped
2 tablespoons honey
2 tablespoons white wine vinegar
⅔ cup water
1 teaspoon cornflour

PUT the chillies, garlic, ginger and onion in a food processor and blend to a paste. Put this in a saucepan with the honey and vinegar. Mix the water and cornflour together and gradually add it to the heated mixture. Bring to the boil and simmer until the sambal has thickened. Spoon it into small warm sterilised jars, bowls or pots. It is best kept refrigerated, and it will last over a month if you can resist eating it.

Fine Spices

A classic combination of pepper and spice. Use it for flavouring terrines, sausages and pies. A pinch of it in a winter's soup is soothing. It can be used much in the same way you use pepper. Sprinkled into a cup of hot water, it was known as a pepper posset and believed to ensure good health. Pepper is a stimulant and aids the digestion.

1 cup black peppercorns
¼ cup cloves
¼ cup nutmeg
½ cup ground ginger
1 tablespoon anise
1 tablespoon coriander seeds

GRIND the spices separately in a food mill or clean coffee grinder. Mix well and spoon into small jars or shallow earthenware dishes that would look nice on the table. Seal and label.

Spiced Salt

Spiced salt is used for the flavouring of charcuterie and stuffings and as a condiment to keep on the table.

2½ tablespoons pepper
1 cup salt
2 tablespoons fine spices (above)

GRIND the pepper in a food mill or pepper grinder and then combine with the salt and fine spice. Mix well and store in small jars or pots. Seal tightly.

Chinese Five-Spice
Powder

It is well worth while investing in a food mill or keeping a coffee grinder just for spices. The difference in taste and aroma between your own freshly ground spices and those stale old powdered spices you buy in packets is enormous. Friends who are too busy to go to a lot of trouble will be especially pleased to receive gifts of your freshly prepared spice powders.

1 tablespoon peppercorns
1 tablespoon star anise

Homemade spicy pastes and powders make curries much faster to prepare. They last to up to six months and taste much fresher than any bought products. The recipes for Thai Green Curry Paste, Harissa, and Garam Masala are on the opposite page.

2 cinnamon sticks
1 tablespoon whole cloves
1 tablespoon fennel seeds

GRIND the spices in a food mill or coffee grinder. Mix well and store in small jars or pots.

Garam Masala

2 tablespoons cardamom seeds
2 tablespoons coriander seeds
1 cinnamon stick
1 tablespoon peppercorns
1 tablespoon cumin seeds
1 tablespoon cloves
1 nutmeg

ROAST separately the cardamom, coriander, cinnamon, peppercorns, cumin and cloves in a dry pan. As the aroma rises, take them off the heat. Remove the husks from the cardamom seeds. Grind all the spices finely in a food mill or coffee grinder. Mix well and grate the nutmeg over the mixture. Store in airtight containers.

Red Curry Paste

1 tablespoon cumin seeds
1 tablespoon peppercorns
1 tablespoon coriander seeds
½ cup chopped red chillies
2 onions, chopped
4 garlic cloves, crushed
3 tablespoons oil
2 tablespoons lemon juice
1 teaspoon turmeric

GRIND the cumin, peppercorns and coriander in a food mill. Combine all the ingredients in a food processor and blend to a smooth paste. Add more oil if necessary. Store in sterilised jars with a layer of oil on the surface and keep refrigerated.

A fast way to make a curry. Just take a tablespoon of red curry paste and put it in a pan with a little oil. Stir for a few minutes and add a chopped onion, a garlic clove, and a cup of chopped mint or coriander leaves. Stir in a chopped tomato and a cup of low-fat yoghurt. Keep stirring for a few minutes, then add lamb or chicken pieces for four. Coat with the sauce; adjust seasoning. Cover and simmer slowly for 60 minutes or until tender.

Green Curry Paste

1 tablespoon coriander seeds
1 teaspoon cardamom seeds
1 tablespoon peppercorns
⅓ cup chopped green chillies
1 small onion, chopped
5 garlic cloves, crushed
1 cup chopped fresh coriander,
    including the washed root
Rind of half a lemon, chopped
1 teaspoon chopped lemon grass
1 teaspoon laos powder
1 teaspoon dried shrimp paste
1 teaspoon turmeric
1 teaspoon salt
2 tablespoons oil

GRIND the coriander and cardamom seeds and the peppercorns in a food mill. Put all the ingredients into a food processor and blend to a smooth paste. Spoon into sterilised jars and pour a layer of oil over the surface of the paste. Cover and store in the refrigerator.

To make a fast Thai curry: Follow the method given with the recipe for the preceding red curry paste, but replace the yoghurt with 2 cups of coconut milk and use green curry paste.

Harissa

This is a hot paste from north Africa.

1 tablespoon coriander seeds
1 tablespoon caraway seeds
1 tablespoon peppercorns
1 cup chopped red chillies
20 garlic cloves
2 tablespoons mint leaves
3 tablespoons fresh coriander leaves
1 teaspoon salt
4 tablespoons oil

GRIND the coriander and caraway seeds and the peppercorns in the food mill. Then put all the ingredients in a food processor and blend to a thick paste. Keep in sterilised bottles in the refrigerator. Pour a seal of oil over the surface after each time you use the paste.

4 Main Courses

In this chapter I have written recipes for large meat and fish dishes for any festive occasion likely to arise. Most dishes are cold, but some can be heated up at the party location. All were chosen for their easiness to transport and because time improves their flavour. There are tarts and pies, terrines and pâtés, sausages, hams, jellied dishes, cold meats, poached fish and mayonnaise dishes.

They could be accompanied by jams, chutneys and pickles from chapter 2 or by sauces and mustards in chapter 3. Arrange them on attractive plates and garnish them when you get to the party. I usually take sharp knives along just in case, as there is nothing worse than trying to carve your wonderful salt-cured leg of lamb with a blunt instrument. Transport the dishes in a portable ice box, as it is unlikely your hosts will have any room in their refrigerator for yet another large dish.

Cheese Tart

With its rustic looks and origins, this is perfect to take as a contribution to a picnic.

Pastry
3 cups flour
1 egg
1 teaspoon salt
7 g ($\frac{1}{4}$ oz) dry yeast
Filling
$\frac{1}{2}$ cup diced bacon
1 cup chopped onions
1 tablespoon butter
1 tablespoon olive oil
1 cup cottage cheese
1 teaspoon salt
1 teaspoon pepper
1 teaspoon chopped sage leaves
$\frac{1}{2}$ cup grated gruyère cheese

To prepare the pastry. Sift the flour into a bowl and make a well in the centre. Add the egg, salt and yeast dissolved in a little warm water. Knead, adding more warm water if necessary. When the pastry is completely smooth, roll it into a ball and cover it with a floured tea-towel. Leave it in a cool place for an hour.

Filling. Fry the bacon and onions in the butter and oil until the onions are translucent. Blend the cottage cheese smooth in a food processor and season with salt, pepper and sage.

Roll out the dough in a circle about 6 mm ($\frac{1}{4}$ in) thick. Put it on a well-greased baking tray in a preheated oven at 250°C (475°F) for 5 minutes. Take it out and sprinkle the bacon and onion mixture over it, then spread the cheese mixture over the top. Sprinkle the gruyère cheese on top and put the tart back in the oven for about 15 minutes.

Onion Tart

This is delicious served cold or at room temperature. Accompanied by a salad, it makes a tasty luncheon dish.

Pastry
2½ cups flour
½ teaspoon salt
150 g (5 oz) butter
1 egg, beaten

Filling
2 cups finely chopped onions
1 tablespoon butter
2 cups fresh cream cheese (page 19)
¼ teaspoon salt
½ teaspoon pepper
1 teaspoon chopped thyme
4 eggs

To MAKE THE PASTRY. Sift the flour and salt into a bowl and make a well in the centre. Add the butter in small pieces. Rub it into the flour until it resembles breadcrumbs. Add the egg. Knead until the dough is very smooth. Shape it into a ball and cover with a floured tea-towel. Let it stand in a cool place for an hour.

Roll out the pastry and line a well-greased flan dish. Rest for half an hour. Bake blind for 20 minutes in an oven preheated to 190°C (375°F). (To bake blind, cover the pastry with greaseproof paper and fill the flan with dried beans to prevent the pastry expanding out of shape. Remove the paper and beans when it has cooled.)

Filling. Put the onions and butter into a pan and cook until the onions are translucent. Drain them on kitchen paper.

Mix the fresh cheese with the salt, pepper and thyme in a bowl and blend until smooth. Add the onions.

Separate the eggs. Whisk the yolks and separately beat the whites until smooth. Add the yolks to the onion and cheese mixture and gently fold in the eggwhites. Pour the mixture into the pastry shell. Bake in a preheated oven at 220°C (430°F) for about 40 minutes.

Pissaladière

This is a French version of the Italian pizza. There are almost as many versions of it as there are pizzas. Experiment—brush on a layer of tomato paste before adding the onions and anchovies, or sprinkle with gruyère cheese as a final topping.

Pastry
2 cups flour, sifted
1 teaspoon salt
1 teaspoon sugar
7 g (¼ oz) dry yeast
¾ cup warm water
3 tablespoons olive oil

Filling
3 cups finely sliced onions
2 tablespoons olive oil
3 garlic cloves, chopped
2 teaspoons chopped rosemary
1 teaspoon pepper
½ teaspoon salt
6 anchovy fillets
20 black olives, stoned and quartered
1 tablespoon rosemary to garnish

To MAKE THE PASTRY. Put the flour, salt and sugar into a bowl. Mix the yeast with the warm water. Make a well in the flour and pour in the yeast mixture and olive oil. Knead to a dough until it is light and elastic. Shape it into a ball, cover with a floured tea-towel and leave in a warm place for an hour. It will double its size.

Filling. Put the onions and oil into a pan and cook until they are very soft and translucent. Add the garlic, rosemary, pepper and salt and simmer for half an hour.

Roll out the dough into a round or rectangular shape. Put it on a well-greased baking tray. Spoon over the onion mixture and smooth it down. Arrange the anchovies in a criss-cross pattern and dot the surface with the black olives. Sprinkle the rosemary over. Bake in a preheated oven at 230°C (450°F) for 20 to 30 minutes or until it is golden and crisp.

ABOVE
A perfect start to a picnic lunch accompanied by a glass of Grape Ratafia (page 151). The recipe for Onion Tart is on page 87.

RIGHT
The Raised Pie (this page) in the foreground and the Ham and Veal Pie (page 90) were contributions to a large luncheon party.

Raised Pie

A most spectacular looking dish to present as a gift or as an offering for a buffet supper.

Pastry
2½ cups flour
1 teaspoon salt
4 tablespoons water
⅔ cup butter, soft
1 egg, beaten
Filling
750 g (1½ lb) pork belly

6 rashers of bacon, diced
1 teaspoon chopped thyme
1 teaspoon chopped sage
1 teaspoon chopped parsley
2 bay leaves
1 onion, chopped
2 garlic cloves, crushed
1 teaspoon salt
1 teaspoon pepper
1 cup thick veal stock
1 egg

To MAKE THE PASTRY. Sift the flour and salt into a bowl and make a well in the centre. Rub the butter into the flour until it resembles breadcrumbs. Add the cold water, butter and egg and gradually work into the dough, mixing as fast as possible. Keep kneading until the paste is smooth. Wrap in plastic and refrigerate for 2 hours.

Roll out the pastry and line a pie mould, leaving a quarter of the pastry for the lid.

Filling. Mince half the pork belly and cut the rest into strips. Mix the minced pork with the bacon, herbs, onion, garlic, salt and pepper. Lay down a layer on the pastry, then a layer of the strips of pork. Keep layering until the pie is full. Put on the pastry cover, pinch the edges together and decorate the top with pastry roses and leaves. Put a few slashes into the pastry to let the steam out. Brush the cover with an eggwash to glaze it. Make the eggwash from the egg and half an eggshell of water. Mix well. Cook in a preheated oven at 180°C (360°F) for 1½ hours. When the pie has cooled, warm the veal stock and pour it into one of the vents. Store in the refrigerator.

Chicken Pie

Chicken pie is very special family dish. It is the perfect gift to take along to a family get-together for Mother's Day or a birthday. It tastes delicious cold with its chicken jelly adding moisture.

Pastry
See the recipe for Raised Pie
(opposite)

Filling
2 slices raw ham
2 bay leaves
750 g (1½ lb) boneless chicken meat
½ cup chopped celery
1 cup chopped mushrooms
1 tablespoon chopped rosemary
1 tablespoon chopped parsley
1 onion
2 garlic cloves, crushed
1 teaspoon spiced salt (page 83)
1 teaspoon pepper
1 cup chicken stock
1 sachet gelatine
1 egg

Mᴀᴋᴇ the pastry as for Raised Pie. Roll it out and line a pie dish, leaving one-third of the pastry for the lid to cover. Lay the ham and bay leaves on the bottom of the pie. Place the chicken meat in layers in the pie, sprinkling celery, mushrooms, herbs, onion, garlic, salt and pepper as you layer. Bring the chicken stock to the boil and mix in the gelatine. Pour over the chicken. Cover with the pastry crust. Pinch the edges well and slash some vents to allow the steam to get out. Brush the cover with an eggwash made from an egg and half an eggshell of water; mix well. Cook in a preheated oven at 180°C (360°F) for 1½ hours.

Ham and Veal Pie

Eat this festive pie cold; it tastes best after two days. It looks wonderful on a winter's picnic table.

Pastry
See the recipe for Raised Pie
   (page 88)
Filling
300 g (10 oz) ham or pickled pork,
   diced
500 g (1 lb) veal, diced
1 cup white wine
1 cup finely chopped onions
3 garlic cloves, chopped
½ cup brandy

2 tablespoons chopped thyme
2 bay leaves
½ cup chopped parsley
1 teaspoon salt
1 teaspoon pepper
1 egg, beaten
1 cup veal stock (optional)
1 sachet gelatine (optional)
1 egg

Mᴀᴋᴇ the pastry as for Raised Pie and leave for two hours in the refrigerator wrapped in plastic film. At the same time marinate the ham and veal in the wine with the onion, garlic, brandy, thyme, bay leaves, parsley, salt and pepper.

Roll out the pastry and line a pie dish with two-thirds of it; reserve one-third for the cover. Add the egg to the meat mixture and then pack the mixture into the pie dish. Cover with the pastry lid, pinching the edges together. Decorate with pastry leaves. Slash a few vents to allow steam out during the cooking. Brush the cover with eggwash made from the egg and half an eggshell of water; mix well. Cook in a preheated oven at 180°C (360°F) for 1½ hours. The pie cover should be browned.

Cool for half an hour. If there is still room for more liquid, heat the veal stock and dissolve the gelatine in it. Pour it through a vent to bring the liquid neatly to the top of the pie.

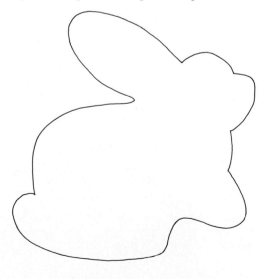

Mutton Pie

A friend gave me this recipe for an old-fashioned mutton pie from her great-grandmother's collection of recipes, written when she helped run a vast property.

Pastry
See the recipe for Raised Pie
    (page 88)
Filling
750 g (1½ lb) mutton or lamb, diced
1 cup chopped onion
2 garlic cloves, crushed
1 tablespoon curry powder
1 tablespoon chopped rosemary
1 teaspoon salt
1 teaspoon pepper
1 cup lamb or chicken stock

MAKE the pastry as for Raised Pie, roll it out and line a pie dish; reserve a quarter of the pastry for the cover. Mix together the lamb, onion, garlic, curry powder, rosemary, salt and pepper. Pack the mixture into the pie case until it reaches the top. Roll out the remaining pastry and cover the pie, pinching the edges together. Cut a hole in the centre. Decorate the cover with curls and leaves and brush with an eggwash as described in Raised Pie (page 89). Cook in a preheated oven at 180°C (360°F) for 1½ hours or until well browned.

Cool the pie for half an hour, then warm the stock and pour it through the hole until the pie is filled.

Pork and Veal Terrine

Terrines make beautiful presents given away with the terrine dish. There are many shapes and sizes with imaginative lids. Watch out for them in antique shops as well as kitchen supply shops. They will become heirlooms.

1 kg (2 lb) pork and veal mince
1 cup chopped bacon
2 onions, chopped
3 garlic cloves, crushed
2 cups fresh breadcrumbs
3 tablespoons brandy
3 eggs, beaten
2 tablespoons Dijon mustard
6 juniper berries, crushed
1 tablespoon salt
1 tablespoon fine spices (page 83)
1 tablespoon chopped thyme
1 tablespoon chopped tarragon
1 cup clear stock
1 tablespoon gelatine
6 bay leaves
Sprigs of thyme and tarragon to
    garnish

COMBINE all the ingredients except for the last four in a large bowl and mix well. Pack the mixture into a greased terrine dish. Smooth the top and cover with a lid or foil. Place the dish into a bain-marie or baking dish with 2.5 cm (1 in) of boiling water in it. Bake in a preheated oven at 180°C (360°F) for 1½ hours or until it is thoroughly cooked. Remove from the heat and cool.

Bring the stock to the boil and simmer. Add the gelatine and stir until it thickens. Arrange the bay leaves, thyme and tarragon lavishly across the top of the terrine and pour the gelatine stock over the herbs. Don't move the terrine until it is set. Keep refrigerated.

Rabbit Pâté

500 g (1 lb) rabbit
Rabbit liver
500 g (1 lb) pork belly
4 bacon rashers
1 tablespoon chopped parsley
1 tablespoon chopped marjoram
½ cup fresh breadcrumbs
60 g (2 oz) butter
⅓ cup finely chopped onions
1 egg, beaten
4 juniper berries
1 teaspoon salt
1 teaspoon peeper
2 garlic cloves, chopped
3 tablespoons port

Dɪᴄᴇ half the meats. Mince the rest through a food processor along with the herbs and breadcrumbs.

Melt the butter in a saucepan and cook the onions until translucent. Combine the meats, onion, beaten egg, juniper berries, salt, pepper, garlic and port. Mix thoroughly and pack the mixture into a large terrine or several small terrine dishes. Cover with the lid or aluminium foil and put into a baking dish of hot water. Bake in a preheated oven at 180°C (360°F) for 1 to 1½ hours, depending on the size of the terrine. Test with a needle; it comes out clean when the pâté is cooked. If you would like the surface browned, take the lid off 15 minutes before the end of the cooking time. If you prefer to decorate the top with herbs and jelly, see the instructions for Pork and Veal Terrine on page 91.

Pâté de Campagne

A classic cold meat dish to serve at a picnic.

500 g (1 lb) minced pork
500 g (1 lb) minced veal
300 g (10 oz) minced bacon
250 g (8 oz) pig's liver
3 cloves of garlic, crushed
Salt and pepper
1 teaspoon ground allspice
4 juniper berries
½ cup brandy
4 bacon rashers
2 bay leaves

Pᴜᴛ all the pork, veal and bacon mince into a mixing bowl. Remove the skin from the liver and mince in a food processor. Add it and the garlic, salt and pepper, allspice, juniper berries and brandy to the bowl and mix well.

Line the terrine dish with the bacon slices, leaving enough hanging over the side to cover the top. Press the meats in and arrange the bay leaves on top, then cover with the ends of the bacon slices.

Put the lid on and place in a bain-marie or baking dish with 2.5 cm (1 in) of water in it. Place in a preheated oven at 180°C (360°F) for 1½ hours. Press the pâté down with a weight until it is cold in order to compress the meats and obtain the delicious jellied juices. Refrigerate.

Pork Liver Pâté

This is a large quantity, so fill several small terrines or cook in preserving jars to give away as gifts. They will keep well in the refrigerator if the lids of the preserving jars are firmly sealed with new rubber rings.

1 kg (2 lb) pig's liver
300 g (10 oz) lean pork
750 kg (1½ lb) belly of pork
6 shallots
2 tablespoons sherry
2 garlic cloves, chopped
1 tablespoon chopped thyme
1 tablespoon chopped marjoram
1 teaspoon salt
1 teaspoon fine spices (page 83)
3 tablespoons cornflour
6 bay leaves
100 g (3½ oz) pork fat

Mɪɴᴄᴇ all the ingredients except for the last two in a food processor. Make sure the mixture is fine and smooth. Put it into a large greased terrine dish or fill several lidded heat-proof glass storage jars, leaving 2.5 cm (1 in) space at the top. Arrange the bay leaves on top. Cover the containers with their lids or aluminium foil and place them in a bain-marie or a baking dish containing 2.5 cm (1 in) of water. Place in a preheated oven at 200°C (400°F). The smaller jars should take about an hour and a large terrine 1½ to 1¾ hours. The pâté is cooked when you can insert a skewer into the centre of the terrine

Pâté de Campagne (this page), baked in a splendid duck terrine, makes a very special present.

and it comes out clean. Remove the lids and put a weight on top while it cools. When it is cold, pour the melted pork fat over the surface to seal the terrine.

Chicken Liver Pâté

250 g (8 oz) chicken livers
125 g (4 oz) butter
1¼ cup finely chopped onion
3 tablespoons brandy
2 garlic cloves, crushed
1 teaspoon parsley
1 teaspoon chopped chives
1 teaspoon chopped thyme
1 teaspoon orange rind
1 teaspoon salt
1 teaspoon pepper
Chives to garnish

CLEAN the livers, removing any yellow spots. Wash and chop them. Melt half the butter in a saucepan and cook the onion until it is translucent. Add the livers, brandy, garlic, herbs, orange, salt and pepper. Stir well and cook, covered, for another 4 minutes.

Remove from the heat and blend in a food processor. Pour into pâté pots or small soufflé dishes. Smooth the surfaces and garnish with chopped chives. Melt the remaining butter and pour over the surface of the terrines to seal.

Potted Beef

1 kg (2 lb) lean beef
1 kg (2 lb) lean pork
Vine leaves
6 bay leaves
1 teaspoon chopped thyme
1 teaspoon chopped marjoram
1 teaspoon juniper berries, crushed
1 teaspoon spiced salt (page 83)
1 teaspoon pepper
1½ cups red wine
1 cup lard

SLICE the beef and pork. Grease an earthenware pot or terrine dish and line it with vine leaves. Put the bay leaves on the bottom and place in layers of the meat, sprinkling with the herbs and spices as you go. Pour in the wine—just enough to cover the meat.

Put the dish into an oven preheated to 180°C (360°F) for 1½ hours or until the contents have reduced by half. When it has cooled, melt the lard and pour over the meat to seal it. Cover with waxed paper and keep refrigerated.

Lamb Meat Loaf

Shoulder of lamb is the most tender, but it requires patience to cut up and take all the fat off. Present the meat loaf in the loaf tin, which makes it easy to transport. To add a touch of extravagance, wrap your gift in a new tea-towel and tie it with thick gardening string.

1 kg (2 lb) lamb shoulder
1½ cups breadcrumbs
1 egg
1 teaspoon Tabasco sauce
3 tablespoons white wine
1 tablespoon Dijon mustard
1 tablespoon honey
1 tablespoon chopped rosemary
1 tablespoon chopped parsley
3 garlic cloves, crushed
1 teaspoon salt
1 teaspoon pepper
5 or 6 bacon rashers, rinds removed.

MINCE the lamb and put it into a bowl with the other ingredients except for the lard. Mix well. Line a loaf tin with the bacon rashers, leaving enough hanging over the edges to cover the meat. Pack in the meat mixture and cover with the overhanging bacon rashers. Bake for 1 hour in an oven preheated to 180°C (360°F). Check if it is cooked by inserting a thick needle; if it comes out clean, the meat is done. Remove from heat and place a weight on top while it cools. Refrigerate.

Jellied Ham

One of the most spectacular and delicious ways to serve ham. This dish will make any table or picnic a festive occasion. It can also be made in a cheaper but just as tasty version using cooked pickled leg of pork instead of ham.

2 cups veal stock
1 cup dry white wine
1 kg (2 lb) cooked ham, cubed or
   shredded
1 teaspoon black pepper
1 cup chopped parsley
2 tablespoons gelatine
½ cup hot water
1 tablespoon tarragon vinegar

Bring the stock and wine slowly to the boil. Add the ham and pepper and cook for 10 minutes. Drain and reserve the liquid. Put the ham into a glass bowl, adding parsley to each layer. Soften the gelatine in the hot water and stir it into the reserved liquid until it dissolves, then add the rest of the parsley and vinegar. When the liquid is cool, pour it over the ham. Refrigerate until serving. It may be served in the bowl or unmoulded.

Jellied Veal Loaf

2 kg (4 lb) knuckle of veal in 2 or 3
   pieces
A bouquet garni of thyme, tarragon
   and parsley
1 onion
1 teaspoon salt
1 teaspoon pepper
4 hard-boiled eggs
1 cup chopped parsley
1 tablespoon capers
1 teaspoon fine spices (page 83)

Cook the veal in enough cold water to cover it. Remove the scum and add the bouquet garni, onion, salt and pepper. Simmer for 2 hours. Take the meat out of the pan and, when cool enough to handle, chop it finely. Strain and reserve the stock.

Slice the eggs and decorate the bottom of a bowl with them. Cover in layers with the veal, parsley, capers and fine spices. Reduce the stock by fast boiling until it is half its size. Pour over the meat. Lay a weight on top to keep the meat pressed down. When the jelly is set, store in the refrigerator.

Jellied Chicken

Present this in the mould it was made in, for easy transport. Decorate the top with a few sprigs of watercress and wrap in clear cellophane.

1 large chicken
1 onion
2 carrots
2 stalks of celery
A bouquet garni of bay leaf, thyme
   and parsley
1 teaspoon salt
1 teaspoon pepper
1 cup watercress sprigs
½ cup chives
Spiced salt (page 83)
2 gelatine sachets
2 tablespoons sherry

Put the chicken in a pot with enough water to cover. Bring to the boil, remove the scum and add the vegetables, herbs, salt and pepper. Simmer until the chicken is tender, about 1 hour.

Remove the chicken, strain the stock and boil fast until it is reduced to about 3 cups.

Meanwhile, remove the best meat from the chicken and shred it. Layer it into a bowl or mould, sprinkling watercress sprigs, chives and spiced salt over the layers. Dissolve the gelatine in the stock, add the sherry and pour over the chicken to cover. Lay a weight on top to keep the chicken pressed down. Store in the refrigerator when cold, after removing the weight.

Sausages can be made with endless variations of meats, herbs and spices. On the left are Pork and Sage Sausages; Spicy Beef Sausages are on the right (the recipes are on the opposite page). The fiery Harissa (page 85) on the far left is used to flavour the spicy beef. If you haven't time to make sausages, use the mixtures for meat balls and rissoles.

96

Pork and Sage Sausages

Traditional pork and sage sausages are not difficult to make, though I'd advise having a helper for stuffing the sausages at your first attempt. Keep everything sterile. Use this mixture to make meatballs and rissoles.

1 kg (2 lb) lean pork
500 g (1 lb) pork belly
1 tablespoon salt
1 teaspoon pepper
1 teaspoon fine spices (page 83)
1 cup breadcrumbs
½ cup red wine
1 tablespoon chopped sage
2 tablespoon chopped parsley
Sausage casings

MINCE the meat and put it into a bowl with all the other ingredients. Mix well. Soak the sausage casings in warm water, then hold them under a cold tap to let the water run through. First knot one end, then tie the other to a large funnel and ram in the meat mixture, or use a sausage-filling machine. Twist the casings at intervals and pierce with a fine needle to let the air escape. Knot the top end and hang up in a cool place for 24 hours, then refrigerate. They won't last longer than 4 days. If it is hot weather, refrigerate immediately.

Spicy Beef Sausages

You will be the star of the barbecue with these fiery sausages. Take some extra harissa (page 85) along for brave souls and chutney for everyone else. Serve in warmed pita bread with a yoghurt and cucumber salad to cool down the chilli.

500 g (1 lb) beef
1 teaspoon harissa
½ teaspoon chopped thyme
½ teaspoon chopped oregano
1 teaspoon chopped parsley
⅓ cup breadcrumbs
1 tablespoon tomato paste
1 teaspoon salt

1 teaspoon pepper
Sausage casings

MINCE the beef and combine all the ingredients in a bowl. Mix well. Push the mixture into the sausage casings as described in the recipe for Pork and Sage sausages and follow the further instructions.

Both these recipes work just as well with lamb.

Pork and Beef Sausages

Robust meat sausages for a hearty eater. They taste best char-grilled or barbecued. The finer the ingredients, the finer the sausages will taste, so try making them with minced leg of pork and rump steak.

750 g (1½ lb) pork mince
250 g (8 oz) beef mince
3 garlic cloves
1 tablespoon spiced salt (page 83)
2 tablespoons paprika
1 tablespoon pepper
1 tablespoon sugar
Sausage casings

MIX all the ingredients together well. Push the mixture into the sausage casings as described in the recipe for Pork and Sage Sausages on this page and follow the instructions from there on.

Chicken Mayonnaise

This is always a popular dish at a picnic. It is easy to transport in a plastic container or, better, a wooden bowl. On very hot days I make a yoghurt dressing, which is lighter than mayonnaise: take a cup of plain yoghurt, squeeze in the juice of a lemon, add pepper and a little Dijon mustard and mix well.

1 large chicken
A bouquet garni of bay leaf, thyme, tarragon, parsley and carrot
1 teaspoon salt

1 tablespoon pepper
2 stalks celery, chopped
2 apples, sliced
1 cup walnuts
$\frac{1}{2}$ cup chopped chives
Watercress
Mayonnaise
2 egg yolks
1 teaspoon salt
1 tablespoon Dijon mustard
1 cup olive oil
1 tablespoon lemon juice

Put the chicken into a saucepan and cover with water. Add the bouquet garni, salt and pepper. Cover the saucepan and slowly bring the water to the boil. Simmer the chicken for 50 to 60 minutes until tender. Take off the heat and leave to cool in the stock.

When cool, shred the chicken into a bowl. Add the celery, apples, walnuts, chives and mayonnaise. Mix gently, garnish and serve with sprigs of watercress.

To make the mayonnaise: Put the egg yolks into a bowl, add the salt and mustard and mix well. Add the oil, drop by drop, until it begins to emulsify, then you can put the oil in faster. Add the lemon at the end with a wooden spoon.

Chicken in a Bread Loaf

This is an old recipe from the Middle East. It looks very beautiful and is easy to transport. Choose a loaf with an attractive shape. When presenting it as a gift, decorate it with fresh herbs, flowers and pistachio nuts.

1 large chicken
A bouquet garni
Pepper and salt
$\frac{1}{2}$ cup dried apricots
1 bread loaf
1 cup chicken liver
1 teaspoon butter
1 teaspoon ground cinnamon
1 teaspoon ground cumin

$\frac{1}{4}$ teaspoon ground cloves
1 teaspoon pepper
1 teaspoon salt
3 tablespoons chopped pistachio nuts
3 tablespoons chopped parsley
1 tablespoon chopped mint
2 tablespoons lemon juice
Herbs for garnish

Cook the chicken in water with the bouquet garni, pepper and salt the same way as for Chicken Mayonnaise (page 97). Strain the stock and reserve. Soak the apricots in a cup of stock.

Cut off the top or side of the loaf and keep it aside. Take out all the soft bread from within the loaf, leaving the crust whole.

Shred the chicken into bite-size pieces into a bowl. Remove any yellow pieces from the chicken livers and cook the livers in butter for a few minutes. Add half a cup of chicken stock and season with the spices and salt. Put the liver mixture through a food processor.

Add the liver to the chicken and mix in the pistachio nuts, apricots, parsley, mint and lemon juice. Mix well, adding more stock if it is too dry. Brush the outside of the loaf with a little stock. Now fill the cavity with the chicken mixture. Replace the top or side you cut off. Keep refrigerated. Serve in slices.

Roast Turkey

Roast turkey is always appropriate for a festive occasion—Christmas, Thanksgiving, birthdays or weddings. This turkey stuffed with celery, apple and walnuts tastes delicious cold and sliced as required at a buffet. Serve with the peach sauce on page 76.

Stuffing
2 onions, chopped
1 tablespoon butter
2 cups breadcrumbs
1 cup chopped celery
2 apples, chopped
$\frac{1}{2}$ cup walnuts

1 teaspoon chopped sage
1 tablespoon chopped rosemary
1 tablespoon chopped tarragon
1 tablespoon chopped parsley
1 tablespoon allspice
2 eggs

1 turkey
Pork belly skin with fat
Pepper
Sprigs of rosemary

COOK the onions in the butter until translucent. Put them into a bowl with

This roast turkey was timed to finish cooking just before I left for a picnic. I covered it in foil and wrapped it in a towel to keep it warm, so that by the time we got to the picnic spot the turkey was still a good temperature to eat.

the rest of the stuffing ingredients and mix well.

Wash and dry the turkey. Pack it with the stuffing and sew up the openings. Gently rub pepper over the skin and under the skin. Put sprigs of rosemary under the skin and tie some on top and under the legs and wings. Place the pork skin all over the turkey and tie it in place with string. This will keep the turkey very moist and will also save you having to baste, which I find difficult with such a heavy bird. Place the turkey in a baking dish and pour in 2 cm (1 in) of water, which also helps to keep such a dry bird moist. This way the turkey roasts and steams simultaneously.

Place the turkey in a preheated oven at 160°C (320°F).

Cooking time: birds under 7 kg (15 lb), 40 minutes to the kilogram (20 minutes to the pound); birds over 7 kg (15 lb), 30 minutes to the kilogram (15 minutes to the pound).

When the cooked turkey has cooled, keep it wrapped in a clean pillowcase. If it is to be eaten the same day, don't refrigerate.

Cassoulet

An easily transported winter dish which you can present as a whole or packed in portions with a little confit d'oie *on top of each portion. This recipe has the authentic texture of the traditional dish from the Languedoc area in France. Its only drawback is the rather volatile nature of the beans.*

1 kg (2 lb) white haricot beans
500 g (1 lb) belly of pork, including skin
1 teaspoon salt
2 onions, diced
4 garlic cloves
2 large tomatoes, diced
A bouquet garni
Pepper and salt
500 g (1 lb) bratwurst sausage
1 kg (2 lb) lamb or mutton
Confit d'oie or some goose, turkey or duck
1 cup goose fat
3 cups fresh breadcrumbs

Soak the beans overnight. Take the skin off the pork belly and make a stock by boiling the skin for several hours with 1 teaspoon of salt.

Next day put the beans in a large pot along with the onions, garlic, tomatoes, bouquet garni, pepper and salt and pork stock. Boil until the beans are almost cooked. Save all the stock. Take out the bouquet garni. At the same time roast the pork, sausage, lamb and poultry (if not already cooked) in the goose fat.

Put all the meats, cut into bite-size pieces, in the bottom of a deep earthenware pot. Cover with the beans and goose fat. Pour the stock over the beans to within 4 cm (2 in) of the top of the beans. Spread a layer of breadcrumbs on top and put the pot into a slow oven (160°C; 320°F). Every hour stir the brown crust into the beans and add another layer of breadcrumbs. The breadcrumbs gradually soak up the surplus liquid and give the dish the right texture. Keep the remainder of the bean stock to add more liquid if necessary or for reheating the next day. The last crust should remain intact for serving. The whole process takes 4 to 5 hours.

Pork with Dates

A wonderful dish to serve cold for a buffet meal. Present whole on a platter surrounded by hazelnuts and sage leaves. The spicy plum sauce on page 76 would be tasty with it.

$\frac{1}{2}$ cup lime or lemon juice
1 cup large fresh dates, stoned
2 pork fillets
500 g (1 lb) pork mince
2 garlic cloves, crushed
1 tablespoon chopped thyme
1 teaspoon chopped sage leaves
2 tablespoons chopped parsley
$\frac{1}{4}$ cup white wine
1 teaspoon salt
1 teaspoon pepper
1 cup grated carrot
$\frac{1}{4}$ cup hazelnuts

POUR the lime or lemon juice over the dates and leave to steep for several hours. Pound the pork out as flat as you can to about 1 cm ($\frac{3}{8}$ in) thick. To help flatten it out, you will need to make several incisions in the meat. Most butchers will flatten the fillets for you.

Put the pork mince, garlic, herbs, wine, salt and pepper into a bowl and mix well to make a stuffing.

On each pork fillet place one-third of the dates and sprinkle with hazelnuts. Then put half the stuffing on top of the dates and hazelnuts on each fillet. Top one of the fillets with the remaining dates. Carefully invert the other fillet on top of the date layer so that you have meat on the top and bottom in a kind of sandwich. Tie it with string at intervals of about 3 cm ($1\frac{1}{4}$ in). Roast in a preheated oven at 190°C (375°F) for 50 to 60 minutes or until cooked. Serve cold, cut in slices.

Christmas Ham

If you are feeling energetic, try pickling a ham and taste the huge difference between homemade and commercial. Otherwise buy a ham and use this recipe (disregarding the first paragraph) for baking and glazing the ham. It is very delicious and very dramatic. Serve cold.

5 kg (11 lb) leg of pork
500 g (1 lb) salt
1 cup brown sugar
8 cups beer
8 cups water
1 tablespoon peppercorns
1 tablespoon juniper berries
Cloves as needed
1 cup brown sugar for glazing

RUB the leg of pork with a handful of salt and sugar all over. Leave overnight. Make the marinade by boiling the rest of the salt, sugar, beer and water. Stir until the salt and sugar have dissolved. When the marinade is cool, pour it over the leg of pork placed in a large sterilised pickling crock. Hold the pork down with a sterilised weight so that it is covered by the marinade. Leave it to stand for 12 days in a cool place.

To cook the leg, place it in a large stockpot or boiler and cover it with cold water. Bring to the boil, skimming the impurities off. Put in the peppercorns and juniper berries and simmer for three hours or until tender.

Remove the ham from the stockpot and let it cool. Remove the rind. Slash the fat diagonally into diamonds and stick a clove into the middle of each. Place in a preheated oven at 180°C (360°F) and bake for half on hour. Remove, sprinkle with the additional brown sugar and return to the oven for half an hour or until the glaze is shiny and golden.

Salt-Cured Lamb

I don't know why this has been so slow coming onto the market commercially. It is relatively easy to make and can be eaten like prosciutto with fresh melon or figs. It is a change from the usual Christmas ham. I sometimes take a leg of cured lamb as a contribution when staying with friends on holidays.

1.5 kg (3 lb) salt
2 tablespoons honey
4.5 litres (8 pints) water
1 teaspoon juniper berries
3.5 kg (8 lb) leg of lamb

DISSOLVE the salt and honey in the water and add the juniper berries. Put the lamb into a large sterilised crock and pour the brine over, covering it completely. Use a sterilised weight to keep the meat under the brine. Let it stand in a cool place, covered, for two weeks.

Take the leg out, rinse and pat dry. Wrap it in a bag of three layers of muslin to protect it from flies. Hang it in a cool, airy place for three months. It is served finely sliced.

Saddle of Lamb

A very special joint of meat for a large party, served rare at room temperature. It is precarved and put back into shape with the meat juices. This is a rather unusual cut, so ask your butcher in advance to prepare a whole saddle of lamb. Make sure he trims away the fat, leaving only a thin protective layer on top of the meat. Skewer the kidneys on.

3–5 kg (6–10 lb) saddle of lamb
1 tablespoon salt
1 tablespoon pepper
Sprigs of rosemary
6 bay leaves
2 onions, chopped
1 cup red wine
2 tablespoons butter
2 cups clear chicken stock
$\frac{1}{2}$ cup port
Watercress to granish

SALT and pepper the lamb and tuck sprigs of rosemary and the bay leaves all over. Tie the lamb together with kitchen string. Place the trussed lamb in a greased roasting pan with the onions, wine and butter. Bake in a preheated oven at 190°C (380°F) for about 1$\frac{3}{4}$ to 2 hours. The meat should be a delicate pink; check when basting occasionally with the pan juices.

When it is cooked, remove it from the oven and let it cool. Carve it the following way: slice down the length of the fillet on each side of the backbone, remove the meat and cut it into slices, then replace it on the bone. Bring the stock and port to blood heat in a saucepan and then brush the meat with this glaze. Decorate with watercress and serve with mint or redcurrant jelly.

PREVIOUS PAGES
An idyllic picnic spot for Christmas Day or a birthday picnic. Each friend can bring a dish of food and something to drink. The picnic becomes a memorable occasion if you present it with silverware, crystal glasses and a damask cloth and napkins.

Roast Fillet of Beef

1.25 kg (2$\frac{1}{2}$ lb) fillet of beef
2 tablespoons oil
1 cup port
1 tablespoon chopped thyme
1 tablespoon pepper
1 teaspoon salt

TRIM the fillet and tie it at regular intervals so that it is a good shape. Preheat the oven to 200°C (400°F). Heat the oil in a baking dish, put the fillet in to brown over a high heat. Never pierce the meat, as this will loose the juices. Brown it all over. Pour the port and sprinkle the thyme over the meat and put it in the oven. Roast for 25 minutes, basting three times. Take it out of the oven and put the meat on a dish. Mix the salt into the pan juices and pour over the beef. When it has cooled, wrap in foil ready to transport. Don't refrigerate if you are giving it away the same day.

Spiced Beef

$\frac{1}{2}$ teaspoon ground cloves
1 teaspoon ground cinnamon
1 teaspoon ground nutmeg
1 tablespoon ground coriander
2 tablespoons pepper
1 tablespoon ground ginger
2 tablespoons chopped thyme
1 cup dark brown sugar
3 kg (7 lb) topside or brisket beef
1 cup salt
15 g ($\frac{1}{2}$ oz) saltpetre
10 bay leaves
15 juniper berries, crushed
2 carrots, chopped
2 sticks celery, chopped
2 onions, chopped
1 orange, quartered
4 garlic cloves, crushed
2 cups port
2 cups beef stock

MIX the spices, thyme and parsley together. Put half of them with the sugar and mix well. Reserve the other spices for a week in an airtight jar. Rub the spicy sugar into the beef and let it rest in a shallow dish. Cover and refrigerate for 24 hours.

Now rub over the salt, saltpetre, bay leaves and juniper berries. Cover and put back into the refrigerator. Turn the meat over every day and rub the spices in. After 5 days remove the meat, rinse it well and soak it in clean water for an hour. Pat it dry with kitchen paper. Rub the reserved spices over it, roll it up and tie with string. Put it into a large pot with a tightly fitting lid. Put in the vegetables, orange, cloves, port and beef stock. Cover and cook in a preheated oven 150°C (300°F) for 4 to 5 hours or until the meat is tender. Let it cool in the cooking juices. Put a board and a weight on top of the meat to press it while it cools. Leave overnight. It is ready to eat the next day. Remove the fat from the juice and use the liquid to moisten the meat.

Poached Snapper

A grand dish for a very special occasion. The recipe works as well for salmon, trout, coral cod or pearl perch.

1 snapper 1.5–2 kg (3–4 lb)
2 cups white wine
Court bouillon
3 small onions, chopped
3 carrots, chopped
4 bay leaves
½ cup chopped fennel leaves and stalk
½ cup chopped parsley
2 slices lemon
1 teaspoon salt
6 peppercorns
5 litres (9 pints) water

To make the court bouillon. Put all the *court bouillon* ingredients in a large saucepan or fish kettle, cover and simmer for 20 minutes. Strain and cool to blood heat. Return the liquid to the pan.

Wash the snapper and slide it into the pan. Add the wine and bring the liquid back to simmering point. Simmer for 5 minutes per 500 g (1 lb). The *court bouillon* should never boil.

Lift the fish out and let it drain and cool on a serving dish. Wipe the serving dish clean around the fish and surround it with sliced cucumber and sprigs of watercress. Serve with mayonnaise (page 98); squeeze in lime juice instead of lemon for a change. Freeze the *court bouillon* to use again.

Seafood with Mayonnaise

30 mussels, in the shell
Court bouillon (see previous recipe)
1.5 kg (3 lb) green prawns
20 scallops, in the shell
2 boiled crabs
4 lemons, cut in wedges
30 oysters, in the shell
A bunch of fresh dill
Mayonnaise (page 98; twice the quantity)

Scrub the mussels and put them into the *court bouillon*. Bring to the boil and cook for 7 to 10 minutes until the shells open. Remove them and leave to cool.

Add the prawns and simmer for just a few minutes until they turn pink. Remove and cool. Peel and de-vein the prawns. Add the scallops and let them cook for 8 minutes. Remove and cool. Remove the meat from the crabs. Rinse and clean out the carapaces and put the crab meat back in.

Arrange some crushed ice on a large platter. Put the crabs in the centre and arrange the legs around each crab as if it were intact. Arrange the prawns and lemon wedges around the edge as a border. Keep the oysters, mussels and scallops on the shell and place decoratively around the crabs. Arrange sprigs of dill in empty places. Serve with bowls of mayonnaise mixed with chopped dill.

5 Bread, Biscuits and Cakes

Easter buns and breads, Stollen (German Advent cake), almond Christmas biscuits, champagne biscuits, simnel cake for Mothering Sunday, birthday cakes—baking to celebrate festive occasions is a traditional social activity.

Bread in particular is a sacred part of life, part of religion, folklore and our communal eating. A loaf of homemade bread passed around the dinner table is appreciated by friends; it makes a meal more special. To buy satisfactory bread is often difficult, but to make it is pleasurable and relatively easy. Most of the bread recipes given in this chapter are for long-lasting loaves. If you are a newcomer to bread baking, start with the soda breads.

Biscuits make an easy and inexpensive gift. Even just half a dozen in a cellophane bag can be a pleasant thought for a neighbour or a great-aunt. You'll find a recipe here to suit most occasions.

Some of the cakes, such as teacake, are easy and fast to make for a picnic or afternoon tea. But most of the recipes are for rich, dense and special occasion cakes. There is nothing more satisfying at the end of a meal than to bite into a sweet chocolate and walnut cake. Forget about diets when you are celebrating.

Easter Nests

Make an Easter nest as the table centrepiece for Easter Sunday lunch. Tell the hostess you are bringing the centrepiece, so that she'll leave space for it. Gather vines and attractive grasses and ferns, and interweave them around a basket to make a nest. Add feathers, shells, gumnuts and tiny flowers that won't die quickly. Make sure it is large enough to contain a dozen eggs.

Make the marbled eggs from the recipe on page 21 or a variety of colours with different food colourings as described here.

Salt
Food colourings
12 eggs
Oil

Put 1 to 2 teaspoons of food colouring into a saucepan with some cold water and salt. Add the eggs and gradually bring the water to the boil. Simmer for 10 minutes, then remove the saucepan from the heat. Let the eggs sit in the water until cold. Dry the eggs and rub them with oil to give them a glossy look. Arrange the eggs attractively in your nest so that some are half hidden.

Banana and
Walnut Bread

A quick, easy soda bread to make.

3 large ripe bananas
$\frac{1}{2}$ cup walnuts
$\frac{1}{2}$ cup unsalted butter
$\frac{1}{2}$ cup vanilla sugar
2 eggs
1 cup plain flour
1 cup wholemeal flour
1 teaspoon bicarbonate of soda
$\frac{3}{4}$ teaspoon baking powder
1 teaspoon salt

This is my contribution to an Easter Sunday lunch. I made a Chicken Liver Pâté (page 94), Easter Bread (page 109) and an Easter nest for the centrepiece of the table (opposite page), filled with coloured eggs.

To make the eggs, wrap ferns around the eggs, hold the ferns in place with muslin and tie with string. Put them into three saucepans each with a different food colouring and cold water. Bring to the boil and simmer for ten minutes. Turn off the heat and let the eggs sit in the water until cold. Unwrap the eggs and rub them with a little oil. I used brown eggs to get this effect; it would be much brighter with white eggs.

PEEL and mash the bananas and chop the walnuts. Cream the butter and sugar in a bowl until light and fluffy. Gradually add in the eggs, beating constantly. Into this mixture sift the flours, soda, baking powder and salt. Mix well and add the bananas and walnuts.

Pour the mixture into a greased bread tin and bake in a preheated oven at 180°C (360°F) for 50 to 60 minutes. Cool in the pan for 10 minutes before turning out on a wire rack.

Yoghurt and Honey Bread

Be sure to choose a cultured yoghurt rather than a thickened one. This is a lovely healthy bread and very easy and fast to make.

2 cups plain yoghurt
$\frac{1}{4}$ cup honey
4 cups wholemeal flour
2 tablespoons cracked wheat, soaked
1 teaspoon salt
1 tablespoon bicarbonate of soda
$\frac{3}{4}$ teaspoon baking powder
1 tablespoon olive oil
$\frac{1}{3}$ cup whole wheat grains

PUT the yoghurt and honey in a bowl and mix well until the honey dissolves. Combine the flour, cracked wheat, salt, soda, baking powder and oil in another bowl. Make a well in the centre and pour in the yoghurt mixture. Fold in the dry ingredients and stir into a dough. Knead for a few minutes on a floured board.

Shape into a round about 20 cm (8 in) and place on a well-greased baking tray. Cut a deep cross 1 cm ($\frac{1}{2}$ in) on top of the dough. Sprinkle wheat grains on top and press in very lightly. Bake in a preheated oven at 190°C (375°F) for 45 minutes or until the loaf sounds hollow when tapped on the bottom.

Black Bread

This is very similar to pumpernickel and has the advantage of lasting up to two weeks. It is terribly simple and fast to make and very nutritious. Serve or give with liptauer cheese (page 20) or a caviar dip (page 17).

1 teaspoon baking soda
2 tablespoons hot water
1 kg (2 lb) cornmeal
2 cups wholemeal rye flour
$\frac{2}{3}$ cup molasses
3 cups buttermilk
1 teaspoon salt

DISSOLVE the soda in the water. Combine all the ingredients and beat to a thick batter.

Pour into well-greased tins and bake in a preheated oven at 160°C (320°F) for 60 minutes or until firm.

Whole-Wheat Bread

This basic dough recipe can also be used to make pizzas. It will make quite a few, so keep some frozen; they always come in handy.

3 cups warm milk
$\frac{3}{4}$ cup honey
15 g ($\frac{1}{2}$ oz) dry yeast or 30 g (1 oz) fresh yeast
2 tablespoons butter
5 cups whole-wheat flour
1 teaspoon salt
2 cups whole-wheat flour

COMBINE the milk, honey and yeast. Allow to stand for 20 minutes. Into a large bowl put the butter, 5 cups of flour and salt; mix the butter into the flour with your fingertips until it resembles breadcrumbs. Add the yeast-and-milk mixture and mix to a dough.

Add the other two cups of flour and knead well. Shape the dough into a ball, put it into a greased bowl, cover and let it stand in a warm place for an hour until it has doubled in size.

Knead the dough well again and let it stand for another hour in a warm place. Knead once more and then put the dough into greased loaf pans or shape into rounds or sticks. Let the dough rise again and put into a preheated oven at 175°C (350°F) for 50 to 70 minutes depending on how large you made the loaves. Let them cool on wire racks. Brush the top of each loaf with butter while it is still hot to make a crisp crust.

Brown Rolls

These rolls are great for hamburgers and meat kebabs at a barbecue. It seems to me I can never make enough of them when we eat outdoors. Why does eating outdoors increase our appetite?

2 cups warm water
¾ cup honey
15 g (½ oz) dry yeast or 30 g (1 oz)
    fresh yeast
½ cup olive oil
2 eggs, beaten
3 cups wholemeal flour
1 cup wheat germ
1 cup cracked wheat, soaked
1 tablespoon salt
⅔ cup buttermilk

Put the water, honey and yeast into a large bowl and mix. After 20 minutes add the oil, eggs and wholemeal flour. Thoroughly mix and add the wheat germ, cracked wheat, salt and buttermilk. Knead until it is a stiff dough. Roll into a ball and place in a greased bowl. Cover and leave in a warm place for an hour.

Knead the dough again and leave to rise for another hour. Pull off pieces of dough the size of an egg, roll them and place them on greased oven trays. Bake in a preheated oven at 180°C (360°F) for 20 minutes. Cool on wire racks.

Easter Bread

Easter bread is a rich bread baked in many European countries with endless variations. The one given here is derived from a Greek recipe. In Russia they would add ½ cup candied fruit. This mixture makes 2 loaves.

15 g (½ oz) dry yeast or 30 g (1 oz)
    fresh yeast
¼ cup warm water
½ cup sugar
½ cup butter
3 eggs
1 cup warm buttermilk
6 cups flour
Zest of 1 orange
1 egg yolk
½ cup sesame seeds
½ cup slivered almonds

Dissolve the yeast in the water and add a teaspoon of sugar. Leave for 20 minutes until the yeast is frothy.

Cream the sugar and butter until light and fluffy, gradually adding the eggs. Slowly add in the buttermilk and the yeast mixture, mixing thoroughly. Now add the flour and orange zest gradually until you have a soft dough. Knead the dough until it is firm and elastic, about 15 minutes. Place in a greased bowl and let it stand, covered, for an hour in a warm place to rise to twice its size.

Knead the dough again and let it rise for another hour in a warm place. Knead once more and then divide the dough into 2 equal parts. Cut 3 strands out of each piece of dough, leaving them joined at one end. Plait the strands together to make 2 loaves. Brush the top with egg yolk and sprinkle with sesame seeds and lightly press in the slivered almonds.

Put into a warm place to rise again, about an hour. Place in a preheated oven at 190°C (375°F) and bake for about 50 minutes or until the loaves are golden brown and sound hollow when tapped. Leave to cool on wire racks.

Fruit Bread

⅓ cup dried apricots, chopped
⅓ cup raisins
⅓ cup prunes, stoned
1 cup rolled oats
½ cup orange juice
1¼ cups buttermilk
1 tablespoon butter
½ cup molasses
30 g (1 oz) fresh yeast or 15 g (½ oz)
    dry yeast
½ cup warm water
8 cups wholemeal flour
1 cup bran
1 teaspoon salt
1 teaspoon ground cinnamon
1 teaspoon ground cardamom
3 eggs, beaten
½ cup chopped walnuts
⅓ cup poppy seeds

Pᴜᴛ the dried fruit and rolled oats into a bowl and pour over the orange juice. Let it soak for an hour. Heat the buttermilk, butter, and molasses to blood heat. Dissolve the yeast in the warm water and leave for 20 minutes.

Into a large bowl put the flour, bran and salt. Gradually add the milk mixture, then the yeast, spices and eggs. Knead for 10 minutes until the dough is elastic. Roll into a ball and place in a greased bowl, covered. Leave in a warm place for an hour until it has doubled in size. Knead for a few minutes to knock it down in size, then mix in the fruit mixture and walnuts. Divide it into

Delicious and healthy Fruit Bread (this page), full of apricots, raisins, prunes and spices. The pattern and instructions for making the kangaroo-stencilled paper are on page 123.

halves. Shape into two round loaves, cut a deep slash across the top of each, sprinkle the poppy seeds over and leave the loaves in a warm place to rise for an hour. Bake on a well-greased tray in a preheated oven at 190°C (375°F) for about 45 minutes or until crusty. Cool on baking racks.

Pita Bread

Flat breads of many kinds are made through-out the Middle East. They have become popu-lar to use with dips, and the pouches are ideal to fill instead of a sandwich for lunch or a snack. The variations suggested at the end of the recipe make attractive and unusual-looking breads to give as presents.

> 7 g ($\frac{1}{4}$ oz) dry yeast or 15 g ($\frac{1}{2}$ oz)
>   fresh yeast
> A pinch of sugar
> 1 cup warm water
> 4 cups wholemeal flour
> $\frac{1}{2}$ teaspoon salt
> 2 tablespoons olive oil

P<small>UT</small> the yeast and sugar into a bowl and pour the water over. Leave in a warm place for about 20 minutes until it becomes frothy.

Put the flour and salt into a bowl and make a well in the centre. Pour in the yeast. Knead to a soft, elastic dough for about 15 minutes. Then knead in the oil. Make the dough into a ball and brush with oil. Cover with a floured cloth and put in a warm place for about 2 hours or until it doubles in size.

When the dough is ready, knead it again for a few minutes and take off pieces of dough the size of an egg. With a floured rolling pin roll them out into circles until they are 6 mm ($\frac{1}{4}$ in) thick. Flour again and leave them all to rise again on oiled baking sheets in a warm place.

Preheat the oven to 240°C (465°F). When the bread has risen again, brush lightly with water and bake for 8 to 10 minutes. Transfer the bread to wire racks to cool. Keep the pitas in plastic bags to keep them soft for serving or giving away.

VARIATIONS
I use wholemeal flour, but plain flour will work just as well. For a change sprinkle poppy seeds and sesame seeds on them just before they go into the oven. Or press pitted olives into the dough. For a *fruity bread*, dimple the dough after you have brushed it with water, put raisins, walnuts and almonds into the dimples and sprinkle with sugar, then proceed with the recipe.

Olive Bread

> 7 g ($\frac{1}{4}$ oz) dried yeast or 15 g ($\frac{1}{2}$ oz)
>   fresh yeast
> 1$\frac{1}{4}$ cups warm water
> 4 cups flour
> 1 teaspoon salt
> 1 onion, chopped finely
> 1 tablespoon olive oil
> 1$\frac{1}{2}$ cups black olives, stoned and
>   chopped

M<small>IX</small> the yeast in the water and allow to stand for 20 minutes. Sieve the flour and salt into a bowl. Make a well in it and pour in the yeast mixture. Mix well and knead the dough until it is quite elastic and smooth. Put it into a greased bowl, cover and let it stand in a warm place for an hour to double its size.

Cook the onion in the oil until it is translucent. Add the olives for five minutes and then transfer the onion and olives to the bowl with the dough. Mix all together well. Shape the dough into a round loaf and put it onto a well-greased tray. Leave it in a warm place for an hour to rise.

Bake in a preheated oven at 190°C (375°F) for 30 to 40 minutes or until it is golden brown. The bottom should be firm when tapped. Cool on a wire rack.

Hot Cross Buns

Hot cross buns are part of a very old festive tradition dating from ancient Greek times. The Greeks marked a cross inside a circle on their buns to denote the sun and four seasons, as a celebration of spring. We now interpret the cross as a Christian symbol. Hot cross buns are traditionally served on Good Friday.

15 g ($\frac{1}{2}$ oz) dry yeast or 30 g (1 oz) fresh yeast
$\frac{1}{2}$ cup warm water
4 cups flour
1 teaspoon mixed spice
$\frac{1}{2}$ teaspoon ground cinnamon
$\frac{1}{2}$ teaspoon ground ginger
1 teaspoon salt
$\frac{1}{2}$ cup sugar
$\frac{1}{3}$ cup butter
1 cup buttermilk
1 egg, beaten
$\frac{3}{4}$ cup sultanas
$\frac{1}{4}$ cup mixed peel
Cross decoration
$\frac{2}{3}$ cup flour
$\frac{2}{3}$ cup milk
1 tablespoon oil
$\frac{1}{4}$ teaspoon baking powder
Glaze
4 tablespoons caster sugar
4 tablespoons hot water

Mix the yeast with the water and leave for 20 minutes until it is frothy. Put the flour, spices, salt and sugar in a large bowl and mix thoroughly. Make a well in the flour mixture and pour in the yeast. Melt the butter in a saucepan, add the buttermilk and heat until luke-warm. Add the egg and pour the mixture into the flour. Work the dough until it is stiff. Add the sultanas and peel and knead the dough until it is smooth and elastic. Form the dough into a ball and put it into a greased bowl, cover and leave in a warm place for an hour.

Punch the dough and knead it again. Divide the dough into 18 equal pieces and mould them into balls. Put them on a well-greased oven tray and leave to stand in a warm place until they have doubled their size. Make sure they are not too close together.

To make the cross decoration, place all the ingredients for it in a bowl and stir until it is a smooth paste. Use a piping bag to form a cross on each bun.

Bake the rolls in a preheated oven at 230°C (450°F) for 10 to 15 minutes until golden brown. Dissolve the caster sugar in the hot water to make a glaze and brush a thin layer over each bun as soon as you take them out of the oven. Sprinkle with extra cinnamon.

Scones

2$\frac{1}{2}$ cups self-raising flour
$\frac{1}{4}$ teaspoon bicarbonate of soda
1 teaspoon salt
2 tablespoons soft butter
1 cup buttermilk or cream

Sieve the flour, soda and salt into a bowl and rub in the butter with your fingertips until the texture resembles breadcrumbs. Make a well and add the buttermilk and mix to a dough.

Put the dough onto a floured board and roll out to 1 cm ($\frac{3}{8}$ in) thick. Cut the dough with a floured biscuit cutter or glass. Brush a little milk on the tops of the scones and transfer them to a well-greased baking tray. Bake in a preheated oven at 230°C (450°F) for 10 to 15 minutes until golden brown.

Pikelets

2 cups flour
2 tablespoons caster sugar
A pinch of salt
$\frac{1}{2}$ cup buttermilk
1 teaspoon bicarbonate of soda

Sift the flour into a basin and mix in the sugar and salt. Gradually add the buttermilk to make a thick batter. Dissolve the soda in a little hot water and add to the batter.

Take a tablespoonful of batter and drop it onto a lightly greased frying pan. When the underneath is lightly browned, turn with a palette knife and cook the other side.

Peppernuts

4 cups flour
3 cups caster sugar
4 eggs
1 teaspoon ground cinnamon
$\frac{1}{2}$ teaspoon ground cloves
$\frac{1}{2}$ teaspoon ground cardamom
$\frac{1}{2}$ teaspoon grated nutmeg
$\frac{1}{2}$ teaspoon pepper
1 teaspoon baking powder
3 tablespoons chopped citrus peel
Zest of half a lemon

Sift the flour into a bowl and mix in the caster sugar. Whip the eggs and gradually add the flour mixture. Fold in all the other ingredients and mix well. Roll into small balls 4 cm (1$\frac{1}{2}$ in) across. Place onto well-greased baking trays and put into a preheated oven 150°C (300°F) and bake until golden brown. Cool on wire racks.

Salt Dough Decorations

These decorations will last for years. All sorts of decorative items can be cut from salt dough: sheaves of corn for the harvest festival, Easter bunnies, baskets of fruit, a dove of peace, amusing animal shapes for children, even napkin rings. Hang them up in the kitchen to decorate any time of the year. Use the designs scattered throughout the book to cut your shapes. There is a same-size pattern for the fruit basket on page 171.

2 cups flour
1 cup salt
1 teaspoon oil
Warm water
1 eggwhite

Have biscuit cutters or template ready to cut the dough and a small sharp knife to add further decorative pieces.

Mix the flour, salt and oil together until a dough is formed. Add some warm water and keep kneading until the dough is stiff. Roll out the dough to 6 mm ($\frac{1}{4}$ in) thick and cut it to the desired shapes. If you are doing a complicated design, like the basket of fruit, be sure to have the base pattern outline ready; cut this out first and then add the intricate shapes on top of it. Glue them on

with watered-down dough. Put the base outline on a well-greased tray first and then decorate. Remember a short straw to make a hole to hang it from. Brush

with eggwhite to glaze the surface and place your dough decorations in a preheated oven at 120°C (250°F).

Remove from the oven and when cool paint with three layers of clear varnish to ensure a long life.

Almond Cake Decorations

Use biscuit cutters to shape these almond cake decorations. They look amusing and taste wonderful. If you want to hang them up, insert a piece of straw near the top of each one before you bake them.

2 cups flour
1 teaspoon baking powder
½ cup ground almonds
2 cups sugar
5 eggwhites
1¼ cups blanched almonds
3 tablespoons lemon juice
1 egg yolk

Mix the flour, baking powder, ground almonds and sugar. Make a well and fold in the eggwhites one at a time. Then fold in the blanched almonds and lemon juice. Mix until it is a smooth dough.

Roll out the dough to 13 mm (½ in) thick and cut into shapes. Put them on well-greased oven trays and bake in a preheated oven at 220°C (430°F) for 15 minutes. Cool on wire racks and gently remove the straw.

Iced Biscuit Shapes

This is a great recipe to use for making decorations for your Christmas tree or biscuits for a children's birthday party. Choose a theme and cut the biscuits with different-shaped cutters. Or better still, draw up your own shapes on thin cardboard and cut around them. Decorate with different-coloured icing sugar. Great fun on a rainy day—get the whole family to help.

2 cups flour
½ teaspoon salt
½ teaspoon baking powder
½ cup butter
1 cup sugar
1 egg
2 tablespoons rum
Icing
1 cup icing sugar
1 eggwhite
¼ teaspoon lemon juice
Food colouring

Sift the flour, salt and baking powder. Cream the butter and sugar until light and fluffy. Add the egg and rum and mix well. Start adding the flour mixture gradually and keep mixing until it is well blended. Make a ball, wrap it in plastic film and refrigerate for an hour.

Roll out the dough to 3 mm (⅛ in) thickness. Cut out your amazing shapes and put them on well-greased baking trays. Bake in a preheated oven at 200°C (400°F) for 10 minutes. Cool on wire racks.

Mix the icing ingredients together until smooth. Divide the mixture into the number of colours you want and colour them. Pipe the designs onto the biscuits. Who said you are not artistic?

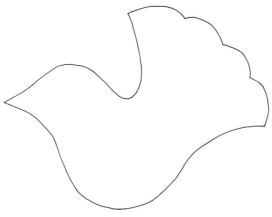

Iced Biscuit Shapes (recipe opposite) ready for a crowd of little boys and girls to devour. You can hang these biscuits on the Christmas tree as well; just be sure to make a hole with a straw before baking. White paper bags are an attractive way to wrap individual gifts of sweets.

Cheese Biscuits

Delicate tasty little biscuits to serve with drinks at any time of day or night, especially if there is a feast to come. Put them in a pretty box lined with tissue paper to present as a gift.

1 cup flour, sifted
2 tablespoons butter
$\frac{2}{3}$ cup parmesan cheese
$\frac{1}{2}$ teaspoon cayenne
1 teaspoon salt
1 egg yolk
1 tablespoon water

PUT the flour and butter into a bowl and rub the butter into the flour until it resembles breadcrumbs. Add the cheese, cayenne and salt. Mix the egg yolk with the water and add to the bowl. Mix into a soft dough. Roll out thinly and cut into rounds 2.5 cm (1 in) across. Bake on greased baking trays in an oven preheated to 180°C (360°F) for 15 minutes or until golden brown. Cool on a wire rack.

Easter Biscuits

Spicy, fruity biscuits rich in butter to feast on after the Lenten fasting. Blessed by the priest at midnight mass on Easter Saturday night, they were often consumed as soon as the congregation was outside the doors of the church.

2 cups flour
$\frac{3}{4}$ cup butter
$\frac{2}{3}$ cup caster sugar
2 tablespoons currants
1 egg, beaten
1 teaspoon ground cinnamon
1 teaspoon grated nutmeg
$\frac{1}{4}$ teaspoon ground cloves
Zest and juice of 1 lemon

MIX all the ingredients together in a bowl until you get a smooth dough. Roll it out on a floured board to a thickness of about 6 mm ($\frac{1}{4}$ in). Cut into rounds, or fluted rounds if you have a fluted biscuit cutter. Put them onto a well-greased baking tray and bake in a pre-

heated oven at 190°C (375°F) for 10 minutes or until golden brown. Let the biscuits cool on a wire rack and sprinkle them with caster sugar.

Walnut Biscuits

2 tablespoons peanut oil
1 tablespoon molasses
$\frac{2}{3}$ cup sugar
$\frac{1}{2}$ cup chopped walnuts
2 eggs
1 cup wheat germ
1 teaspoon cinnamon
$\frac{1}{2}$ teaspoon salt
$\frac{1}{2}$ cup skim milk
$\frac{1}{2}$ teaspoon baking powder

COMBINE all the ingredients in a bowl and stir well. Spread the mixture over well-greased waxed paper on a 20 × 20 cm (8 in × 8 in) baking tray. Bake in a preheated oven at 175°C (350°F) for 30 minutes or until cooked. Turn out of baking tray immediately and remove the paper. Cut into bars while still hot.

Muesli

As well as being a most nutritious start to any day, muesli can be used to make muesli bars and biscuits (see the following recipes). As a breakfast food you can serve it with milk, although I prefer it dry. There are many recipes for muesli. This one is full of goodness and fibre.

6 cups rolled oats
$\frac{1}{2}$ cup sunflower seeds
$\frac{1}{2}$ cup sesame seeds
$\frac{1}{4}$ cup desiccated coconut
1 cup wheat germ
2 cups bran
$\frac{1}{3}$ cup oil
$\frac{2}{3}$ cup honey
1 cup chopped dried apricots
1 cup chopped dried apples
$\frac{1}{2}$ cup chopped dried prunes

Mɪx together the oats, seeds, coconut, wheat germ and bran, then stir in the oil followed by the honey. Bake in a baking tin in a preheated oven at 200°C (400°F) for 45 minutes or until it begins to brown. Stir twice while it is cooking. Let it cool and add the dried fruits. Store in large screw-top jars.

Muesli Bars

6 cups dry muesli mixture (opposite page).
1 egg, beaten
1 cup milk
½ cup honey

Pᴜᴛ the muesli into a bowl and stir in the egg, milk and honey. Mix well. Press the mixture into a greased Swiss roll pan and bake in a preheated oven at 200°C (400°F) until golden brown. Remove from the oven and cut into bars. Take them out of the tray when cold. Wrap in cellophane or waxed paper and twist the ends.

Muesli Biscuits

1 cup muesli (opposite page)
1 cup wholemeal flour
½ cup sugar
4 tablespoons butter
1 tablespoon honey
¼ cup hot skim milk
1½ teaspoons bicarbonate of soda

Pᴜᴛ the muesli, flour and sugar into a bowl and stir well. Melt the butter and honey together. Mix the milk and the bicarbonate of soda together and mix this into the butter and honey. Stir the liquids into the muesli in the bowl.

Place spoonfuls of the mixture on a greased baking tray. Bake in a pre-heated oven at 150°C (300°F) for about 20 minutes, until the biscuits are golden brown. Remove them from the oven and let them stand for a few minutes, then transfer them to wire racks to cool.

Lemon Shortbreads

Cut these into different shapes for a change. Use candied lemon peel as the eyes or a mouth or just for decoration. Children love them, so I make them to break the ice at a party.

1 cup butter
2 cups flour, sifted
½ cup sugar
Zest of 1 lemon
Candied lemon peel

Pᴜᴛ the butter and flour into a mixing bowl and rub the butter into the flour until the mixture resembles bread-crumbs. Stir in the sugar and lemon. Mix to a stiff dough. On a floured board knead the dough until it is smooth. This may take 10 to 15 minutes. Roll the dough out thinly and cut it into rounds or different shapes with biscuit cutters. Prick evenly with a fork. Press one or two pieces of candied peel onto each biscuit. Bake on a greased oven tray in a preheated oven at 180°C (360°F) until golden brown. Cool on a wire rack.

Almond and Hazelnut Slices

Excellent stand-by Christmas presents wrapped in cellophane bags or boxes.

½ cup blanched almonds
½ cup hazelnuts
2 cups flour, sifted
2 eggs, beaten
1 cup vanilla caster sugar
½ teaspoon baking powder
A pinch of salt
1 eggwhite, beaten

Cʜᴏᴘ the almonds and hazelnuts roughly. Put the flour into a bowl and make a well. Add the nuts, eggs, sugar, baking powder and salt. Mix and form into a smooth dough. Roll the dough on a floured board into flattened sausage shapes about 8 cm (3 in) long and 1 cm (½ in) in diameter. Place on greased baking trays.

117

Bake in a preheated oven at 190°C (375°F) for 15 minutes. Remove from the oven, cool slightly, then cut at a 45-degree angle into 1 cm ($\frac{1}{2}$ in) slices. Return to the baking trays and cook for a further 25 minutes until they are golden brown.

Champagne Biscuits

12 eggs
2 cups caster sugar
1$\frac{1}{2}$ cups flour, sifted
$\frac{1}{2}$ teaspoon salt

2 tablespoons caster sugar
Zest of 1 lemon

SEPARATE the eggs. Put the yolks into a bowl with the cup of caster sugar and mix well. Whip the eggwhites until light and fluffy. Fold the eggwhites into the egg-yolk mixture very gently. Then stir in the flour, salt, 2 tablespoons of sugar and lemon very gradually so the egg-whites remain frothy. Pour into buttered sponge finger tins, just half-filling the moulds. Bake in a preheated oven at 200°C (400°F) until the biscuits turn a lovely yellow. Cool on a wire rack.

Gingerbread Tree Decorations

My husband's family in northern Germany always make these biscuits to hang from their Christmas tree. They are made in all sorts of shapes—angels, stars, hearts and bears, to name a few. The decorations are hung up with thin cotton cord or silk ribbon. See the designs throughout this book for cutting your own templates for a variety of shapes.

2 tablespoons golden syrup
2 tablespoons brown sugar
1 teaspoon water
$\frac{1}{2}$ teaspoon ground cloves
2 teaspoons ground ginger
1 teaspoon ground nutmeg
2 teaspoons ground cinnamon
3 tablespoons butter
$\frac{1}{2}$ teaspoon bicarbonate of soda
$\frac{1}{2}$ teaspoon baking powder
1$\frac{1}{2}$ cups flour

HEAT the golden syrup in a saucepan with the sugar, water and spices. Mix

well while the syrup melts. Bring to the boil, then remove from heat. Add the butter, soda and baking powder to the pan. Stir until the mixture is clear and smooth. Put the flour in a bowl and blend in the hot mixture until a dough is formed.

Roll out the dough on a floured board until it is 6 mm ($\frac{1}{4}$ in) thick. Press out the desired shapes with biscuit cutters or cut around cardboard templates. Put a piece of straw where you want a hole to hang the biscuit from. Put the shapes on well-greased oven trays and cook in a preheated oven at 180°C (360°F) for about 10 minutes or until golden brown.

Hanging up the Gingerbread Tree Decorations (this page), on the Christmas tree. There are plenty of shapes to copy throughout the book. They smell delicious while baking; the spiciness penetrates the whole house.

Macaroons

Macaroons will keep for weeks in an airtight tin. They taste delicious as a dessert crumbled into the centre of poached peaches and placed under the griller to lightly toast.

> 4 eggwhites
> 1½ cups slivered almonds
> 1½ cups icing sugar
> Juice of 1 lemon

BEAT the eggwhites until light and frothy. Fold in the almonds, sugar and lemon juice very gradually so that the eggwhites remain frothy. Cover baking trays with greaseproof paper and place teaspoonfuls of the mixture onto it. Keep some space between each, as they will expand. Bake in a preheated oven at 190°C (375°F) for 25 minutes or until the macaroons are lightly coloured. Allow to cool before removing them from the paper.

Nutcake

A rich and absolutely delicious cake which is quick and easy to make.

> ½ cup sultanas
> ½ cup rum
> 2 cups stale sponge cake
> ¾ cup walnuts
> ½ cup pine nuts
> ½ cup slivered almonds
> ⅓ cup candied peel
> ½ cup honey

SOAK the sultanas in the rum for half an hour. Crumble the sponge cake into a mixing bowl. Roughly chop the walnuts, pine nuts and almonds and the candied peel and mix with the sponge. Add the honey, sultanas and rum and mix together. Pour into a well-greased rectangular cake tin and bake in a preheated oven at 180°C (360°F) for 25 to 30 minutes. Test by inserting a toothpick; if it comes out smooth, the cake is cooked. Turn out of the tin when cool.

Apple Teacake

Teacakes were the first cakes I learnt to make as a child. They are foolproof and delicious.

> ⅔ cup butter
> 1 cup caster sugar
> 2 eggs
> ½ cup buttermilk
> 2 cups self-raising flour, sifted
> 1 teaspoon ground cinnamon
> 1 cup fresh apples, peeled, cored and
>   chopped finely
> *Decoration*
> 1 tablespoon butter
> 1 teaspoon cinnamon
> 1 teaspoon caster sugar

CREAM the butter and sugar. Add the eggs gradually, beating all the while. Stir in the buttermilk. Mix in the flour and cinnamon. Add the chopped apples. Pour the mixture into a well-greased loaf tin that has been lined with greaseproof paper. Bake in a preheated oven at 180°C (360°F) for 50 to 60 minutes. Brush the top with melted butter and sprinkle with cinnamon and caster sugar. Remove from the tin when cool.

Lemon Syrup Cake

Serve this delicious cake with little glasses of the homemade lemon liqueur. The glasses could be part of the gift. Decorate the plate with fresh lemon leaves and blossoms. Use gin if you don't have lemon liqueur.

> Zest of 1 lemon
> ¾ cup sugar
> 1½ cups butter
> 4 eggs
> 2 cups self-raising flour, sifted
> 1 teaspoon baking powder
> ½ teaspoon salt
> ¼ cup lemon juice
> *Syrup*
> Juice of one lemon
> 2 tablespoons caster sugar
> 2 tablespoons lemon liqueur
>   (page 151)

COMBINE lemon zest, sugar, and butter and beat until it is light and fluffy. Add the eggs, one at a time, and mix well. Fold in the flour, baking powder, salt and lemon juice. Mix well and pour into a cake tin or Gugelhupf mould which has been buttered and lightly floured. Put into a preheated oven at 180°C (360°F) for 45 to 60 minutes or until cooked. Test by inserting a toothpick; if it comes out smooth, the cake is cooked.

Make the syrup by mixing the lemon juice and sugar in a saucepan. Heat until the sugar is dissolved. Pour in the liqueur. Remove the cake from the tin onto a wire rack. Place a plate under the rack and cake and pour the syrup over the cake. When the cake is cool, sit it on the plate to soak up the rest of the syrup. Store in the refrigerator.

Rich Pound Cake

This cake should be baked at least a day ahead of the celebration. After two days it is just as wonderful. Store in the refrigerator. I prefer to cook it in a Gugelhupf mould.

$\frac{3}{4}$ cup butter
3 eggs
1 cup sugar
Zest of one orange
1$\frac{1}{4}$ cups flour, sifted
$\frac{1}{2}$ cup sherry
1 tablespoon vanilla sugar

CREAM the butter until it is light and fluffy. Mix together the eggs, sugar and orange zest and blend until the mixture is pale and fluffy. Gradually add the flour and then quickly add the butter. When well mixed, spoon it into a well-greased and lightly floured cake tin or Gugelhupf mould.

Put into a preheated oven at 175°C (350°F) for about 40 minutes or until golden brown. Turn out of the cake tin after 10 minutes onto a wire rack.

Now to add the sherry. Dissolve the vanilla sugar in the sherry and pour it onto a plate that has high sides. Put the cooled cake on the plate in the sherry. It will take a day to soak up the sherry. Keep refrigerated.

Yeast Cake

An old-fashioned European cake baked with yeast. It takes longer to make, but what is time if you are making it as a gift for a special person. There are many variations to the flavours, so experiment. Add almonds, raisins or treacle as a change.

15 g ($\frac{1}{2}$ oz) dried yeast or 30 g (1 oz) fresh yeast
1 tablespoon sugar
1 cup warm milk
4 cups sifted flour
1 teaspoon salt
1 egg, beaten
$\frac{2}{3}$ cup butter
1 cup currants
$\frac{1}{2}$ cup lemon and orange peel
1 tablespoon honey
1 tablespoon caraway seeds

PUT the yeast into a bowl with a sprinkling of sugar and half the milk. It is ready when it begins to bubble. Into a mixing bowl put the flour and salt. Make a well and pour in the yeast mixture. Mix well. Sprinkle with a little flour and put in a warm place for 15 minutes.

Add the rest of the milk, the egg and mix to a smooth dough. Put in a warm place for an hour to rise.

In the meantime, melt the butter. Flour the fruit lightly; this prevents them from falling to the bottom of the cake. Butter and lightly flour a cake tin.

Knock down the dough and gradually add the butter, fruit, honey and caraway seeds. Press the dough into the cake tin and leave to stand in a warm place until it doubles its size. Bake in a preheated oven at 180°C (360°F) for an hour or until risen and golden brown. Turn out onto a wire rack to cool.

Printing Paper

Hand-printed paper is a very special wrapping for a gift—it immediately gives a message that a lot of thought and originality has gone into the gift, even before the receiver knows what's inside. If you are in the mood when printing paper, make an additional amount and roll up to give as drawer liners. Sprinkle some oil of lavender or roses on the paper to give it that extra touch. This paper would be excellent to cover the homemade boxes that some of you might want to make. Don't forget to make gift cards and tags at the same time to match the paper.

Potato Printing

You may remember this from childhood. If you don't, and my instructions aren't enough, call in a child to help out. It's better fun with company.

Materials
Firm potatoes
Tubes of artists' acrylic paints
Brown paper, butchers' paper or
    newspaper
Knife and scalpel

Design a simple pattern on paper before you start, and work out how it will fall over the whole sheet. Do you want to add the same design in a different colour? Or add a different design in the same colour? There are endless permutations, and you'll save a lot of wastage if you experiment first, get your design and colour right and then proceed to print up the whole sheet.

Choose your potato carefully. A large, firm new potato gives the best results. Clean the potato and cut it in half. Now draw the simple design to size on a piece of paper (it must, of course, be smaller than the potato half). Cut the shape out of the paper and place it on the cut surface of the potato; the moisture of the potato will hold it in place. With a scalpel, carefully cut away the potato where it does not form part of the design. When you've finished, remove the paper shape and dry the potato on kitchen paper.

Get to know the contours and imperfections of your potato half, as this will help with placement of the shape on the paper. For example, if the potato folds in at one edge, then use that edge to help you place the shape each time you make a print.

Have the acrylic paint mixed in a bowl. Very little water is needed to give the paint the consistency required. Test on some waste paper before starting the main sheet to see if the consistency seems right. If it is too thick, mix in a little water.

To print, place the face of the potato in the paint and then lay it carefully on the paper. Press firmly and evenly, and lift off neatly. Repeat according to your overall design until the whole sheet is printed. Don't forget to sign it! Hang to dry on the clothesline.

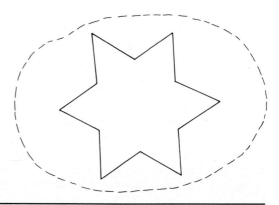

Paper Stencilling

Draw up a design motif of your choice or copy mine. It takes patience to cut out a stencil, but once you have, you can use it many times. Use the same motif in different colours for printing birthday cards, tea-towels, oven gloves, gift boxes, tablecloths and napkins as well as wrapping paper. Ezi-cut, a plastic stencil sheet, is available from art supply shops.

Materials
Ezi-cut stencil sheet
Cutting board
Scalpel
Pencil
Brushes for mixing paint
Natural sponge
Artists' acrylic paints
Paper

TRACE your chosen design onto the Ezi-cut sheet. Make a block of up to 8 repeats of the design to save time when printing. Place the Ezi-cut on a cutting board and cut out the areas with the scalpel, leaving a good-sized margin around the designs to avoid mistakes.

Mix the paint, using a small amount of water. Place the stencil on the paper to be printed on and hold it firmly in place with one hand. With the other

Printing paper can be lots of fun. In the foreground, three kangaroos are being stencil-printed in gold paint onto brown paper. You can also see how the other stencils were cut in blocks. In the background is a sheet of butchers' paper printed with a potato. The potato moulds can be seen under the lamp. If you choose a theme such as kangaroos for Christmas, you can stencil gift paper and gift tags, make labels and cards in the shape of a kangaroo, and even make gingerbread or biscuit kangaroos.

hand, dip the dry sponge into the paint and dab the paper firmly with it. Do not rub. Too much water in the paint or sponge will cause the design to bleed and the clean line of the shape to be lost. Carefully remove the stencil from the paper, reposition it and repeat until the sheet is covered.

Experiment first on newspaper. When you have finished stencilling, let your stencils dry out so that you can use them again with different colours on different papers.

Fabric Stencilling

You need the same materials as for paper stencilling except that you will need fabric paint instead of acrylic and, of course, fabric to print on. Follow the same instructions. Pin or tape your fabric to the table so that it doesn't move.

Almond Meringue Cake

This is an excellent cake to give away as a dessert. It is actually two cakes held together in the middle with jam and cream. Choose amongst the homemade jams in chapter 2; apricot, strawberry, raspberry or nectarine could be just as good as peach jam. You could add more jam on the side when serving. The cake without the filling can be made the day before.

4 eggwhites
1½ cups vanilla caster sugar
½ teaspoon lemon juice
⅔ cup ground almonds
Icing sugar as needed
½ cup thick cream
½ cup brandied peach jam (page 38)

Whisk the eggwhites until they are stiff. Gradually beat in the caster sugar and continue to beat until the mixture is very stiff. Add the lemon juice, then fold in the ground almonds. Grease and lightly flour two 20 cm (8 in) sandwich tins. Line the bottom with buttered greaseproof paper. Pour the meringue mixture into the tins and bake in a preheated oven at 150°C (300°F) for 40 minutes. Remove the paper 10 minutes after taking the meringues out of the oven. Cool on a wire rack.

Whip the cream stiff and fold in the jam gently. Spread onto one of the cakes and put the other on top. Dust the top with icing sugar. Place a paper doily underneath when presenting the cake.

Fairy Cakes

These are perfect little cakes for a young child's birthday party. They are iced with pink and white icing.

4 eggs
½ cup sugar

1 cup plain flour, sifted
¼ teaspoon baking powder
Icing
1 cup icing sugar
Red food colouring

Beat the eggs and sugar until the mixture is stiff. With a wooden spoon, gradually fold in the flour and baking powder.

Spoon the batter into trays or patty tins which are well greased and lightly floured. Fill just to the top.

Bake in a preheated oven at 210°C (410°F) for 15 minutes or until golden brown. Turn them out onto wire racks to cool. Make the icing by mixing water with the icing sugar until the icing is thin enough to spread. Divide in half and add a few drops of food colouring in one batch—just enough to make it pale pink. Ice half of each cake pink and the other half white.

Chocolate Birthday Cake

When we are young we always had a rich chocolate cake for our birthday cake. No other cake ever came up to our expectations as a birthday cake. This recipe has the added treat of walnuts. It will last for a week stored in the refrigerator.

250 g (8 oz) cooking chocolate
1 cup honey
1½ cups butter, soft
6 eggs, separated
1 cup flour
2 teaspoons baking powder
1 cup walnuts, finely chopped
Icing
90 g (3 oz) cooking chocolate
2 tablespoons hot water
1 cup icing sugar
Walnut halves to decorate

To melt the chocolate, put it in a bowl standing in a saucepan of warm water. Simmer the water until all the chocolate is melted. Remove from heat and pour the chocolate into a mixing bowl, add the honey, and then add the butter and the egg yolks. Stir until smooth, then sift the flour and baking powder into it and mix in the walnuts. Beat the egg-whites stiff and gently fold them into the cake mixture. Pour into a well-greased cake tin that has also been dusted with flour. Put the cake into a preheated oven at 200°C (400°F) for an hour or until cooked. Test by inserting a tooth-pick into the cake; when it comes out clean, the cake is done. Let it cool on a wire rack.

If you would like to ice it, melt the chocolate with the hot water in a bowl sitting in a saucepan of simmering water. Add the icing sugar and gradually add extra water until the icing is thin enough to spread. Ice when the cake is cool. Decorate with the walnut halves. Chocolate swirls also make a marvellous decoration extravagantly piled on top of the cake.

Cheesecake

This is an old recipe for cheesecake which is more wholesome than some of the oversweet cheesecakes available these days. It makes a simple and delightful luncheon dish. Add more sugar if you'd prefer a sweet cake. I take it along for a girls' lunch when we are too busy talking to want to cook.

Pastry
½ cup butter
2 eggs, separated
2 cups flour, sifted
2 teaspoons baking powder
1 cup milk
Filling
500 g (1 lb) cottage cheese
1 egg, separated
½ cup sultanas
1 tablespoon vanilla sugar
3 apples
Juice of 1 lemon
2 teaspoons ground cinnamon

To MAKE the pastry, cream the butter and beat in the egg yolks until the mixture is light and fluffy. Mix in the the flour, baking powder and milk. Beat the eggwhites until fluffy and fold into the mixture. Knead and roll out the dough on a well-floured board; line a 23 cm (9 in) flan tin or springform tin.

If you are using cottage cheese for the filling, cream it in a food processor until it is smooth. Into a bowl put the cheese, egg yolk, sultanas and sugar. Mix well and then gently fold in the stiffly beaten eggwhite. Pour the mixture into the flan tin.

A perfect cake for afternoon tea, Gugelhupf (opposite page), always looks charming with its attractive moulding and a delicate dredging of icing sugar.

Grate the apples into a bowl with the lemon juice. Mix well to prevent the apples from discolouring. Cover the cheese with the apples and sprinkle with the cinnamon. Bake in a preheated oven at 180°C (360°F) for 45 minutes or until the filling is firm. Remove from the flan tin when cold.

126

Gugelhupf

Gugelhupf is a breadlike cake that is immensely popular throughout Austria, Germany and Alsace, where there are as many variations of the recipe as there are variations of the spelling of the name. One thing that has changed little over the centuries is the shape of the mould in which the cake is cooked. It has slanting, furrowed or moulded sides and a central funnel through which the oven heat is able to penetrate the cake's centre. A Gugelhupf is traditionally made with yeast, but here is a simpler version that is just as good.

175 g (6 oz) butter
1¼ cups icing sugar
3 eggs
½ cup milk
2½ cups self-raising flour
½ teaspoon vanilla essence
Grated rind of 1 lemon
¾ cup sultanas
A little icing sugar to dredge

CREAM the butter and icing sugar together until light and fluffy. Beat in the eggs one at a time. Gradually mix in the milk alternately with the sieved flour, being careful not to let the mixture curdle. Add the vanilla essence, grated lemon rind and cleaned sultanas. Mix well until the mixture is smooth and well blended. Turn into a well-greased Gugelhupf tin and bake in a moderate oven 185°C (370°F) for about 1 to 1¼ hours or until well risen and firm to touch. Turn onto a wire rack until cold. Dredge with icing sugar.

Polish Easter Cake

Polish Easter cakes are rich flat loaves baked with nuts and dried fruit. They traditionally end the Lenten fast at midnight on Easter Saturday. They are also eaten for Christmas and other special occasions.

1 cup butter
1 cup sugar
1½ cups flour, sifted

¼ teaspoon salt
6 egg yolks
½ cup ground almonds
½ cup finely chopped hazelnuts
2 tablespoons finely chopped orange
    and lemon peel
2 tablespoons sultanas

CREAM the butter and sugar until light and fluffy. Add the flour and salt, then gradually add the egg yolks. Stir in the ground almonds, hazelnuts, peel and the sultanas. Roll out the dough on a floured board and shape into two long loaves. Bake in a preheated oven at 180°C (360°F) for about 40 minutes or until they have turned golden brown. Cool for 10 minutes on a wire rack, then cut into slices.

Simnel Cake

This is the traditional cake to give to mothers on Mothering Sunday, the Sunday in mid-Lent on which it is customary for Britons to visit their mothers with a small gift.

⅓ cup butter
½ cup sugar
4 eggs
⅔ cup flour, sifted
1 teaspoon baking powder
⅔ cup orange and lemon peel
1½ cups sultanas
1½ cups currants
1 cup ground almonds
½ teaspoon ground cinnamon
½ teaspoon ground ginger
½ cup brandy
1 eggwhite
Caster sugar
Angelica to decorate
Almond paste
1½ cups ground almonds
1½ cups brown sugar
1 egg
1 tablespoon brandy

CREAM the butter and sugar together until they are light and fluffy. Gradually beat in the eggs, one at a time. Mix in the flour and baking powder and then add the fruit, spices and brandy.

Mix all the almond paste ingredients together until smooth. Divide the paste into three equal portions.

Pour half the cake mixture into a cake tin that has been greased and lined with buttered greaseproof paper. Then spread a layer of one portion of the almond paste and cover that with the rest of the cake mixture. Bake in a pre-heated oven at 160°C (320°F) for about $1\frac{1}{2}$ hours. Test if it is cooked by inserting a toothpick; when it comes out clean the cake is ready. Cool on a wire rack.

When cool, cover the top of the cake with another portion of almond paste. Roll the remaining portion into balls and place them around the edge of the top layer as a decoration. Brush the paste with eggwhite and dust with caster sugar. Put the cake back in the oven at 100°C (200°F) until the paste has set. Decorate with angelica.

Stollen
(German Advent Cake)

This is a German cake or sweet bread that is eaten on the first Sunday in Advent. The shape is meant to represent the Holy Child in a swaddling cloth. It makes perfect gift to take to a first Advent celebration, but I wouldn't suggest waiting till Advent to make one.

7 g ($\frac{1}{4}$ oz) dry yeast or 15 g ($\frac{1}{2}$ oz)
   fresh yeast
$\frac{3}{4}$ cup warm milk
4 cups flour
1 cup butter
$\frac{1}{2}$ teaspoon cinnamon
$\frac{2}{3}$ cup slivered almonds
1 cup vanilla sugar
2 tablespoons rum
$\frac{1}{2}$ cup currants
$\frac{1}{2}$ cup sultanas
$\frac{1}{2}$ cup candied orange and lemon peel
$\frac{1}{2}$ cup melted butter
$\frac{1}{2}$ cup icing sugar

Put the yeast into the milk, sprinkle in a little sugar and let sit until it is bubbly. Combine the flour, butter, cinnamon, almonds, sugar and rum in a bowl and mix in the yeast mixture. Knead until the dough is smooth and elastic. Leave it covered to rise in a warm place for an hour. Knock down the dough, sprinkling all the fruits through as you go. Form the dough into an oval shape with a pouch tucked into the top, so one side is higher than the other—that is, try to make it look like a swaddled child. Put it on a greased

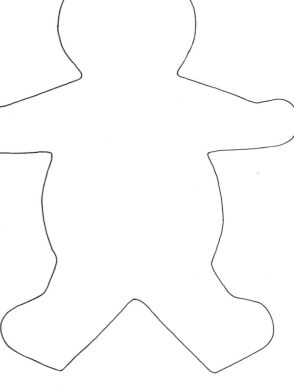

baking tray. Brush with the melted butter and leave to rise for 15 minutes.

Brush with butter again. Bake in a preheated oven at 180°C (360°F) for 40 minutes or until it is cooked. Brush with melted butter and sprinkle with icing sugar.

Christmas Cake

This is my old family recipe. It makes two to three cakes or a very large one. It works just as well halved, if you prefer to make a smaller cake. It is rich and dark and has been known to last up to two years; and that was only because we misplaced some. Ice the cake with royal icing if you wish. Of course, this same cake is used for weddings and special anniversaries. Just vary the decoration.

2 cups sultanas
2 cups raisins
1 cup currants
$\frac{1}{2}$ cup dates
$\frac{1}{2}$ cup mixed peel
$\frac{1}{2}$ cup glacé cherries
$\frac{1}{4}$ cup slivered almonds
$\frac{1}{4}$ cup glacé fruit
$\frac{1}{2}$ cup dark rum
$\frac{1}{2}$ cup brandy
1 cup butter
1 cup brown vanilla sugar
6 eggs
1 tablespoon golden syrup
$2\frac{1}{2}$ cups flour, sifted
2 teaspoons mixed spice
1 teaspoon ground cinnamon
1 teaspoon grated nutmeg
$\frac{1}{4}$ teaspoon ground cloves
$\frac{1}{2}$ teaspoon bicarbonate of soda
$\frac{1}{2}$ teaspoon salt
Whole almonds and glacé cherries to
    decorate

Prepare the fruit by chopping them and macerate in half the spirits for 24 hours.

Cream the butter and sugar until light and fluffy. Gradually add the eggs, one by one, then add the golden syrup and half the fruit. Add half the flour and spices and mix well. Add the rest of the rum and brandy and the remainder of the flour and fruit.

Butter the cake tin or tins and line them with buttered brown paper. Spoon in the take mixture. Decorate the top with the almonds and half-cherries. Bake in a preheated oven at 180°C (360°F) for 3 to $3\frac{1}{2}$ hours. Turn the oven down to 150°C (300°F) after the first half-hour. After $2\frac{1}{2}$ hours, cover the top of the cake with greased brown paper.

When the cake is cooked, remove it from the tin immediately and wrap aluminium foil around it, then 5 layers of newspaper so that it cools very slowly. Tie with string and leave in a cool place.

Royal Icing

A traditional icing to put over a Christmas or wedding cake. It is a simple recipe; spend the extra time on creative ideas for decorating, marzipan Christmas tree or Holy Family silhouette, perhaps. First cover the cake with a layer of marzipan 1 cm ($\frac{3}{8}$ in) thick. Read the marzipan recipes on page 163.

2 eggwhites
Salt
2 teaspoons lemon juice
3 cups icing sugar, sifted

Whisk the eggwhites until they are stiff. Add the salt and lemon juice and then gradually whisk in the sugar until the mixture is smooth and thick. Put the icing on the cake immediately with a spatula. It will dry in about 10 hours. Decorate with holly flowers and ribbon on the day you are giving it away.

6 Desserts

ALL THESE FOLLOWING recipes are for portable desserts: flans and pies, puddings, and fruit in alcohol. Some are traditional dishes for special occasions, such as mince pies, walnut tart and plum pudding for Christmas, pumpkin pie for Halloween and strawberries in eau de vie for Saint Valentine's Day. Others can be enjoyed any time with any excuse.

The fruit in alcohol recipes are terribly easy to make and cheap if you make them when the fruit is readily available. You do not need expensive wines and spirits; buy the cheapest brands. Make large quantities and you will always have plenty of jars to give as presents. There is a recipe for Summer Fruits in a Pot from my husband's German family. The summer fruits gradually fill up a huge earthenware pot and are covered with more and more rum as the pot fills. By Advent the pot has been sitting, sealed, for over three months. Traditionally it is opened up on the first Sunday in Advent. It is gradually eaten and drunk during the festive season and finished off on New Year's Eve. The huge pot sits on a dresser with a silver ladle and everyone is free to take a nip or a bite any time of the day, even the children. It can get very cold in the north of Germany at Christmas, and after a brisk walk in the snow carrying the last of the Christmas shopping it is wonderful to be greeted by a warm apartment made warmer still with a bite of the summer fruits.

Grape Flan

An attractive all-green flan: the green grapes sit in lime and ginger marmalade. For a gift, put the flan on a layer of grape leaves with a few tiny bunches of grapes. You could still make this flan in the depth of winter using the preserved grapes in brandy on page 139.

Shortcrust pastry
1½ cups plain flour
A pinch of salt
¼ teaspoon baking powder
3 tablespoons butter, chilled and diced

1 egg yolk
2 teaspoons iced water
A squeeze of lime juice
Filling
750 g (1½ lb) green seedless grapes
1 cup lime and ginger marmalade
   (page 42)
Juice of 1 lime

Apple Pie (page 132), about to be wrapped up to take along to a Fathers Day dinner. The wrapping paper has been printed with a potato (page 122).

Sift the flour, salt and baking powder together. Rub in the butter until the mixture resembles coarse breadcrumbs. Mix the egg yolk, iced water and lime juice together, and stir them quickly into the flour mixture with a knife to form a dough. Shape into a ball, wrap in plastic film, and chill for 20 minutes. This recipe makes enough pastry to line a 20 to 23 cm (8 to 9 in) flan ring or pie plate.

Roll out the pastry and line a buttered and floured flan ring. Chill for 30 minutes. Bake blind—that is, cover the pastry with greaseproof paper and fill the flan with dried beans, then put it into a preheated oven at 190°C (375°F) for 20 to 25 minutes or until the pastry is golden brown.

Remove the flan from the oven; when it is cool, remove the beans and paper. Fill the flan with the grapes. Melt the marmalade with the lime juice and spoon it over the grapes.

Apple Pie

Pastry
2½ cups flour
½ cup butter, chilled and diced
¼ cup vanilla caster sugar
A pinch of salt
2 eggs
1 tablespoon water
A squeeze of lemon
Filling
1 kg (2 lb) cooking apples, peeled, cored and sliced
½ cup vanilla sugar
3 tablespoons cornflour
1 tablespoon lemon juice
1 teaspoon lemon zest
½ teaspoon chopped ginger
½ teaspoon ground cinnamon
¼ teaspoon ground cloves
1 tablespoon butter
1 tablespoon milk

To make the pastry: Put the flour, butter, sugar and salt in a mixing bowl.

Mix well and rub the butter through with your fingers until the mixture resembles breadcrumbs. Mix the eggs, water and lemon together and then add them to the flour mixture. Stir in quickly with a knife to form a dough. Shape into a ball, wrap in plastic and chill for 30 minutes.

Roll out two-thirds of the pastry to line a 23 cm (9 in) buttered pie dish.

Mix the sliced apples with the sugar, cornflour, lemon juice and zest, ginger and spices. Put the mixture into the pie dish and dot with the butter. Roll out the remaining pastry. Cover the pie dish, trim the edges and crimp them together. Decorate with left-over pastry. Prick the top of the pie with a fork so that the steam can escape. Brush the pastry with a little milk. Bake in a preheated oven at 180°C (360°F) for 45 to 60 minutes or until the pie is golden brown.

Prune Flan

A rich, glossy cream and black flan to enliven a winter's day lunch. Present it in the flan dish, wrapped in glossy black paper and tied with a shocking pink satin ribbon.

Shortcrust pastry (see the recipe for Grape Flan, page 130)
Filling
1 tablespoon Yunnan tealeaves
400 g (12 oz) pitted dried prunes
1 egg
1 teaspoon cornflour
3 tablespoons caster sugar
2 tablespoons lemon liqueur (page 151)
¾ cup cream

Make 2 cups of Yunnan tea and soak the prunes in it for 3 hours. Roll out the pastry and line a buttered and floured flan dish. Chill for 30 minutes.

Drain the prunes and fill the flan dish with them. Bake in a preheated oven at 190°C (375°F) for 10 minutes. In the meantime, beat the egg, cornflour, sugar and liqueur into the cream. Take the flan out of the oven, pour the cream mixture over the prunes and return the flan to the oven. Bake for another 15 to 20 minutes or until the filling is set and the pastry golden brown.

Pumpkin Pie

A homely pie to take to a Thanksgiving or Halloween celebration. Leave the pumpkin shell intact when you remove the edible layer and carve a Halloween pumpkin face. Put candles inside it and use it for the centrepiece of the table.

Shortcrust pastry (see the recipe for
　　Grape Flan, page 130)
Filling
3 eggs
½ cup sugar
2 cups puréed pumpkin
1 teaspoon grated nutmeg
½ teaspoon ground cloves
½ teaspoon ground cardamom
1 teaspoon salt
1 cup thick cream
Walnut halves for decoration

Roll out the pastry and line a buttered and floured pie dish. Chill the pastry while you make the filling.

Beat the eggs and sugar together until they are light and then stir in the pumpkin purée, spices and salt and mix well. Stir in the the cream and pour the mixture into the pie dish.

Bake the pie in a preheated oven at 190°C (375°F) for 40 to 50 minutes until the filling is well risen and golden.

Decorate with walnut halves around the edge and in the centre.

Walnut Pie

In some European countries walnut pie is a traditional dish to eat as part of the Christmas Eve feast. It certainly tastes like a special treat with its rich dense filling and rich shortcrust pastry.

Shortcrust pastry (see the recipe for
　　Grape Flan, page 130)
Filling
4 egg yolks
⅔ cup sugar
2 cups finely ground walnuts
1 tablespoon julienne lemon peel
6 eggwhites
Juice of 1 lemon

Roll out the pastry and line a buttered and floured flan ring or pie plate. Chill.

Beat the egg yolks with the sugar until pale and fluffy. Fold in the walnuts and lemon peel. Beat the eggwhites until stiff. Fold them into the egg and walnut mixture. Now fill the pastry case.

Bake in a preheated oven at 190°C (375°F) for 35 to 40 minutes until the filling is well risen and golden.

Mincemeat

Mincemeat makes a thoughtful gift to a busy cook at the beginning of Advent. It has to macerate for a month, so all the cook has to do on Christmas Eve is to make the pastry for the mince pies. It can be very delicious as a filling for a sweet dessert omelette, or serve with ice-cream. Give serving suggestions and the recipe for mince pies with the jar of mincemeat. This is a large quantity, so halve if liked.

2½ cups finely chopped suet
3 cups currants
3 cups raisins
3 cups grated apple
2 cups sugar
1½ cups sultanas
⅔ cup candied orange peel, chopped
⅔ cup slivered almonds
1½ cups rum
Juice and chopped rind of 1 orange
1 teaspoon cinnamon
1 teaspoon grated nutmeg
½ teaspoon ground cloves

Put all the ingredients into a bowl and mix thoroughly. Spoon into sterilised jars, seal and label. Store for one month.

Mince Pies

Mince pies make a handy small gift to give to neighbours and acquaintances. Wrap a few in a handkerchief tied with ribbon and a piece of holly. I have read that mince pies were originally oval shaped to represent Christ's crib.

1 slab short or puff pastry
4 cups mincemeat (page 133)
1 eggwhite
Caster sugar to decorate

Roll out the pastry and cut into rounds to line buttered and floured muffin pans. Fill them up with the mincemeat. Brush the edge with a mixture of egg and water. Cover with smaller rounds of pastry. Pinch the edges together well and trim. Slash the pies a few times to let the steam out when cooking. Brush the pastry with the eggwhite. Put the pies into a preheated oven at 220°C (430°F) for about 30 minutes or until the tops are golden bown. Halfway through the cooking, remove the pies and dredge them with caster sugar, then return them to the oven.

Store in an airtight container and you'll find they keep very well.

A Halloween barbecue dinner which started and ended with pumpkin. There is pumpkin soup in the charming terrine; the recipe for the Pumpkin Pie is on page 133.

Summer Pudding

You need enough fruit to fill a soufflé dish or a pudding basin. Vary the combination of fruits. Add stoned cherries, blackcurrants, boysenberries, blackberries or blueberries. Just use what is available. It is best kept for a day in the refrigerator, so it makes an easy gift for a summer's day picnic or outdoor lunch.

    750 g (1½ lb) mixture of summer
        fruit: raspberries, strawberries,
        redcurrants
    ½ cup caster sugar
    Slices of stale sliced bread, crusts
        removed
    2 tablespoons strawberry liqueur
        (page 153)

PREPARE and wash the fruits and put into a saucepan with the sugar. Cook gently for a few minutes until the sugar melts and the juices begin to flow.

Butter a soufflé dish, line with the slices of bread nearly up to the rim. Fill it up with the warm fruit, pour the strawberry liqueur over it, and cover the fruit with more slices of bread. Cover with a plate. Put a weight on top of the plate and keep in the refrigerator for 24 hours. Save any left-over juice.

Give it as a gift in the soufflé dish and unmould when ready to eat. Check whether the bread has soaked up all the juice before leaving home; sprinkle more juice or liqueur over the bread if the juice hasn't quite soaked through. The pudding is usually served with cream, though I prefer plain yoghurt these days.

Custard

A friend gave me a mug of this custard when I was lying in bed miserable with the flu after a week of teeming rain. He couldn't have thought of a nicer gift; of course I was rallying soon after. He brought the ingredients with him and cooked it quickly on my stove.

    1 egg yolk
    1 cup milk
    2 tablespoons sugar
    A pinch of nutmeg
    1 teaspoon lemon zest
    2 teaspoons Armagnac or cognac

BEAT the egg yolk. Heat the milk and add the sugar, egg, nutmeg and lemon zest. Stir over a low heat for 5 to 10 minutes. Add the Armagnac.

Eggnog

A traditional concoction given to the old and the sick as a restorative. Make the eggnog just before leaving to see your friend, and put it in a warm vacuum flask. Or you could freeze it and give it as an ice-cream. But also prescribe it to yourself any time you need a restorative.

    3 eggs
    3 tablespoons sugar
    2 tablespoons sweet white wine

YOU will need a saucepan large enough to hold a mixing bowl. Put some water into the saucepan and bring it to the boil. Put the eggs and sugar into the mixing bowl and beat until they are light and fluffy. Then beat in the wine. Put the bowl into the boiling water. Keep whisking the eggnog until it is firm.

Rich Plum Pudding

The Sunday before the beginning of Advent used to be called stir-up Sunday. It was the day devoted to making the plum pudding, Christmas cake and mincemeat. This is a family recipe for a huge quantity which we continue to make so as to have enough to give small puddings away to friends. I love the spicy smell of our cellar when all the plum puddings are hanging up. I must admit it is sometimes a wrench to take them down. This sixty-year-old recipe was described as 'serves 12'. They must have had huge appetites those days.

6 cups raisins
3 cups sultanas
3 cups pitted prunes
1½ cups currants
4 tablespoons chopped orange peel
1 cup grated apple
1 tablespoon chopped glacé cherries
½ cup slivered almonds
2 cups brandy
1½ cups butter
1½ cups sugar
6 eggs
6 cups breadcrumbs
4 tablespoons flour, sifted
1 teaspoon grated nutmeg
1 teaspoon ground cinnamon
1 teaspoon ground ginger
1 teaspoon ground cardamom
½ teaspoon ground cloves
½ teaspoon bicarbonate of soda
1 teaspoon salt

Cʜᴏᴘ up the larger fruits and combine with all the other fruits, almonds and brandy. Mix well, cover and macerate for 5 days.

Cream the butter and sugar together until the mixture is light and fluffy. Add the eggs, one by one, getting each one incorporated before adding another. Add the breadcrumbs, a cup at a time, mixing well. Now add the flour, spices, soda and salt and mix well. Lastly mix in the macerated fruit. If it gets too hard to stir such a large quantity with a wooden spoon, the hands work wonders.

Cut a piece of previously boiled calico into squares of the size required. Sprinkle each piece with flour around the area the pudding will take up. Put some pudding mixture in the centre and form into a ball. Draw up the calico around the pudding and tie tightly at the top with kitchen string, leaving enough to hang up later.

Place the puddings in a large saucepan of boiling water—you may need two pots. Simmer for 6 hours. Keep checking the level of the water and replenish when necessary. Less cooking is needed for smaller puddings.

I hang the puddings in the garden to cool and drip dry, then transfer them to hang in the cellar.

Reheat in simmering water on Christmas Day for 1½ to 2 hours.

Hard Sauce for Plum Pudding

½ cup caster sugar
½ cup milk powder
⅓ cup melted butter
3 tablespoons rum

Mɪx the sugar and milk powder together. Add the butter and rum and mix well. Chill and serve cold with the hot pudding.

Rum Butter

Rum butter can be made weeks before Christmas and stored in the refrigerator.

1 cup unsalted butter
1½ cups soft brown sugar
1 cup brown rum
1 teaspoon ground cinnamon
1 teaspoon grated nutmeg
½ teaspoon grated ginger

Pᴜᴛ the butter into a bowl and place the bowl in simmering water. When the butter has melted, stir in the sugar. When the sugar has dissolved, pour in the rum slowly, whisking all the time. Add the spices. Pour into a butter dish and, when cool, cover and refrigerate.

Light Christmas Pudding

A low-fat Christmas pudding that is still very rich in fruit and nuts. I find this an excellent pudding to make for friends on a cholesterol-free diet. Make it a month in advance if you have the time. It really improves with ageing.

1½ cups prunes
2 tablespoons chopped mixed peel
½ cup raisins
1 cup sultanas
½ cup currants
1 grated apple
1 grated carrot
½ cup brandy
Zest and juice of 1 lemon
Zest and juice of 2 oranges
2 tablespoons sugar
2 eggs
1 teaspoon grated nutmeg
1 teaspoon ground allspice
1 teaspoon ground cinnamon
3 cloves, ground
1 cup fresh wholemeal breadcrumbs
1 cup wholemeal self-raising flour
½ cup slivered almonds
Butter as required

SLICE the prunes and put the peel, raisins, sultanas, currants, apple and carrot in a bowl. Pour the brandy over and stir well. Cover and leave to macerate for several days.

Into a bowl but the zest and juices of the lemon and the oranges, the sugar and the eggs. Whisk and then stir into the mixed fruit. Add the spices, breadcrumbs, flour and almonds. Let stand for an hour.

Meanwhile, double-grease the pudding basin to ensure that the pudding turns out easily. Smear the basin well with butter, refrigerate for 15 minutes, then grease it again and refrigerate until you put the pudding mixture in.

After filling the basin, smooth the top of the pudding flat. Cover the top of the basin with two layers of aluminium foil and tie with string; make a handle of string across the top so that you can lift the pudding in and out of a saucepan. Steam in a large saucepan of simmering water, covered, for 4 hours. Check the level of the water regularly and top up when necessary.

Refrigerate the pudding when it has cooled down. On Christmas Day, boil for another 1½ hours before eating.

Cherries in Eau-de-Vie

This combination makes an excellent change from the better-known cherry brandy. Use only the best-quality cherries without blemishes and not too ripe. I collect old and well-shaped bottles so that I always have an attractive bottle to give away. If you cannot buy eau-de-vie, use flavourless vodka.

4 cups eau-de-vie
2.5 kg (5 lb) cherries
2 cups caster sugar

CUT off half the stalk of each cherry. Wash and dry the cherries and put them into sterilised jars. Put the sugar in and stir or shake to cover the cherries. Pour in eau-de-vie to cover, seal and label. Shake the bottles every week to disperse the sugar. They will be ready in two months. Store in a cool, dark place.

Cumquats in Brandy

Brandied cumquats are a delicious dessert with ice-cream, and the left-over syrup can be drunk as a wonderful fruit liqueur after a festive meal.

750 g (1½ lb) firm cumquats
1 cup vanilla sugar
2 cups water
4 cups inexpensive brandy

CAREFULLY wash the cumquats and prick them eight times with a needle to prevent them from bursting.

Put the sugar and water into a saucepan and bring slowly to the boil. Simmer for 15 minutes and add the cumquats. Bring the syrup back to the boil and simmer for 5 minutes. Take from the heat and ladle the cumquats into a sterilised jar. Reduce the syrup by half and when cool pour in the brandy. Pour the mixture over the cumquats.

Seal immediately, label and store away for at least a month or two before giving it away or opening.

Prunes in Red Wine

This is a quick and easy recipe.

5 cups red wine
2 cups sugar
1 vanilla pod
1 cup rum
4 cups pitted prunes

Put the wine, sugar and vanilla pod into a saucepan and bring to the boil. Keep boiling until the syrup thickens.

The preparation for Plum Pudding (page 135) together with a pudding dressed up as a gift with a recipe for Rum Butter (page 136) to accompany the gift.

Remove from the heat, let it stand for 5 minutes and then pour in the rum and take out the vanilla pod.

Fill warm sterilised jars with the prunes and pour the wine liqueur over them to cover. Leave for three weeks before opening.

Grapes in Brandy

The best way to eat these is in small glasses with some of the liqueur. Pick the grapes up by the stem to eat, then drink the liqueur. They'll be ready towards the end of winter.

> 1 kg (2 lb) large firm grapes
> 1½ cups caster sugar
> 4 cloves
> 10 peppercorns
> 1 teaspoon fennel seeds
> Peel of half a lemon
> 1 bottle brandy

Wash and dry the grapes and cut them off the branches, leaving the stem on. Put them into a bowl, cover with the sugar, spices and lemon peel. Stir the grapes so that they are all coated. Spoon into sterilised jars along with all the flavourings. Pour the brandy over to cover. Seal, label and store for 6 months. Shake the jars occasionally.

The fruits of summer preserved in brandy and syrup: Grapes in Brandy (this page), Cumquats in Brandy (page 137) and Green Figs in Syrup (this page).

Green Figs in Syrup

I was lucky enough to be able to pick small green figs from a friend's trees for this recipe. You need to catch them just before they begin to soften. The liqueur that results is as delicious as the figs.

> 1 kg (2 lb) small green figs
> 2 cups sugar
> 2 cups water
> Zest and juice of 1 orange
> 2 tablespoons brandy

Wash the figs carefully, because they are quite fragile. Leave the skins on and just trim the stems. Make a syrup by heating the sugar and water in a saucepan. Add the orange as soon as it begins to thicken, then take the pan off the heat. Put the figs in the syrup and let them sit there overnight.

The next day bring the syrup to the boil and let it simmer until the figs are soft. Lift them out and put them into warm sterilised jars. If the syrup isn't luscious and thick, boil fast until it is. Remove from heat and let it sit for 15 minutes. Stir in the brandy and pour over the figs. Seal and label.

Dried Fruit Compote

This compote can be eaten the day it is made or sealed away in jars to be kept and used as gifts. The recipe is for a large quantity so that you can have plenty to give away. Halve it if you want a smaller amount. Glass compote dishes are usually lovely designs, so comb the second-hand shops and give a compote dish as part of the gift.

$1\frac{1}{2}$ cups sugar
6 cups water
Zest of 1 orange
Zest of 1 lemon
3 cloves
1 cinnamon stick
$\frac{1}{2}$ cup dried pears
$\frac{1}{2}$ cup dried figs
$\frac{1}{2}$ cup dried peaches
$\frac{1}{2}$ cup dried prunes
3 cups dried apricots
$1\frac{1}{2}$ cups dried apples
$1\frac{1}{2}$ cups dried sultanas
3 cups marsala

MAKE a syrup by heating the sugar, water, zest and spices in a saucepan. When it comes to the boil, add all the dried fruit and simmer for half an hour. Remove from heat and let it stand for 20 minutes.

Spoon the fruit into sterilised jars or a compote dish. Bring the syrup back to the boil and boil hard until it is nice and thick. Let it cool for 20 minutes, add the marsala and stir well. Pour the syrup over the fruit to cover. Seal the jars and label.

Peaches in Vodka

The peaches and syrup will be in their prime two months after they are bottled, so write the opening time on the label.

2 kg (4 lb) peaches
1 kg (2 lb) sugar
5 cups water
3 cloves
2 cups vodka

RUB the fuzz off the peaches and prick them about six times with a skewer right through to the stone. Put the sugar and water into a saucepan and bring to the boil. Add the peaches and cloves and as soon as it comes to the boil again take them out. When the peaches cool, remove the skins. Leave the peaches whole or cut them in half.

Bring the syrup to the boil again and put in the peaches. When the syrup comes to the boil once more, remove the peaches and put them into warm sterilised jars. Continue to cook the syrup until it is nice and thick. Let it cool a little, add the vodka and pour over the peaches to cover them. Seal, label and store in a dark, cool place.

Summer Berries in Rum

People often ask me for the recipe, or another jar, of this. It is a dark rich red preserve and looks beautiful spooned over mascarpone accompanied by homemade macaroons.

$1\frac{1}{2}$ cups raspberries
$1\frac{1}{2}$ cups strawberries
1 cup blackcurrants
1 cup vanilla sugar
3 cups dark rum

HULL the strawberries and stem the currants. Wash and dry the fruits and put them in a bowl. Sprinkle with the sugar and mix well. Put the fruit into sterilised jars and pour the rum over to cover the fruit. Seal and store at least for two months before eating.

Strawberries in Eau-de-Vie

I always associate strawberries with romance. After all, they are red, representing passion, and heart-shaped when cut into two. Which makes this preserve an ideal Saint Valentine gift. Prepare it when strawberries are cheap. The strawberries are delicious to eat and the liqueur is heavenly. Use as a flavouring for champagne or serve as a dessert with strawberry ice-cream and mint leaves. If you cannot buy eau-de-vie, use flavourless vodka.

    4 cups strawberries
    2 cups vanilla caster sugar
    4 cups eau-de-vie

Hull the strawberries, wash and dry them. Pack them into sterilised jars, pour the sugar over them and shake. Cover the fruit with the eau-de-vie. Seal and store in a cool, dark place for 3 weeks before opening.

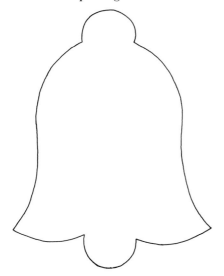

Summer Fruits in a Pot

There are many versions of this recipe. The fruits vary according to what is available, as does the liquor. You can use brandy or even eau-de-vie instead of rum. In Germany they have a special pot, a Römertopf, which is like a soup tureen, to make it in. The idea is to conserve the summer fruits in alcohol and sugar as they become available and, when the container is full, seal it up for three months before opening. If you make a huge quantity, you can ladle out small measures to give away as presents. Use a glazed bread crock, a soup tureen, or very large jars. If the container doesn't have a lid, put two layers of plastic film over the top and cover with a tea-towel.

To start
    2 cups white rum
    3 cups sugar
    2 cups fruit

Put the rum into the container with 2 cups of the sugar. Add the washed and dried fruit, stir and sprinkle on the other cup of sugar. Cover well. As other fruits become available, put them in and add sugar and rum in the same proportions as at the start.

Choose from strawberries, cherries (stoned), currants, raspberries, grapes, prunes, cumquats, and blackberries, which should be whole. Cut peaches, apricots and plums in half, and quarter apples and pears.

Tamarillos in Strawberry Liqueur

This preserve has the most beautiful colour; it will give your friends much pleasure just looking at it. Serve with natural vanilla ice-cream—or hokey pokey ice-cream, which apparently New Zealand gave the world as well as the fancy name for this South American tree-tomato.

    2 cups sugar
    1½ cups water
    1 cinnamon stick
    Zest of 1 lemon
    12 tamarillos
    2 cups strawberry liqueur (page 153)

Make a syrup by heating the sugar, water, cinnamon stick and lemon zest in a saucepan. Cook until the syrup thickens. Meanwhile, wash the tamarillos, remove the stems and cut the fruit into halves. Put them into the syrup and simmer for 10 minutes.

Spoon the tamarillos into warm sterilised jars. Pour the strawberry liqueur into the syrup and then pour over the fruit to cover. Seal and store for at least two months before opening.

7 Drinks

Fruit syrups, herbal teas, barley water, tomato juice, mulled wines and punches, fruit liqueurs and ratafias—all delicious drinks to make and give away as presents. Some last for only a week or so, but those preserved in a sterilising bath or alcohol will last for months or indefinitely.

Most of these homemade beverages are made by macerating good-quality fruit in syrup or alcohol for some time and then straining, bottling and storing in a cool, dark place. Remember to keep everything spotlessly clean and to sterilise the jars and bottles. Read the instructions that follow before embarking on the recipes for fruit syrups, punches and fruit liqueurs.

Fruit Syrups and Squashes

Making syrups and squashes is a very useful way of preserving fruit. Fruit syrups are usually made from berry fruits. The finely strained juice is sweetened with sugar. Squashes are made mainly from citrus fruit, and the fruit tissue is included.

Besides making splendid drinks, syrups and squashes can be used to flavour jellies, sweets, puddings and sauces. If the sterilising method is correctly followed, the bottles will last for several weeks. The flavour deteriorates after that. Refrigerate once a bottle is opened.

For syrup drinks, use one or two tablespoonfuls of syrup for each cup of water, soda or mineral water. When making milk or yoghurt drinks, add the syrup slowly while stirring rapidly to prevent curdling.

The most suitable fruits for syrups are blackberries, blackcurrants, raspberries and strawberries. The fruit should be ripe, fresh and clean.

To extract the juice from the fruit, cut up the fruit into small pieces and put in a bowl, then mash with a potato masher. Stand the bowl in a pan of simmering water and leave it there until the juices flow freely. Remove from heat and mash

A delicious display of fruit liqueurs: Passionfruit Gin (page 152), Blackberry Liqueur (page 149) and Orange Ratafia (page 152). An antique decanter can be part of the gift of a homemade liqueur. On the left is a Victorian set of fruit liqueur decanters.

again. To press out the juice, put the fruit into a jelly bag and leave for 2 to 3 hours or overnight; squeeze the jelly bag to extract as much juice as possible.

The amount of sugar added varies, but I usually add one cup of sugar for each cup of juice. I prefer to use sugar as a sweetener, as it helps to retain the original flavour of the fruit. No heating is needed when adding the sugar to the fruit juice; just stir until it has dissolved. Most citrus squashes are improved by adding a little citric acid, but you can please yourself about doing this.

When the sugar has dissolved, the syrup should be bottled at once. Recycle screw-top sauce bottles and bottles with wired-down lids. They should be filled to within 2.5 cm (1 in) of the top and lightly sealed. The syrup needs to be sterilised, together with the bottles and lids, in a hot-water bath. If you don't have a bottling pan, use the largest saucepan you have and put wire racks on the bottom so the bottles aren't sitting on the bottom of the pan. Wrap the widest part of each bottle with a sheet of newspaper—this helps support the bottles and stops them knocking against each other. Stand the bottles upright in the pan, and put in enough water to cover the tops of the caps. Bring the water to the boil and simmer for 20 minutes, after which bottles can be removed and the screw tops tightened.

Fruit Liqueurs and Ratafias

A ratafia is, properly, a fruit liqueur flavoured with almonds or other fruit kernels as well as juice. However, the name is commonly applied to any homemade liqueur of fruit, sugar and brandy or eau-de-vie. Liqueurs are simple to make and delicious to sip. They usually need to mature for two months before they are strained and decanted. The miracle that takes place is wonderful. Basically you just throw fruit into a bottle, pour in a sugar syrup and top up with the cheapest brandy or vodka. In two months time, you can hardly believe the wonderful clear liqueur, the pastel colours and the taste. Generally you end up with double or triple the volume of alcohol you originally purchased, which makes it a pretty good bargain. Watch out for bottles, large and small, to decant the liqueur in, or buy antique decanters as part of the gift. For a small gift I pour some into old perfume bottles and tie a ribbon around the neck.

Oh yes, I nearly forgot—they are also good for you. They were originally justified as medicine. Ratafias were prescribed for melancholy, gout and fainting fits, among other things. So if you are feeling a little anxious or tired of life, an orange ratafia may be just the thing.

Punches and Cups

The very word *punch* conjures up festive occasions and warm hospitality. What can be more welcoming than a large, attractive bowl filled with champagne and fruit, and the colours of the fruit—eye-catching reds, pinks, purple and green—which are stirred up as each guest is given some. The recipes here can be assembled at home hours before and the champagne or soda poured in when you arrive at the celebration. Keep an eye out for punchbowls or any large attractive bowls. Victorian wash bowls are a perfect size.

Now for a few helpful hints. Make the punch with the appearance in mind as well as the taste. It is very important that it looks attractive and not like the leftovers from the fruit market. Only use fresh fruits. Add the sparkling drinks at the last minute. Keep the prepared punch refrigerated. Only use one large block of ice to keep the punch chilled, as it melts very slowly. Make an attractive piece of ice by putting flowers, herbs or fruit in a plastic jelly mould or ice-cream container of water and freezing. If the punch is potent, give your guests the opportunity of diluting it with soda or mineral water.

Apricot Syrup

Peaches and nectarines will work just as well with this recipe

$\frac{1}{2}$ cinnamon stick
2 cloves
1.5 kg (3 lb) apricots
1 cup water
Sugar to measure

PUT the cinnamon stick and cloves in a muslin bag. Cut the fruit up into small pieces and put in a bowl and mash. Add the water and the muslin bag. Stand the bowl in simmering water and leave until the juices flow freely and the fruit is softened. Remove the muslin bag. Mash again.

Strain the juice through a jelly bag. Measure the juice, and for each cup of juice add one cup of sugar. Stir until the sugar is dissolved. Pour into warm sterilised bottles. Seal and sterilise in a hot-water bath.

Blackcurrant Syrup

I haven't used any sugar in this recipe. It makes a nice change to taste the natural sweetness of the blackcurrants. Sugar can always be added later if preferred.

$4\frac{1}{2}$ cups blackcurrants
$2\frac{1}{2}$ cups boiling water

PUT the blackcurrants into a bowl and mash. Pour the boiling water over them, cover and leave in a cool place to ferment. It will take 1 to 3 days; you know when bubbles of gas begin to form on the surface.

Mash again and strain. Pour into warm sterilised bottles. Seal and sterilise in a hot-water bath.

Carnation Syrup

Old-fashioned clove pink gillyflowers were used for soups, sauces, syrups, salads, vinegars and as 'sops in wine'—that is, they were floated in the drinks of betrothed couples. Carnations were also one of the most popular flowers to use in wreaths to celebrate weddings. This carnation syrup would be an old-fashioned gourmet gift to present at a wedding with a posy of carnations. It is a very pleasant-tasting syrup and believed to be 'a strong comforter of the heart'.

3 cups carnation petals
6 cloves
6 cups boiling water

CUT the white heels off the petals; they are bitter. Put the petals and cloves into a bowl and pour the boiling water over them. Cover and leave for 12 hours.

Strain through a jelly bag, but do not squeeze it; this way you will get a very clear syrup. Measure the liquid, and for every cup of juice add 1½ cups of sugar. Stir the syrup until the liquid is dissolved. Pour into warm sterilised bottles. Seal and sterilise in a hot-water bath.

Lemon Squash

Handy to carry on a picnic, as all you have to do is add water at the picnic spot. Make with orange or lime as an alternative.

3 cups lemon juice
Zest from half the lemons squeezed
6 cups sugar
4½ cups water
1 tablespoon citric acid (optional)

PUT the lemon zest, sugar and water in a bowl, stir until the sugar has dissolved and then strain. Add the lemon juice (and citric acid, if used) to the syrup. Mix well, pour into warm sterilised bottles and sterilise in a hot-water bath.

Rose Hip Syrup

Lots of vitamin C in this syrup; a spoonful each day will keep several doctors away.

10 cups water
4 cups ripe rose hips
2 cups sugar

PUT 7 cups of water in a saucepan and bring to the boil. Chop the rose hips in a food processor and put them in the boiling water. As soon as it comes to the boil again, remove from heat. Let it stand for 20 minutes and strain through a jelly bag. Return the pulp to the pan, add another 3 cups of boiling water and reboil. Let it stand for 10 minutes and strain.

Pour both lots of juice into a clean saucepan, boil it down until it measures 3 cups. Add the sugar and boil again for 5 minutes. Pour into warm sterilised jars, seal and sterilise by simmering for 20 minutes in a hot-water bath.

Strawberry Syrup

Use this syrup for drinking with champagne: 1 teaspoon per glass and pour the champagne over. Perfect for a romantic evening.

5 cups strawberries
Juice of 1 lemon
2 cups water
Sugar to measure

CUT the strawberries into small pieces and put in a bowl. Add the lemon juice. Mash, then stand the bowl in a pan of simmering water and leave until the juices flow freely. Remove from heat and mash again.

Strain the juice through a jelly bag. Measure the juice and for each cup of juice add one cup of sugar. Stir until the sugar is dissolved. Pour into warm sterilised bottles, seal and sterilise in a hot-water bath.

Ginger Beer

This is a fast method for making homemade ginger beer.

1 tablespoon bruised and chopped ginger
1 tablespoon sultanas
1½ cups sugar
1 tablespoon cream of tartar
Rind and juice of 1 lemon
4 litres (7 pints) boiling water
30 g (1 oz) yeast
⅔ cup warm water

INTO a large bowl put the ginger, sultanas, sugar, cream of tartar and lemon rind. Pour on the boiling water. Mix well, cover and leave to cool.

Dissolve the yeast in the warm water and leave until it begins to froth. Pour it into the ginger mixture along with the lemon juice. Cover and let it stand overnight. Strain and pour into sterilised screw-top bottles. Store in a cool, dark place. The ginger beer will be ready to drink after 3 or 4 days.

Lemon Barley Water

Add serving suggestions when giving away the barley water. You may like to dilute it with mineral water and add some mint leaves. Or add the juice of three oranges or half a cup of passionfruit pulp. It is an excellent drink as a pick-me-up.

½ cup pearl barley
7 cups water
Rind and juice of 3 lemons
2 tablespoons sugar or honey

Wash the barley and put it into a saucepan with the water and lemon rind. Bring to the boil and simmer for 2 hours. Remove from heat, strain and allow to cool. Add the lemon juice and sugar. Stir to dissolve the sugar. Pour into sterilised attractive cordial bottles and refrigerate.

Ginger Beer and Lemon Squash (opposite page) ready to be drunk at an outdoor luncheon party.

Apple Juice

2.5 kg (5 lb) apples
3 cups water
Sugar to measure

Cut the apples into chunks; don't bother to peel or core them. Put them into a saucepan with the water and stew until they are soft. Strain the juice through a jelly bag. Squeeze to extract all the juice. Measure the juice and for every cup of juice add one cup of sugar. Bring the juice to the boil and simmer until the syrup clears. Pour into warm sterilised bottles, seal and sterilise in a hot-water bath.

Homemade Tomato Juice

5 kg (11 lb) tomatoes will make 8 cups of tomato juice. I make the juice without any condiments; when you open the bottles you can add salt, pepper, sugar, chilli, Worcestershire sauce or a slice of lemon.

5 kg (11 lb) ripe tomatoes

Skin the tomatoes, first putting them into boiling water for 5 to 10 minutes, depending how ripe they are, to make the skin easier to remove. Chop them roughly and put into a large saucepan. Gently bring to the boil and simmer until the tomatoes are soft. Strain the pulp through a sieve.

Put the tomato juice into a saucepan and bring to the boil, then remove from the heat. Pour into warm sterilised screw-top bottles and seal. Read the instructions for fruit syrups in the introduction, and sterilise the bottled tomato juice in a boiling-water bath.

Billy Tea

We give this as a farewell gift to overseas friends when they come to visit us. Buy a billy from the local hardware shop. Pick some perfect eucalyptus leaves and dry them in the sun for a few days along with pieces of lemon peel.

1 cup Billy Tea or Darjeeling
   tea-leaves
½ cup dried eucalyptus leaves
1 tablespoon dried lemon peel
1 cup ironbark honey or sugar

Wrap the tea-leaves, eucalyptus leaves and lemon peel separately in twists of waxed kitchen paper. Pour the honey into a small bottle. Pack them all in a billy can with the instructions for making billy tea. You can also add 2 enamel mugs to complete the nostalgic trip. Only the blowies are missing, but they are not for export.

Preparation instructions included in billy
Take one or two teaspoons of tea-leaves and one gum leaf and put them into a billy almost full of hot water. Cover. Put on to the heat. When it comes to the boil again, remove immediately. Making sure the lid is on tight, swing the billy two times in a complete circle.

Let it stand for a minute. As you pour it into the mugs, add lemon peel and honey as desired.

Herb Teas

Flowers, seeds and leaves of herbs make very pleasant hot and chilled drinks. They are also valued for their medicinal properties.

Dry the herbs yourself: tie the up in bunches and leave them to dry hanging in a cool, airy place. Package them attractively in boxes, tins or cellophane bags to give away. You could make the box yourself (page 159). Mention their medicinal values on the label.

Make the tea by infusing a teaspoon or two of the dried herb in a teapot of boiling water for no more than 10 minutes. Sweeten, if necessary, with sugar or honey. Or serve iced with a fresh sprig of the herb or a slice of lemon, lime or orange.

Borage tea is made from the flowers and is excellent as a tonic and to clear colds.

Chamomile tea is made from the flowers: it is an aromatic and used as a tonic to calm the nerves.

Dill seed tea is excellent for the digestion and relieves wind.

Lemon grass has a soothing effect on the nerves and helps to keep the skin clear.

Fennel tea is made from the leaves and stimulates the kidneys.

Mint tea is a digestive, helps clear a cold and sweetens the breath.

Rosemary tea is drunk as a headache cure and is also reputed to strengthen the memory ('rosemary for remembrance').

Sage tea has aromatic properties and is said to relieve liver complaints and increase longevity.

Thyme tea is a tonic used for relieving tension.

Peppery Tea

Peppery brews like this are believed to keep you in good health. Take a cup when you are feeling a bit listless.

2 cups orange pekoe tea-leaves
10 peppercorns
1 clove
1 cinnamon stick, broken up
6 coriander seeds

Mix all the ingredients together and store in an airtight container.

Blueberry Ratafia

A delightful aperitif to sip in the late afternoon on the terrace.

1 cup blueberries
4 cups brandy
1½ cups sugar

Wash and crush the berries gently so that the juice will be released. Put the berries and juice into a saucepan with half a cup of water. Bring to the boil and simmer for 10 minutes. When cool, pour into a warm sterilised jar and pour the brandy over. Seal and store for one week in a dark place.

Strain the juice off the fruit, pressing the fruit hard to extract all the juice. Put the sugar in a saucepan with half a cup of water and boil until the syrup begins to thicken. Mix it into the berry liquor. Pour into bottles and seal. Store in a dark, cool place for a month before opening.

Blackberry Liqueur

A thoughtful winter's gift to savour the delights of last summer's fruits. Fruit liqueurs are wonderful as a happy ending to a large, rich meal or as an aperitif mixed with wine. Only the cheapest kirsch or flavourless vodka needs to be used, as the blackberries transform the flavour.

1 kg (2 lb) firm blackberries
1 cinnamon stick
2 cloves
1½ cups vanilla sugar
4 cups kirsch

Carefully sterilise a large earthenware crock. Put in all the ingredients and leave the fruit to macerate for six to eight weeks. Keep the crock carefully covered with a sterilised lid. When you lift it to check the maceration, be careful to sterilise the lid again.

Strain the liquid and store in sterilised bottles.

Cherry Brandy

Morello cherries, if you can get them, are by far the best to use for cooking or bottling. This is an old recipe requiring a year's ageing. I can guarantee total success with this classic liqueur. So it's worth waiting for it to mature.

2.5 kg (5 lb) cherries
3 cups sugar
1 tablespoon chopped bitter almonds, if available
8 cups brandy

Mash the cherries and crush the stones with a rolling pin. Put into a large stone jar, or any large jar. Add the sugar and almonds. Pour the brandy over and mix well. Seal and store in a dark, cool place. Stir or shake every day for a month, then occasionally for the next three months.

After four months, strain through a jelly bag. Bottle and seal and try to keep for another eight months before tasting.

Crème de Cassis (Blackcurrant Liqueur)

Another old recipe for this well-known drink from France. To make the aperitif Kir, put one teaspoon in a glass of white wine.

  4 cups blackcurrants
  1 teaspoon ground cloves
  1 cinnamon stick
  4 cups brandy
  2 cups sugar

PUT all the ingredients into a large jar and mix well. Seal and store away, being sure to stir or shake the ingredients every day for two weeks. (If you go away on holidays you will have to get someone to mind the liqueur as well as the cat and the garden.)

Strain through a jelly bag. When it has settled and is perfectly clear, bottle.

Grape Ratafia

A drink for taking to friends to sit and sip on the veranda on a hot summer's day. Serve chilled.

  6 cups grapes, green or red
  1 cup sugar or to taste
  Brandy to measure (about 3 cups)

WASH the grapes and take them off the branches. Chop them up roughly in a food processor; be careful not to chop too fine. Strain through double muslin into a large bowl, squeezing the mash hard to extract all the juice. Measure the juice and for every cup of juice add a

Fruit liqueurs in attractive bottles dressed up for Christmas Day. From left, Blueberry Ratafia (page 149), Lemon Liqueur (this page), Grape Ratafia (this page) and Quince Ratafia (page 153). The bottles are all recycled from vinegar and commercial liquor bottles. I have covered up the commercial caps. If you have trouble getting off stubborn labels, use lighter fluid or eucalyptus oil to remove them.

cup of brandy. Add sugar to taste. Cover and leave the liqueur to clear, then pour it off into sterilised bottles.

Lemon Liqueur

A friend arrived on my doorstep with a bottle of this lemon liqueur and strict instructions that I must put the recipe in the book. This is a simple and fast liqueur to drink while you wait for the others to mature. My friend drank it in Italy and experimented with making it on returning home. Here is his splendid recipe.

  6 lemons
  Peel of 1 lime
  $1\frac{1}{2}$ cups sugar
  4 cups vodka

SCRUB the lemons to remove any wax. Peel them finely with a vegetable peeler. Put the lemon peel and lime peel in a jar and pour 2 cups of the vodka over. Seal the jar and let it stand in a cool, dark place for 3 days.

Make a syrup by heating the sugar and $2\frac{1}{2}$ cups of water in a saucepan. Remove from heat after it has come to the boil and let it cool. Add it to the lemon vodka mixture and mix well. Filter the contents, then put back the filtered liquid and the peel and the other 2 cups of vodka. Seal and store for 2 more days. Strain the liqueur through a jelly bag, bottle and seal. Let it stand for another week before tasting.

Nutmeg Brandy

Nutmeg is a narcotic and is excellent to induce sleep. Have a teaspoon of nutmeg brandy in a mug of hot milk or water before retiring.

  $\frac{1}{3}$ cup grated nutmeg
  1 bottle brandy

PUT the nutmeg into the brandy. Shake every day for 3 weeks. Strain into smaller bottles and label with instructions for use.

Orange Ratafia

A nice big quantity to start you off, as you'll have to drink some yourself if you want to be an expert on ratafias. This one is a digestive; and if you are sick in bed with flu, just a few nips at five o'clock are prescribed. Apricots and peaches are also excellent made with this recipe.

9 oranges
3 cups sugar
1 cup coriander seeds
2 cinnamon sticks
1 bottle brandy

SCRUB the oranges to get rid of any wax. Peel off the skin finely with a vegetable peeler; julienne. Squeeze the oranges and put the juice in a large bowl. Add the zest, sugar, spices and brandy. Stir well and pour into large jars. Seal and store for 2 months in a dark, cool place. Strain the liqueur and decant into suitable bottles or decanters. Seal, label and keep in a cool place until making a present of them.

Orange Wine

This is a sweet and exceedingly pleasant wine to serve with a dessert course. Take it to a dinner party as a change from sauterne or champagne. The recipe is for a large quantity, but it will work well halved. Serve chilled.

6 oranges
1 lemon
5 bottles dry white wine
1 cup vanilla sugar
1 bottle brandy

SCRUB the oranges and lemon. Take off the zest. Cut the fruit into quarters and put into large jars or a crock. Add the zest, wine, sugar and brandy. Seal and store in a cool, dark place for 2 months.

Strain through a jelly bag or muslin, squeezing hard to extract all the juice. Pour into sterilised bottles and seal.

Passionfruit Gin

I collected this recipe in the South of France. The aroma of the liqueur is heavenly before you even get to taste it. Not much of it gets given away at our place. I put down a lot at the end of summer when passionfruit become cheap in the markets.

3 cups passionfruit pulp
1½ cups sugar
6 cups gin

PUT the passionfruit pulp into a sterilised jar. Dissolve the sugar in half a cup of water in a saucepan. Pour it over the passionfruit and then pour in the gin. Seal and store in a dark, cool place for two months.

Pear Ratafia

Pears make a very delicate-flavoured liqueur. I first drank this in France as well and have been enthusiastic about it ever since.

6 ripe pears
1 cup sugar
1 bottle vodka

WASH the pears, cut them into quarters and fill a large jar with them. Make a syrup with the sugar and 1½ cups of water. Cook until the syrup thickens, then pour over the fruit. Add the vodka, seal tightly and store in a cool, dark place for two months. Strain the liquid off the fruit and pour it into sterilised bottles, label and seal.

Plum Liqueur

A Polish friend gave us a bottle of this one birthday celebration, and we have been making it ever since. It really lifts the spirits on a cold, rainy autumn afternoon.

750 g (1½ lb) plums
1 cup sugar
4 cups gin

WASH the plums and prick each 6 times with a skewer, going right through to the stone. Put them into a sterilised jar and pour the sugar over them. Cover tightly and let them stand for 3 days or until the juices begin to flow. Shake or stir every day.

Pour the gin over the plums and seal the jar. Stand it in a warm, sunny place for 2 months. Strain the plums through a jelly bag or muslin, squeezing hard to extract all the juice. Pour the liqueur into sterilised bottles, seal and label.

Quince Ratafia

This liqueur is a pale yellow, a most delicate clear liquid. It is pretty potent, too, so it's best not to have too many nips.

    4 quinces
    2 cups sugar
    3 cloves
    2 cinnamon sticks
    1 bottle white rum

WASH the quinces, cut them up and remove the seeds only. Put the fruit into a large sterilised jar and pour over the sugar, spices and rum. Seal well and leave for 3 months in a dark, cool place. Strain and decant into suitable bottles, seal and label.

Spicy Ratafia

This is a very old recipe for what was used as a digestive in Victorian times. I have a cousin who doesn't drink alcohol but makes this ratafia to give to family and friends. The first encounter with a glass made our heads reel.

    Threads of saffron
    2 tablespoons raisins, chopped
    1 tablespoon ground coriander seeds
    1 tablespoon ground cinnamon
    3 cloves, ground
    3 cups sugar
    4 cups water
    6 cups brandy

MIX together the saffron, raisins, and spices and put them into a large jar. Heat the sugar and water in a saucepan to dissolve the sugar. Pour the syrup over the raisin mixture in the jar and add the brandy. Seal and let it infuse for a month, stirring every second day. Strain, bottle and store in a cool, dark place.

Strawberry Liqueur

    4 cups strawberries, hulled
    4 cups brandy
    2 cups sugar
    ½ cup water

PUT the strawberries into a jar and cover with the brandy. Seal and store on a sunny windowsill for 2 months.

Put the sugar in a saucepan with the water and heat only enough to dissolve the sugar. Pour the syrup onto the strawberry liqueur. Strain and bottle. The liqueur is a fine pale pink.

Fish House Punch

I've come across this recipe in quite a few books. It seems to originate in America and claims to have made thousands of people happy, including George Washington and Lafayette.

    1 cup caster sugar
    7 cups mineral water
    3 cups lemon juice
    4 cups rum
    2 cups brandy
    ½ cup pear liqueur (opposite)

DISSOLVE the sugar in 2 cups of the mineral water, add the lemon juice and the remaining mineral water. Mix well. Add the rum, brandy and liqueur and stir well. Cover and let it infuse for 3 hours. Put in a large block of ice when ready to serve.

Kirsch Punch

'Punch cures the gout, the Cholic,
and the Phtistic,
And it is to all men the very best Physic.'
An excellent warm punch to drink in the middle of winter, sitting around the fire with friends. This is one to assemble at the party in front of the fire.

4 cups water
1 tablespoon tea-leaves
1 cinnamon stick
2 cups caster sugar
3 cups kirsch

BOIL the water and throw in the tea and cinnamon. Let it infuse for 10 minutes. Put the sugar into a punchbowl and pour the strained hot tea over it, dissolving the sugar. Add the kirsch and set alight.

Mulled Wine

Take this in a vacuum flask for a winter's day picnic. It will keep all of you warm while you light the fire.

1 bottle red wine
1 cup sugar
Zest of 1 orange
$\frac{1}{2}$ stick cinnamon
$\frac{1}{2}$ teaspoon grated nutmeg
1 clove
1 lemon, thinly sliced

INTO a saucepan put the wine and sugar. Stir until the sugar dissolves and add the zest and spices. Heat the wine until it is almost boiling. Remove from heat and strain into a warm vacuum flask. Serve with a slice of lemon in each mug.

Pineapple Punch

3 pineapples
2 cups caster sugar
2 cups lemon juice
1 cup mint leaves

$\frac{1}{2}$ cup cherry brandy (page 149)
2 cups brandy
2 cups rum
4 bottles champagne
Mint leaves to decorate

PEEL and roughly chop the pineapple. Purée it in a food processor, then put it in a bowl and cover with the sugar. Let is macerate for 2 hours. Add the lemon juice, mint and spirits. Stir, cover and let it stand for 12 hours.

When ready to serve, add a large block of ice, the champagne and mint leaves to decorate.

Wassail Bowl

Drinking spiced ale from a wassail bowl is traditional on Christmas Eve in England.

8 cups ale or beer
2 cups raw sugar
$\frac{1}{2}$ teaspoon grated nutmeg
$\frac{1}{2}$ teaspoon ground ginger
3 cups sherry
1 lemon, sliced
2 apples, sliced

PUT the ale, sugar and spices into a large saucepan. Dissolve the sugar over a low heat; do not boil. Take off the heat and stir in the sherry, lemon and apples. Pour into a vacuum flask to take to friends.

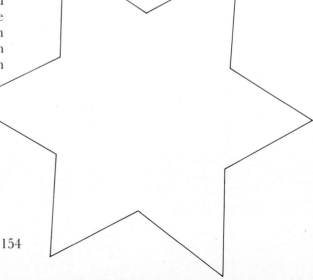

Christmas Day
Champagne Punch

½ cup quartered strawberries
1 orange, peeled and segmented
Pulp of 2 passionfruit
1 peach, peeled and sliced
2 tablespoons brandy
2 tablespoons pear liqueur (page 152)
1 bottle dry champagne

Christmas Day Champagne Punch ready to serve. I made the ice in a fluted jelly mould and froze clove carnation flowers and buds and ferns in it.

Pᴜᴛ the fruit in a punchbowl and pour the brandy and liqueur over. Mix and keep refrigerated for two hours or until you leave for the celebration. Pour the chilled champagne over just before serving. Remember to take an attractive block of ice.

8 Sweets

Hᴇʀᴇ ᴀʀᴇ some age-old recipes to brighten up everyday living: toffees, chocolates (Why is chocolate so deeply satisfying and soothing?), almond and fruit sweets; recipes from childhood—popcorn, toffee apples and honeycomb—and sophisticated sweets such as exquisite pieces of marzipan, lemon liqueur chocolates, and quince jellies. None of them costs much money to make, but several are very time-consuming.

Old-fashioned candy stored in a pretty box in layers of waxed paper is an attractive present for people of any age and for any occasion. Most people will never have tasted sweets such as barley sugar and fudge made to the original recipe. One hardly dares refer to them by the same name any more, because the commercial product has gone so far from the original.

The sweets in this chapter are all very attractive. After all, visual delight is half the satisfaction of food. Save all small boxes and cover them with paper or cloth. I have always saved jars; I now save boxes to recycle with gifts.

Some of the recipes call for toffee making. You must be very careful when making toffee, because the syrup has to reach a high temperature. Spilt toffee can cause terrible burns. Have all your equipment set out neatly before you start. Place it so that there is little room for error. Make sure there are no pets or small children around the kitchen. Toffee is ready at 140°C (280°F). If you don't have a sugar thermometer, test by dropping a small teaspoonful of the mixture into cold water. It should set instantly and crack if it is ready.

Almond Brittle Centrepiece

A charming offering to take to a hostess at a dinner party. I shape this rich toffee into a round and, when it is cold, decorate it with candied fruit to make a centrepiece on the table for the dessert course. The guests break off pieces to eat with their ice-cream or coffee. It is also ideal for kids' birthday parties, covered with Smarties.

2 cups white sugar
1½ cups honey
½ cup water
1½ cups finely chopped walnuts
250 g (8 oz) butter

Put the sugar, honey and water into a pan and bring to the boil. When the mixture is very hot—150°C (300°F)—add the butter and the walnuts and pour onto a greased heatproof surface. As soon as it is cool enough to handle, smooth it out into a round until the sheet is 7 mm ($\frac{1}{4}$ in) thick. Leave until it is cool. Keep on a flat plate or baking tray and wrap in aluminium foil until you're ready to decorate it and take to the party.

Caramel Walnuts

Walnut and almond balls dipped into caramel.

1 egg
$\frac{1}{3}$ cup icing sugar
$\frac{1}{3}$ cup caster sugar
$\frac{1}{3}$ cup ground almonds
$\frac{1}{2}$ cup halved walnuts
2 cups sugar
1 cup water

Bonbons

This is an exciting way to wrap a small inexpensive or very expensive gift. Use bonbons also as table decorations or as extra gifts filled with apricot jellies, candied fruit or any sweets your friends like best. Layer them in a box of six with a different kind of sweet in each one. The French originally conceived the bonbon as a decorative way of giving sweets.

Materials
Fine wrapping paper
Thin cardboard for inner tubes
Fine cord or ribbon
Double-sided sticky tape

For each bonbon make three tubes from pieces of cardboard measuring 10.5 cm (4 in) × 19 cm (7 in). Roll the cardboard to form a tube about 5 cm (2 in) in diameter; fasten the overlapped ends with double-sided tape. Cut a piece of wrapping paper 19 cm ($7\frac{1}{2}$ in) × 48 cm (18 in). Place the three tubes in a row lengthwise on the bottom edge of the wrong side of the paper, with the ends of the two outside tubes 4 cm ($1\frac{1}{2}$ in) from the edges of the paper and the middle tube in the centre. Keep the tubes in place with some more double-sided tape. Fill the middle tube with sweets (or diamonds!). Roll the paper around the tubes, forming one long paper-covered cylinder, and stick the overlap with double-sided tape. Pinch the paper slightly at both ends of the central tube and tie with cord.

Bonbons make a special gift when arranged in a box and decorated with the biscuit shapes, holly or herbs.

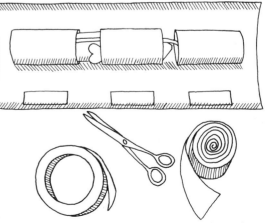

Place the three tubes on the wrong side of the paper and fill the inner tube with sweets. Roll the paper over and secure with double-sided tape.

157

Beat the egg and add the icing sugar and caster sugar and almonds until you have a very stiff dough. Rub a little icing sugar over your hands and roll the dough into balls. Press a walnut piece into each one and leave to harden for a day.

Make a syrup by heating the sugar and water in a saucepan, stirring all the time until the sugar has dissolved. Boil until the syrup begins to brown and caramelise, then stand the saucepan in a basin of boiling water. Skewer the

Nut Clusters (page 160), about to be wrapped up in butterfly boxes. The boxes are very easy to make; see the instructions on the opposite page. Instructions for making the stencilled teddy bear gift cards and tags are on page 65. The travelling flower press is handy for collecting leaves and flowers in order to press them immediately (see instructions page 162).

walnut balls and dip them into the caramel. Leave them to dry on an oiled heatproof surface. Be very careful, as caramel can cause nasty burns. Put the coated nuts into small paper cases.

158

Making Boxes

One of the most attractive ways to present a gift is in a homemade box. I actually consider a box part of the gift, as boxes can be used for so many useful things once you have eaten your way through the contents. Line them with tissue paper.

There are same-size patterns of a variety of boxes at the back of the book: a round box, a square box and a butterfly box. Either choose attractively coloured cardboard to make your box or decorate a plain box in some way— hand paint, stencil a pattern, glue pressed flowers on or cover with homemade wrapping paper. If you want larger boxes, just blow up the pattern on a photocopier. Alternatively, cover commercial boxes with paper or fabric.

The boxes are not just cut out; they are scored as well, in order to fold the cardboard neatly. This may take some practice. Aim to cut through a quarter of the thickness, enough for a sharp edge and not enough to cut through. The scored edges are marked with a dotted line. Use rubber solution for glueing flaps together.

Same size patterns for these three boxes are on pages 172 and 173.

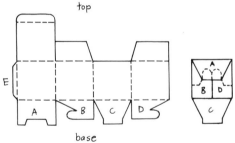

SQUARE BOX. An easy-to-make one-piece box to start. The lid is an extended flap. The pattern is on page 172. Trace the pattern onto the chosen cardboard. Cut along the cut lines and score along the dotted lines. Fold the scores. Then fold the sides around to form the central box shape. Secure by glueing tab E. Position the flaps to make the base as shown in the illustration. The lid folds over and tucks away neatly.

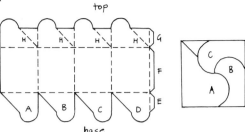

BUTTERFLY BOX. Trace the pattern onto the cardboard. Cut the pattern out and score all the dotted lines except for H. Score them on the other side of the cardboard because they fold inwards.

Form the box first by glueing tabs F and G. When dry, fold up D flap to form the start of the base and glue tab E in place.

Construct the base by folding C flap on top of D. Fold B flap and hold it in place by slipping the straight edge under the circle of D flap. To complete, fold A flap and hold it in place with the curve of C flap.

Keep the top open until the box is filled. Then tuck the flaps into each other to make a butterfly top.

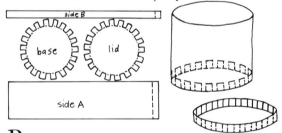

ROUND BOX WITH LID. This is harder to make than the other boxes, but once you have mastered the technique you can make a round box in any size or shape. Use heavier cardboard for the base.

Trace the pattern onto the cardboard. Cut around the outline and score the dotted lines. Make the basic cylinder by overlapping the ends of side A and glueing them together. Bend the tabs of the base upwards. Stick the base to the cylinder with the tabs inside the box. Make the lid the same way as the base using side B.

Honeycomb Toffee

We used to love making honeycomb toffee as children. We were allowed to make large quantities to sell at school and church fêtes.

1 cup sugar
1 cup golden syrup
4 teaspoons bicarbonate of soda

Heat the sugar, golden syrup and half a cup of water in a deep pan and stir until the mixture begins to go brown. Stir in the soda. The mixture will froth and rise up. Remove from the heat and pour into a greased baking tray. When it has cooled down a bit, put it into the refrigerator to set. Break the honeycomb into pieces and store in airtight containers. When giving some as a present, wrap each piece in cellophane paper and twist the ends. Pile them up in a small basket.

Honeyed Toffee Apples

Kids of all ages enjoy toffee apples. The toffee on these is particularly fine, in case one of your small friends is a connoisseur of toffee.

½ cup honey
1 cup hrown sugar
5 tablespoons water
2 tablespoons butter
1 tablespoon golden syrup
2 teaspoons lemon juice
8 small apples
8 wooden meat skewers

Heat the honey until it is runny; reserve. Heat the sugar and water in a large deep pan until the sugar has dissolved, then add the butter, syrup and lemon juice and bring to the boil. Boil until the mixture reaches 140°C (280°F) and begins to go brown. (To test if the toffee is ready, take a spoonful and put it into cold water. It should set instantly and crack.) Turn off the heat. Put a skewer into each apple and dip the apple into the melted honey and then into the toffee. Put the apples on a greased tray to set. When cool, wrap the apples in clear cellophane paper and tie around the stick.

Barley Sugar

This is an authentic recipe for barley sugar twisted into sticks. Turn one end to make a shepherd's crook. Shape into barley sugar bows to decorate a party table. Or make into rounds for bracelets, necklets and crowns.

1 cup barley
20 cups water
5 cups sugar

Simmer the barley and water in a covered saucepan for 5 hours. Strain the barley grains off. Put the barley water back into a deep saucepan and add the sugar. Boil until the syrup begins to darken and a spoonful will crack in cold water. Pour onto a greased baking tray. When it is cool enough to handle, cut it into long strips and twist.

Nut Clusters

1 cup slivered almonds
½ cup chopped hazelnuts
½ cup chopped pistachio nuts
½ cup honey
1½ cups sugar

Mix the nuts together. Put little heaps of them together in paper cups. Gently heat the sugar and honey in a saucepan, stirring well. When the mixture has caramelised let the toffee cool slightly, then pour a little over each of the nut clusters. The toffee will hold the nuts together. Line a tin or box with waxed paper and fill with the nut clusters.

Simple sweets packed in attractive boxes which become part of the gift. The recipe for Apple Candy, on the left, is on page 168 and Almond Paste on page 163.

Pressed Flowers

Pressing flowers is a wonderful way to record a scene of beauty or a floral gift. Just the sight of a few pressed violets can bring back memories of a happy summer's day or a treasured posy. Pressed flowers make beautiful decorations for gift cards, boxes, jars and wrapping paper.

It is best to use a flower press; if you haven't one, use a heap of heavy books to get the necessary weight. The flowers are put very carefully between two layers of blotting paper and corrugated cardboard. The press is then tightened.

Only put flowers of the same thickness in one layer. Arrange them carefully in an attractive way before pressing. Choose only perfect blooms, and press them as soon as possible after picking. Don't forget to pick some leaves as well. Grass, ferns and seaweed can make interesting variations.

As the flowers dry they become thinner, so keep checking and tightening your flower press. Leave the flowers to dry for at least two weeks; they will take from two to six weeks to dry depending on their size. Store them in envelopes until ready to use. Keep a heavy book on top of the envelopes.

Handle pressed flowers very carefully, as they are fragile. Pick them up with tweezers or stick a needle into the centre. Use rubber solution to stick them on paper. You only need a small amount. A palette knife is excellent to use for this.

When making cards, arrange the flowers carefully before glueing them down, so that you know it will be a success. Don't be afraid to experiment. Try to think of a theme, like a heart for Saint Valentine's Day or your boyfriend's birthday, a large 5 (or whatever) made out of daisies for your favourite niece, a wreath for Christmas or a posy for a wedding. Choose attractive thick paper or thin cardboard for making cards. Go to an art supply shop where they have a wonderful range of handmade paper. Use pressed flowers for decorating labels and gift tags as well. For wrapping paper, wrap the present up first and then glue the flowers, leaves or ferns on the paper.

Decorate the top or sides of recycled boxes with pressed flowers and leaves. They are a good way to cover up commercial emblems or wording as well. If there is too much to cover with pressed flowers, paint the whole box. After you have pasted the flowers down, give the whole box a coat of clear varnish; this will make your gift box last for years.

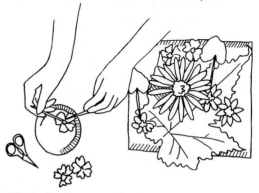

Hold the flower with the tweezers while you apply some glue onto the back of the flower centre with a fine skewer.

Place the flowers between the layers of blotting paper and cover with a sheet of cardboard. Tighten the flower press with strong cord. Hold the tension by securing the cord to the cleats at the top.

Peanut Brittle

An easy sweet to make for school fêtes.

1 cup molasses
2 cups unsalted peanuts

L AY some buttered waxed paper over a baking tray. Cook the molasses slowly to 140°C (280°F) or until it is extremely hot and darkens. Add the peanuts and remove from heat. Be very careful, because sugar at this high temperature can cause serious burns. Pour the brittle on the greased paper. When the toffee is cool enough to touch, break it into pieces. Store in the refrigerator.

Walnut Bars

Children love these bars. Wrap them in attractive paper and twist the ends.

$\frac{1}{4}$ cup boiling water
$\frac{1}{2}$ cup butter
$\frac{1}{2}$ cup brown sugar
$\frac{1}{2}$ cup molasses
1 teaspoon bicarbonate of soda
3 cups flour
1 teaspoon ground ginger
1 teaspoon grated nutmeg
$\frac{1}{3}$ cup sesame seeds
$\frac{2}{3}$ cup chopped walnuts

P OUR the boiling water over the butter and melt. Mix the sugar, molasses, soda, flour and spices together and add to the butter. Knead the paste. Chill the mixture in the refrigerator, then roll it out and cut in strips 9 cm ($3\frac{1}{2}$ in) by 4 cm ($1\frac{1}{2}$ in). Sprinkle the sesame seeds and walnuts over the top and bake in a preheated oven at 160°C (320°F) for 15 minutes.

Almond Bars

Cut into large stars with a biscuit cutter, these tasty confections make easy Christmas presents. Present them in a cellophane bag and tied with a silver ribbon.

$3\frac{1}{2}$ cups vanilla caster sugar
1 cup ground almonds
8 eggwhites
$2\frac{1}{2}$ cups flour, sifted

P UT the sugar and almonds into a bowl. Gradually stir in the eggwhites, one at a time. Stir in the flour and mix well.

Roll it out gently and put onto a greased baking sheet. Cut into bars or press out any shapes with biscuit cutters. Cook in a preheated oven at 160°C (320°F) for 15 minutes. Store in an airtight container.

Almond Paste

The paste is set in little paper cases. They look attractive layered in a cardboard box between waxed paper. Serve them with coffee at the end of a meal or with afternoon coffee.

1 cup ground almonds
2 eggwhites
$\frac{3}{4}$ cup caster sugar
1 teaspoon orange ratafia (page 152)
Icing sugar to decorate

P UT the ground almonds in a saucepan, mix in the eggwhites gradually and then add the sugar. Gently stir the mixture over a low heat until it is thick and begins to come away from the side of the pan, about 5 minutes. Remove from the heat and stir in the orange liqueur.

Spoon the mixture into paper cases then sprinke with icing sugar.

Marzipan Sweets

Marzipan is made from a mixture of ground almonds, sugar and whites of eggs. It can be coloured and shaped into fruit and flowers, anything you wish. It is a very old recipe originally made in France by an order of nuns.

2 cups ground almonds
2 cups caster sugar
Flavouring and colouring
4 eggwhites

MIX the almonds, sugar and drops of your desired flavouring and colouring. Add the eggwhites gradually. Let the mixture stand for 10 minutes. Roll it out until it is 3 mm ($\frac{1}{8}$ in) thick. Cut it into shapes with biscuit cutters or mould by hand. Put on a baking tray and bake in a preheated oven at 120°C (250°F) until they are dry. Pack into cardboard boxes or lay out on a piece of stiff card in a shape suitable for the shapes you have made.

Almond and Pistachio Drops

This is a fast and simple sweet to make. You can use orange ratafia (page 152) instead of orange blossom water if you like.

1 cup ground almonds
1 cup icing sugar
5 tablespoons orange blossom water
$\frac{1}{2}$ cup shelled pistachio nuts
Icing sugar to decorate

MIX the almonds and sugar together in a bowl. Gradually add drops of orange blossom water until you have a thick paste. Knead until it is smooth. Let the pastry rest while you chop up the pistachios.

Shape the paste into balls 2.5 cm (1 in) in diameter, inserting some of the chopped pistachio nuts into the centre of each one. Roll them in icing sugar. Put them into little paper cases and pack into tins or cardboard boxes. Alternatively, cut little squares of coloured paper with fringed edges and wrap up the balls, screwing the paper at two ends to enclose the sweets. They could then be stored in a box.

Nougat (page 166), beautifully laid out in gift boxes between layers of waxed paper, and Walnut Truffles (page 167), in paper cases for easier handling. Sometimes they are hard to part with!

Almond Dates

These dried dates stuffed with an almond mixture are simple to make and delicious with coffee any time of the day. You need whole dates, before they are pitted and broken.

1 cup ground almonds
$\frac{1}{3}$ cup caster sugar
4 tablespoons rum
2 cups dried dates, not pitted

MIX the almonds and sugar together in a bowl and sprinkle in enough rum to make a firm paste. Slit each date and carefully remove the stone. Press into the stone's place as much almond paste as you can get into it, leaving the slit slightly open.

Halva

A sweet enjoyed since medieval times in many countries from India to the Middle East and Central Europe. Take it to a dinner party to serve with coffee and fruit.

$\frac{1}{2}$ cup sugar
$\frac{1}{2}$ cup water
4 tablespoons butter
$\frac{1}{2}$ cup semolina
$\frac{1}{2}$ cup chopped mixed nuts
1 tablespoon cinnamon
Pine nuts to decorate

MAKE a syrup by boiling the sugar and water together, stirring until the sugar has dissolved. In a separate pan melt the butter, stir in the semolina and cook until it begins to turn golden. Mix in the syrup, nuts and cinnamon. Take the pan off the heat, cover and put into a preheated oven at 160°C (320°F) for 15 minutes.

Put the halva into small porcelain pots or moulds that have been brushed with water first. Decorate with pine nuts. Chill in the refrigerator until ready to serve or to take to a dinner party. Unmould just before serving.

Nougat

Nougat can also be shaped into flowers, rabbits, hearts—whatever theme you desire for the occasion you are celebrating: a box of heart-shaped nougat for a wedding anniversary or a box of bears for a child's birthday.

4 cups sugar
1 cup boiling water
$\frac{1}{2}$ cup honey
2 tablespoons cream of tartar
2 cups hazelnuts
2 eggwhites
$\frac{1}{2}$ cup icing sugar

PUT the sugar into a saucepan and pour the boiling water over. Stir until the sugar dissolves, then bring to the boil and when it reaches boiling point add the honey and cream of tartar. Boil for 10 minutes and remove from heat. Leave overnight to cool down.

Meanwhile, toast the hazelnuts in a preheated oven at 180°C (360°F). Rub the skins off and chop roughly. Beat the eggwhites until stiff.

Gradually add the eggwhites to the sugar and honey mixture and then stir in the hazelnuts and icing sugar. Spoon the mixture onto a greased marble slab or flat surface and smooth the top with a spatula. Cut into squares, bars or any desired shape. Let it cool and pack into boxes.

Coconut Apricot Chews

$\frac{2}{3}$ cup sweetened condensed milk
$\frac{1}{4}$ cup powdered milk
$\frac{1}{4}$ cup wheat germ
$1\frac{1}{2}$ cups shredded coconut
$\frac{1}{2}$ cup dried apricots, finely chopped

COMBINE the condensed milk, powdered milk and wheat germ and then add the coconut and apricots. Mix well. Drop teaspoonfuls of the mixture onto greased aluminium foil over an oven tray. Bake in a preheated oven at 160°C (320°F) for about 15 minutes. Remove the sweets from the foil after they have cooled.

Peanut and Sultana Clusters

A favourite sweet among children, these fruit and nut clusters make an over-the-top decoration on a birthday chocolate cake. They also can be made with walnuts instead of peanuts.

500 g (1 lb) milk chocolate
$\frac{1}{2}$ cup unsalted peanuts
$\frac{1}{2}$ cup sultanas

MELT the chocolate in a bowl placed in hot water. Stir until smooth and then add the peanuts and sultanas. Spoon into chocolate moulds or small paper cases.

Popcorn Balls

Popcorn balls are cheap to make and a great favourite with kids. Take some to picnics to keep them happy while you slave over a hot fire.

1 cup popping corn
4 tablespoons vegetable oil
1 cup salted peanuts
1 cup golden syrup
$\frac{1}{2}$ cup sugar
1 tablespoon lemon juice
A pinch of salt
1 tablespoon butter
1 teaspoon cinnamon

TO MAKE POPCORN. Heat the oil in a large pan that can be covered with a tight-fitting lid. When hot, put in the corn and gently shake so that all the corn is coated in oil. Put the lid on immediately. As soon as the corn begins to pop, turn the heat down as low as possible. When the popping stops, remove the pan from the heat, uncover and sprinkle with salt.

To make popcorn balls. Mix together 6 cups of popcorn and the peanuts in a bowl. Combine the golden syrup, sugar, lemon juice and salt in a saucepan; bring to the boil and cook until the syrup begins to darken and a spoonful turns brittle when dropped in cold water. Remove from heat and stir in the butter and cinnamon. Pour it over the popcorn and peanuts. Stir until everything is coated with the toffee. When the mixture is cool enough to handle, press it into popcorn balls.

Peppermint Chocolate

Mints to take to a dinner party to serve with coffee. Layer into an attractive cardboard box lined with waxed paper.

500 g (1 lb) dark chocolate
A few drops of peppermint oil
$\frac{1}{2}$ cup slivered almonds, chopped
Whole almonds to decorate

MELT the chocolate in a bowl placed in hot water. Stir until smooth and add the peppermint oil and almonds. Mix well and spoon into chocolate moulds or small paper cases. Put an almond on top of each one.

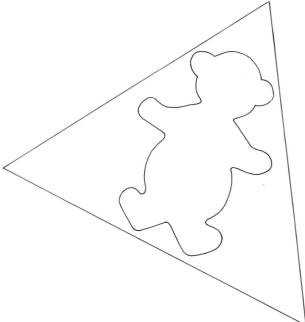

Walnut Truffles

Once, when I was plunged into deepest gloom, a friend gave me some walnut truffles. It is amazing how chocolate can help solve problems or at least arrest gloom with passing indulgence.

500 g (1 lb) milk chocolate
5 tablespoons unsalted butter
$\frac{1}{4}$ cup cream
4 egg yolks
$\frac{1}{2}$ cup finely chopped walnuts
Drinking chocolate

MELT the chocolate and butter in a bowl placed in hot water. Mix together, then add the cream, stirring well. Remove the bowl from the heat and let the mixture cool. Gradually stir in the egg yolks and then the walnuts. Mix well. Put in the refrigerator to harden for 1 to 2 hours. Roll the mixture into small balls and then roll them in cocoa. Put into small paper cases or layer between waxed paper in an airtight container.

Chocolate Almond Balls

This recipe claims to have saved lives otherwise wrecked with cares.

400 g (14 oz) dark chocolate
1 cup icing sugar
$\frac{1}{2}$ cup ground almonds
1 eggwhite
$\frac{1}{2}$ cup cream
1 tablespoon rum
Desiccated coconut

MELT the chocolate in a bowl placed in hot water. Mix the icing sugar and almonds in another bowl. Stir in the eggwhite until it is a firm paste. Add the cream and the melted chocolate and mix well. Stir in the rum. Refrigerate for 1 to 2 hours to harden. Roll into balls and then roll in desiccated coconut. Put into small paper cases.

Lemon Liqueur Chocolates

Serve these with coffee or tea at the end of a dinner, or give as a present with a small bottle of lemon liqueur.

400 g (14 oz) dark chocolate
2 tablespoons unsalted butter
1 tablespoon lemon zest
1 tablespoon lemon liqueur (page 151)
4 tablespoons icing sugar
Chocolate powder or cocoa to decorate

Melt the chocolate and butter in a bowl placed in hot water. Remove from heat, mix and add the zest and lemon liqueur. Then add the icing sugar and mix thoroughly. Refrigerate the mixture for 1 to 2 hours for the chocolate to become firmer. Roll the chocolate into small balls, then roll in chocolate powder. Put each one into a paper case.

Rum and Chocolate Fudge

Adults and children alike love these fudge sweets. Replace the rum with orange juice if preferred. They make a very handsome present in an attractive box or, for children, in a tin they can keep to store special things in.

1 tablespoon dried pears
1 tablespoon dried apricots
2 tablespoons sultanas
1 cup slivered almonds
2 tablespoons pine nuts
1 cup chocolate pieces
1 tablespoon icing sugar
2 tablespoons rum
Cocoa to decorate

Chop up the fruit and nuts in a food processor and then put them in a bowl. Melt the chocolate in another bowl standing in hot water. Stir the chocolate and pour it over the fruit mixture along with the icing sugar and rum. Stir and knead until soft and pliable. Roll the mixture into balls and then roll them in the cocoa. Put the balls into small paper cases and store in layers in a tin or box. They last for ages.

Chocolate Strawberries

Very welcome served with strong coffee at the end of a feast. Cherries in Eau-de-Vie (page 137), taste very good made this way, too. A great treat for birthdays and wedding anniversaries. Use them to decorate a cake, the Chocolate Birthday Cake on page 125, perhaps.

1 cup dark chocolate pieces
$\frac{1}{4}$ cup cream
2 tablespoons unsalted butter
24 strawberries
Toothpicks

Put the chocolate, cream and butter in a bowl and place the bowl in hot water to melt the chocolate. Stir well. Put a toothpick into each strawberry and dip into the chocolate mixture. Place them on a buttered tray. Refrigerate to set the chocolate. Put each one in a small paper case and store in the refrigerator.

Apple Candy

This is a treat that you could almost claim was good for you. Your small friends will love it. For taking to a party, turn the paste onto a flat plate and cut it in squares, keeping it all together. Sprinkle with sugar. It looks spectacular glowing this way.

6 large cooking apples
$1\frac{1}{2}$ cups vanilla caster sugar
1 eggwhite
Caster sugar to decorate

Bake the apples until soft. Remove the skins and cores and mash them in a food processor along with the vanilla caster sugar. Beat the eggwhite until it is stiff and gently fold it into the apple. Spread the purée about 13 mm ($\frac{1}{2}$ in) thick in shallow dishes lined with greaseproof paper that has been smeared with butter. Leave overnight in the oven at 100°C (200°F). The next day cut them into squares and sprinkle with sugar. Store them in layers on waxed paper in an airtight container.

Candied Fruits, with Crystalised or Glacé Finish

A luxurious delicacy, so expensive to buy that you need a very special occasion to justify the expense. It is the lengthy preparation of candied fruits that makes them expensive. You can make them at home at no great cost of money, just time. Make a large batch so that there is plenty to give away as well.

The process consists in covering the fruit with a hot syrup and gradually increasing the sugar content each day until the fruit is impregnated with sugar. You have to do this gradually or the fruit will shrivel.

The most successful fruits to use are apricots, peaches, pineapple, plums, cherries, angelica and citrus peel. Only use one kind of fruit in a syrup, because you don't want the flavours to blend. The fruit should be firm and just ripe. Apricots and plums should be pricked all over with a skewer. Cherries should be stoned, peaches and pears peeled, halved and stoned or cored.

1 kg (2 lb) fruit
1$\frac{3}{4}$ cups sugar
3 cups sugar

COVER the fruit with boiling water and simmer until the fruit is just tender. It will take from 3 to 15 minutes depending on the fruit.

Drain the fruit and reserve the liquid. Make a fruit syrup with 2 cups of the reserved liquid and 1$\frac{3}{4}$ cups of sugar. Heat until the sugar is dissolved and pour over the fruit. If by chance it doesn't cover the fruit, make some more syrup in the same proportion of sugar and water the fruit was cooked in. Leave soaking for 24 hours.

Next day drain the syrup off into a saucepan, add $\frac{1}{2}$ cup of sugar to it and bring to boiling point. Pour over the fruit and leave for 24 hours. This step should be repeated 5 times.

Soak the fruit for another 3 days—or longer if you can't get to it straight away; it will last for 3 weeks. Drain and reserve the syrup and place the pieces of fruit on a wire tray or cake rack. Place in a preheated oven at 60°C (140°F) for several hours until dry. Turn the fruit several times. The fruit is ready when it is no longer sticky. It can also be dried in the sun for 3 to 5 hours. Just be careful of insects.

The fruit is usually given a crystallised or glacé finish before packing.

To get a crystallised finish. Take the candied fruit and dip each piece individually in boiling water. Drain and then dip the fruit in fine granulated sugar.

To get a glacé finish. Make a fresh syrup from 4 cups of sugar dissolved in 1 cup of water and bring it to the boil. Have also a saucepan of boiling water. Holding the fruit with a skewer, dip each piece in the boiling water and drain. Then pour some of the hot syrup into a small bowl, dip the fruit in and place it on a wire rack. It is important that the syrup does not get cloudy; as soon as it starts to cloud, throw it away and take some more syrup from the saucepan, which should be kept hot and covered. When all the fruit is dipped, put the wire rack in a warm place to dry or in the oven at 60°C (130°F).

Pack the crystallised or glacé fruit in boxes. Line the boxes with waxed paper and layer the fruits with the paper. Do not put them in an airtight container, as they might go mouldy. Make paper or cloth covers if you don't have lids.

Silver Pine-Cone Tree

Make a silver tree to decorate the Christmas table. Gather some fresh ferns and leaves on Christmas morning to sit the tree on. Add a few fresh flowers or berries if you like. If you have time, make napkin rings to match the pine tree. I find kids love to help make the decorations and very often have creative ideas to contribute.

> A selection of small pine cones
> Walnuts
> Ferns
> Gumnuts and seed pods
> Bay leaves
> Eucalyptus leaves
> Silver metallic paint
> Cardboard
> Glue

MAKE sure you have covered the floor and a large table with plenty of newspaper, as this process is messy. First dip the found pieces into silver paint, holding each one over the tin until it has stopped dripping and then put to dry on a wire rack.

Make a cone of medium-size cardboard, 30 cm (12 in) high. Glue the pine cones all over it. Now glue the other found pieces in the empty spaces, keeping to the basic shape of the cone, or Christmas tree.

Make the basic napkin ring of the same cardboard, 4 cm ($1\frac{1}{2}$ in) wide with a circumference of 6 cm ($2\frac{3}{4}$ in). Glue well. Dip into the silver paint. Decorate over the seam with a pine cone and some fern or leaves.

Citrus Peel in Syrup

Save all your citrus peel in a plastic bag in the refrigerator for a week or two. Grapefruit, sweet and bitter oranges, and lemons all make good candied peel. It can be served either in a small glass with the syrup or drained and rolled in sugar. Use the spare syrup for fruit compotes, poured over ice-cream or diluted as a drink. Give serving suggestions on the label when you present the citrus in syrup as a gift.

> 1 kg (2 lb) citrus peel, in strips
> 1 kg (2 lb) sugar
> 4 cups water
> Juice of 1 lemon

IF SOME of the peel is thick and pithy, scrape some of the pith off. Boil the peel in some water until soft. Drain and soak in cold water for a day, changing the water several times.

Roll the strips up into curls and thread them on a long piece of cotton to keep them rolled up like a necklace.

Boil the sugar, water and lemon juice until it has become a thick syrup. Put in the citrus necklace and simmer for an hour or so until the peel has absorbed the syrup. Take the necklace out of the syrup and remove the cotton. Put the peel into a sterilised jar and pour the syrup over to cover. Seal and label.

Turkish Delight

Turkish delight is easy to make. Alternate rows of orange and red sweetmeats packed into tins or boxes make special gifts.

> 2 tablespoons gelatine
> 1 cup boiling water
> 2 cups sugar
> $\frac{1}{2}$ cup apricot syrup
> $\frac{1}{2}$ cup strawberry syrup
> Lemon food colouring
> Red food colouring
> Icing sugar to decorate

DISSOLVE the gelatine in the boiling water and pour into a saucepan with the sugar. Bring to the boil and simmer for 10 minutes. Divide the mixture and add the apricot syrup to one half and the strawberry syrup to the other. If the colours aren't bright enough, add red food colouring to the strawberry and lemon to the apricot. Pour the mixtures into separate greased square cake tins. When the Turkish delight is cold and set, cut it into squares with a knife dipped in boiling water. Dust the squares with icing sugar. Store in layers on waxed paper in an airtight tin.

OVERLEAF
The patterns for the boxes: the square box is in blue, the butterfly box in red, and the round box in black. The instructions for making them are on page 159.

BELOW
The pattern for a salt-dough decoration. It can be made larger if desired. The instructions for making it are on page 113.

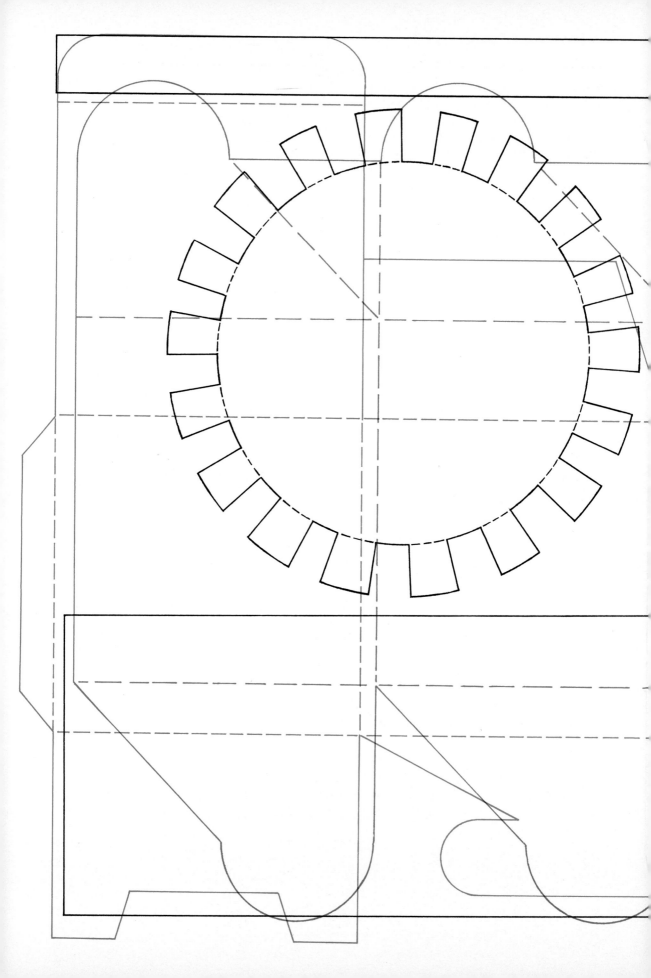

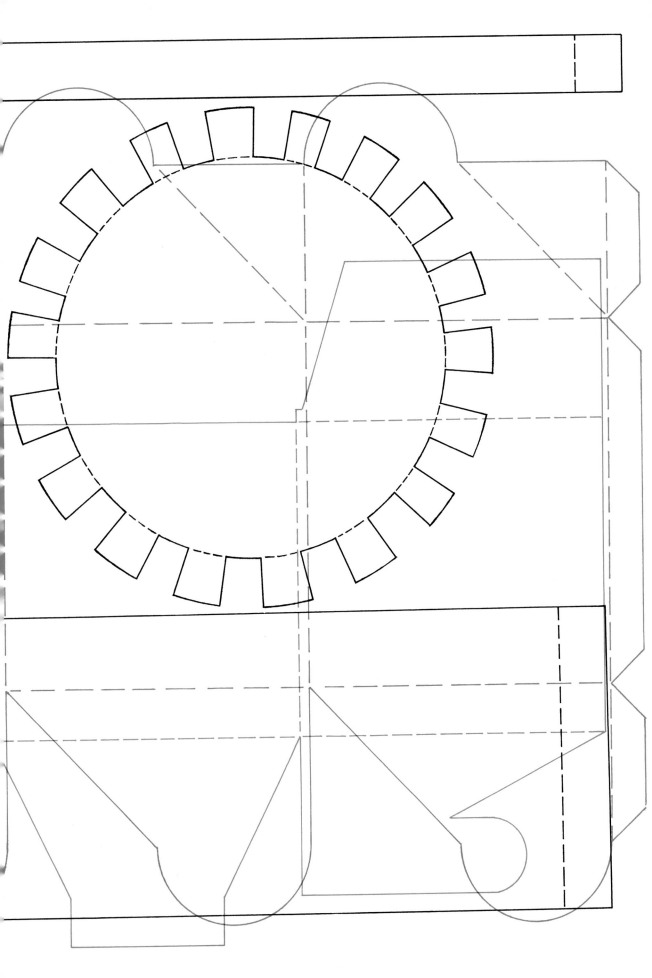

Index

Numbers in italics indicate photographs

ajvar 16
almond: balls, chocolate 167; bars
    163; brittle centrepiece 156; cake
    decorations 114; dates 165; and
    hazelnut slices 117; meringue
    cake 124; paste *161*, 163; and
    pistachio drops 165
almonds, spiced 15
amber marmalade 40, *44*
anchovies, in tapénade 14
anchovy paste 16
apple: and beetroot relish 55; and
    blueberry jelly 47; butter 51;
    candy *161*, 168; jam 33; juice 147;
    and mango chutney 54; and
    orange marmalade 43; and
    passionfruit jam 33; pie *130*, 132;
    and plum chutney 60, *61*; and
    plum jelly 48; pomanders 45; and
    rhubarb jam 39; teacake 120
apples: dried 52; in harmony jam 35;
    spiced 62, *67*; toffee, honeyed 160
apricot: chews, coconut 166; chutney
    54; jam 33; preserve 49; syrup 145
apricots, dried 52
aubergine. *See* eggplant

baby beetroots in raspberry vinegar
    62
banana: chutney 55, *56*; and walnut
    bread 107
bananas, in nine-jewelled chutney
    59
barbecue sauce 74
barley and chicken soup *26*, 27
barley sugar 160
barley water, lemon 147
basil: and chilli oil *81*, 82; and garlic
    sauce 74; sauce, spicy 83
baskets of gifts 22
bean soup 25
beans, dried white: in soup 25
beans, haricot: in cassoulet 100
beef: consommé 25; and pork
    sausages 97; potted 94; roast fillet
    of 104; sausages, spicy *96*, 97;
    spiced 104; tea 25
beetroot: and apple relish 55; baby,
    in raspberry vinegar 62
billy tea 148
birthday cake, chocolate 125
biscuits: almond and hazelnut slices
    117; almond cake decorations
    114; champagne biscuits 119;
    cheese biscuits 116; Easter
    biscuits 116; gingerbread tree
    decorations *118*, 119; iced
    biscuit shapes 114, *115*; lemon
    shortbreads 117; macaroons 120;
    muesli bars 117; muesli biscuits

117; peppernuts 113; walnut
    biscuits 116
bitter orange jelly 47
blackberry: jelly 48; liqueur *142*, 149
blackcurrant: jam 34; liqueur 151;
    syrup 145
black: bread 108; jam 49
blueberry: and apple jelly 47; jam
    34; ratafia 149; soup, iced 24;
    vinegar 77, *78*
bonbons 157
borage tea 148
boxes: instructions for making 159;
    patterns 172–73
brandade de morue 17, *18*
brandied peach jam 38
brandy: cherry 149; cumquat,
    marmalade 41; cumquats in 137,
    139; grapes in 139, *139*; nutmeg
    151
bread 106; banana and walnut 107;
    black 108; Easter *107*, 109; fruit
    110, *110*; olive 111; pita 111; rolls,
    brown 109; whole-wheat 108;
    yoghurt and honey 108
bread cheese 20
brined: black olives 14; green olives
    13
broth: duck 24; wine 27. *See also*
    soup
buns, hot cross 112
butter: apple 51; mango 51; rum
    136

cabbage: pickled Chinese 62;
    sauerkraut 69
cakes 106; almond meringue
    cake 124; apple teacake 120;
    cheesecake 125; chocolate
    birthday cake 125; Christmas
    cake 129; fairy cakes 124;
    Gugelhupf *126*, 127; nutcake 120;
    lemon syrup cake 120; Polish
    Easter cake 127; rich pound cake
    121; simnel cake 127; Stollen 128;
    yeast cake 121
candied fruits 169
candy, apple *161*, 168
capers 14
capsicum (sweet pepper), in ajvar 16
caramel walnuts 157
carnation: syrup 145; vinegar 77
carrot, and pumpkin jam 39
cassoulet 100
cauliflower, pickled 63
caviar cream 17
celery: cream cheese with 21; and
    sweetcorn relish 60
champagne biscuits 119
chamomile tea 148
cheese: biscuits 116; bread cheese

20; cream cheese 20; fresh, with
    herbs 19, *19*; herbed 20; and herbs
    in oil *19*, 20; Liptauer 20; tart 86;
    with celery 21
cheesecake 125
cherries: in eau-de-vie 137; sweet
    and sour 63
cherry: brandy 149; and redcurrant
    jam 34; soup 25
chicken: and barley soup *26*, 27;
    in a bread loaf 98; consommé 25;
    jellied 95; liver pâté 94, *107*;
    mayonnaise 97; omelette, spicy
    22, *23*; pie 89
chickpeas: in hummus bi tahina 16;
    toasted 16
children's birthday party, recipes
    for: almond brittle centrepiece
    156; fairy cakes 124; ginger beer
    146, *147*; iced biscuit shapes 114,
    115; lemon shortbreads 117;
    muesli bars 117; muesli biscuits
    117; nougat 166; walnut bars 163
chilli 4; and basil oil *81*, 82; chutney
    55; sambal 83; sauce 74
Chinese: cabbage, pickled 62;
    five-spice powder 84; vegetable
    pickles *70*, 71
chocolate: almond balls 167;
    birthday cake 125; and rum fudge
    168; strawberries 168; lemon
    liqueur chocolates 168;
    peppermint chocolate 167
Christmas food and decorations:
    almond and hazelnut slices 117;
    almond bars 163; almond cake
    decorations 114; blueberry
    liqueur 151; champagne punch
    155, *155*; Christmas cake 129;
    cumquat brandy marmalade
    41; cumquats in brandy 137;
    gingerbread tree decorations *118*,
    119; grape ratafia 151; ham 101;
    hard sauce for plum pudding 136;
    iced biscuit shapes 114, *115*;
    lemon liqueur 151; marzipan
    shapes 129; mincemeat 133;
    paper stencilling 123, *123*; picnic
    104; pineapple and mint jelly 48;
    pressed flowers 162; printing
    paper 122, *123*; puddings, 135,
    136, *138*; quince ratafia *151*; roast
    turkey 98, *99*; royal icing 129; rum
    butter 136, *138*; salt-cured lamb,
    101; salt-dough decorations 113;
    silver pine-cone tree 170; Stollen
    (German Advent cake) 128;
    walnut pie 133; wassail bowl 154
chutney 32; apple and mango 54;
    apricot 54; banana 55, *56*; chilli
    55; date 57; fiery eggplant

(aubergine) 57; Kashmir 57;
lime and fig 57; mango and date
56, 58; mango and tomato 58;
nine-jewelled 59; onion 59, *61*;
pawpaw 59; plum and apple 60,
61; rhubarb 60; sweet tomato 61;
tamarind 62
citrus peel in syrup 170
coconut apricot chews 166
compote, dried fruit 140
confiture noire 49
conserve, plum 49; raspberry 50
consommé (beef or chicken) 25
crème de cassis 151
cumquat brandy marmalade 41
cumquats in brandy 137, *139*
curry paste, green *84*, 85; red 85
custard 135

damson pickle 63
date: chutney 57; and mango
chutney *56*, 58
dates: almond 165; pork with 100
decorations: almond cake 114;
gingerbread tree *118*, 119; iced
biscuit shapes 114, *115*; pressed
flowers 162; salt-dough 113; silver
pine-cone tree 170
dill tea 148
dips: ajvar 16, anchovy paste 16;
brandade de morue 17; caviar
cream; 17 hummus bi tahina 16;
tapénade 14
dried fruit 52; compote 140
drinks. *See* fruit liqueurs and
ratafias, fruit syrup drinks, ginger
beer, lemon barley water, milk
drinks, mulled wine, punch,
squash, tea, wassail bowl, yoghurt
drinks
duck broth 24

Easter food and decorations: almond
cake decorations 114; brandade
de morue 17; chicken liver pâté
94; Easter biscuits 116; Easter
bread 109; Easter eggs 107;
Easter nests 106, *107*; Easter
Sunday lunch *107*, marbled eggs
21; Polish Easter cake 127;
salt-dough decorations 113
eau-de-vie, cherries in 137;
strawberries in 140
eggnog 135
eggplant (aubergine): in ajvar 16;
chutney, fiery 57; pickle 64
eggs: Easter 106, *107*; marbled 21;
in spicy chicken omelette 22, *23*;
in spinach omelette cake 24

fairy cakes 124
Fathers Day *130*
fennel, pickled gherkins with 66
fennel tea 148
fig: and lime chutney 57; and orange
jam 34; and tomato jam 35
figs, green, in syrup 139, *139*

fine spices 83
fish. *See* seafood
Fish House punch 153
flan, grape 130; prune 132
flour 4
flower pressing *158*, 162
French mustard 82
fresh cheese with herbs 19
fruit: acid in 29; candied 169;
in chutney making 32; in jam
making 28–29; in jelly making 30;
pectin in 29; preserving 28–33,
31; summer berries in rum 140;
summer fruits in a pot 141;
summer pudding 135; vegetable
and fruit pickle 71. *See also* dried
fruit *and under individual fruit
names*
fruit in alcohol 130; cherries in
eau-de-vie 137; cumquats in
brandy 137, *139*; grapes in brandy
139, *139*; peaches in vodka
140; prunes in red wine 138;
strawberries in eau-de-vie 140,
summer berries in rum 140;
summer fruits in a pot 141;
tamarillos in strawberry liqueur
141
fruit bread 110, *110*
fruit butters 51
fruit liqueurs and ratafias 143–44;
blackberry *142*, 149; blackcurrant
(crème de cassis) 151; blueberry
149, *150*; cherry brandy 149; grape
150, 151; lemon *150*, 151; orange
142, 152; passionfruit gin *142*,
152; plum 152; quince *150*, 153;
spicy, 153; strawberry 141, 153
fruit in syrup: citrus peel 170; green
figs 139, *139*
fruit syrup drinks 143, 144; apricot
145; blackcurrant 145; carnation
145; rose and honey 82; rose hip
146; strawberry 146
fruit wine: orange 152

garam masala *84*, 85
garlic: and basil sauce 74; and herb
soup 27; vinegar 79; and walnut
sauce 77
gherkins, pickled 18, 66; with fennel
66
gift baskets 22
gift cards 65
gift paper. *See* packaging
gift tags 65, 122, 123
ginger 4; apple and ginger jelly 46;
Japanese ginger slices 66; lime
and ginger marmalade 42
ginger beer 146, *147*
gingerbread tree decorations *118*,
119
gooseberry and orange jam 35
grape: flan 130; jam 40; ratafia 88,
150, 151
grapes: in brandy 139, *139*; pickled
66

grapefruit jelly marmalade 42
green: curry paste *84*, 85; figs in
syrup 139, *139*; olives in oil 14, *14*;
tomato jam 40; tomato pickle 71
Gugelhupf *126*, 127

Halloween, food for, 133, *134*
halva 165
ham: and veal pie *89*, 90; Christmas
101; jellied 95; potted 18
hard sauce for plum pudding 136
harissa *84*, 85
harmony jam 35
hazelnut honey 82
herb: and garlic soup 27; jellies 46;
teas 148, 149; oil, spicy *81*, 82;
vinegar 79
herbed cheese 20
herbs 4; and cheese in oil *19*, 20. *See
also under individual herbs*
honey: hazelnut 82; and rose syrup
82; and yoghurt bread 108
honeycomb toffee 160
honeyed toffee apples 160
hot cross buns 112
hummus bi tahina 16

invalid food: bean soup 25; beef tea
25; blackcurrant tea 34; carnation
vinegar 77; cherry soup 25;
chicken and barley soup 27;
custard 135; eggnog 135; herb
and garlic soup 27; herb teas
148–49; nutmeg brandy 151;
peppery tea 149; rose hip syrup
146; wine broth 27

jams: making, bottling and storing
28–30; apple 33; apple and
passionfruit 33; apricot 33;
blackcurrant 34; black 49;
blueberry 34; brandied peach 38;
cherry and redcurrant 34; fig and
orange 34; fig and tomato 35;
gooseberry and orange 35; green
tomato 40; harmony 35; kiwi fruit
and melon 37; mulberry 37;
nectarine *36*, 37; pear and vanilla
38; plum and raisin 38; pumpkin
and carrot 39, *41*; rhubarb and
apple 39; strawberry and lemon
39; sultana grape 40; watermelon
40
Japanese ginger slices 66
jars, dressing 67
jellied: chicken 95; ham 95; veal loaf
95
jellies, making bottling and storing
30–32
jelly: apple and ginger *36*, 46; bitter
orange 48; blackberry 48;
blueberry and apple 47;
grapefruit, marmalade 42; mint
46; pineapple and mint 48; plum
and apple 48; quince and orange
36, 47; redcurrant and raspberry
46, rosemary 46

jelly bag 31, 42
juice: apple 147; homemade tomato 148

Kashmir chutney 57
kirsch: in blackberry liqueur *142*, 149; punch 154
kiwi fruit and melon jam 37

labels 65
lamb: meat loaf 94; saddle of 104; salt-cured 101
lemon: amber marmalade 40; barley water 147; curd 51, liqueur *150*, 151; liqueur chocolates 168; and quince marmalade 43; shortbreads 117; squash 146; and strawberry jam 39
lemon grass tea 148
lemons preserved in salt 54
lime: and fig chutney 57; and ginger marmalade 42
limes, preserved 53, *54*
Liptauer cheese 20
liver, in pâté: chicken 94; pork 92, *93*

macaroons 120
mango: and apple chutney 54; butter 51; and date chutney *56*, 58; and tomato chutney 58
mangoes, in nine-jewelled chutney 59
marbled eggs 21
marmalade: making, bottling and storing 30; amber 40, *44*; cumquat brandy 41; grapefruit jelly 42; lime and ginger 42; orange and apple 43; orange and ginger 42, *44*; orange whisky 43, *45*; quince and lemon 43; Seville 46
marzipan: shapes 129; sweets 163
mayonnaise 98; chicken 97; seafood with 105
measurements 4
melon, and kiwi fruit jam 37
meringue cake, almond 124
milk drinks 143
mincemeat 133
mince pies 134
mint: jelly 46; and pineapple jelly 48; tea 148; vinegar, orange 79
muesli 116; bars 117; biscuits 117
mulberry jam 37
mulled wine 154
mushroom ketchup 74
mustard, French 82; grainy 82
mutton pie 91

nectarine jam *36*, 37
nine-jewelled chutney, 59
nougat *164*, 166
nutcake 120
nut clusters 160
nutmeg brandy 151

oil 73; basil and chilli *81*, 82; spicy herb *81*, 82

olive bread 111
olives: brined black 14; brined green 13; green, in oil 14, *14*; spicy black 14; in tapénade 14
omelette, spicy chicken 22, *23*
omelette cake, spinach 24
onion: chutney 59, *61*; sauce 75; tart 87, *88*
onions, pickled 18, 68
orange: and apple marmalade 43; curd 51; and fig jam 34; and gooseberry jam 35; jelly, bitter 47; marmalade *45*; mint vinegar 79; and pineapple relish 59; and quince jelly 47; ratafia *142*, 152; sauce 76; whisky marmalade 43; wine 152
oranges: in amber marmalade 40; as pomanders 45; preserved 49; Seville 46

packaging: bonbons 157; boxes *158*, 159, 172–73; gift cards 65; paper *110*, 122, 123; pressed flowers and leaves 162; tags 122, 123
paper. *See* packaging; printing; stencilling
passionfruit: and apple jam 33; gir *142*, 152
paste: almond *161*, 163; anchovy 16; green curry *84*, 85; harissa *84*, 85; quince 51; red curry 85; spicy 85, tahina 16, tapénade 14
pâté: chicken liver 94, *107*; de campagne 92, *93*; pork liver 92; rabbit 91
pawpaw chutney 59
peach: jam, brandied 38; sauce 76
peaches in vodka 140
peanut: brittle 163; and sultana clusters 166
pear: ratafia 152; and vanilla jam 38
pears: in harmony jam 35; spiced *67*, 68
pectin 29–30
pepper 4
peppermint chocolate 167
peppernuts 113
peppery tea 149
piccalilli 68, *70*
pickled: cauliflower 63, *70*; Chinese cabbage 62; gherkins 66; gherkins with fennel 66; grapes 66; onions 68
pickles 33; Chinese vegetable *70*, 71; damson 63; eggplant (aubergine) 64, *64*; green tomato 71; Japanese ginger slices 66; piccalilli 68, *70*; sauerkraut 69, shallots in vinegar 69; torshi (mixed pickles) 72; vegetable and fruit 71; watermelon chow chow 72
pie (savoury): chicken 89; ham and veal *89*, 90; mutton 91; raised 88, *89*
pie (sweet): apple *130*, 132; mince

134; pumpkin 133, *134*; walnut 133
pikelets 112
pine-cone tree, silver 170
pineapple: and mint jelly 48; and orange relish 59; in nine-jewelled chutney 59; punch 154; spiced 69
pissaladière (French pizza) 87
pita bread 111
plum: and apple chutney 60, *61*; and apple jelly 48; and raisin jam 38; conserve 49; damson pickle 63; in harmony jam 35; liqueur 152; pudding, 135, 137, *138*; sauce, spicy *75*, 76
poached snapper 105
Polish Easter cake 127
pomanders *44*, 45
popcorn 166
popcorn balls 166
pork: and beef sausages 97; in cassoulet 100; with dates 100; liver pâté 92; in pâté de campagne 92, *93*; in raised pie 88, *89*; in rillettes 19; and sage sausages *96*, 97; and veal terrine 91
potato printing 122, *123*, *130*
potpourri, spicy *78*, 79
potted: ham 18; salmon 17
pound cake, rich 121
preserved oranges 49
preserves: apricot 49; black jam (confiture noire) 49; rose petal 50
pressed flowers and leaves 162
printing, paper 122, *123*, *130*
prune flan 132
prunes in red wine 138
pudding: light Christmas 136; rich plum 135; summer 135
pumpkin: and carrot jam 39; pie 133, *134*; soup *134*
punch 144, 145; Christmas Day champagne 155, *155*; Fish House 152; kirsch 154; pineapple 154

quince: and lemon marmalade 43; and orange jelly 47; paste 51; ratafia 153

rabbit pâté 91
raised pie 88, *89*
raspberries, in summer berries in rum 140
raspberry: conserve 50; and redcurrant jelly 46; vinegar 79
ratafias. *See* fruit liqueurs and ratafias
redcurrant: and cherry jam 34; and raspberry jelly 46
red curry paste 85
red wine, prunes in 138
red rose vinegar 78
relishes: beetroot and apple 55; pineapple and orange 59; sweetcorn and celery 60

rhubarb: and apple jam 39; chutney 60
rillettes 19
roast: fillet of beef 104; turkey 98, *99*
rolls, brown 109
rose: and honey syrup 82; vinegar, red 78
rose hip syrup 146
rose petal preserve 50
rosemary: jelly 46; tea 149
royal icing 129
rum: butter 136, *138*; and chocolate fudge 168

saddle of lamb 104
sage: and pork sausages *96*, 97; tea 149
Saint Valentine's Day food and decorations: caviar cream 17; pressed flowers 162; red rose vinegar 78; rose and honey syrup 82; rose petal preserve 50; strawberry syrup 146
salt 4; lemons preserved in 54; spiced 83
salt-cured lamb 101
salt-dough decorations 113, 171
salmon, potted 17
sambal, chilli 83
sauce 73; barbecue 74; chilli 74; chilli sambal 83; garlic and basil 74; hard, for plum pudding 136; mushroom ketchup 74; onion 75; orange 76; peach 76; spicy basil 83; spicy plum *75*, 76; spicy tomato *75*, 77; walnut and garlic 77
sausages: pork and beef 97; pork and sage *96*, 97; spicy beef *96*, 97
sauerkraut 69
scones 112
seafood: caviar cream 17; poached snapper 105; potted salmon 17; salt cod purée 17, *18*; seafood with mayonnaise 105; tapénade 14
setting point, in chutney making 32; in jam making 29
Seville marmalade 46
shallots in vinegar 69
simnel cake 127
snapper, poached 105
soups: bean 25; cherry 25; chicken and barley *26*, 27; consommé 25;

herb and garlic 27; iced blueberry 24. *See also* broth
spiced: almonds 15; apples 62, *67*; beef 104; pears, *67*, 68; pineapple 69; salt 83
spices 73; Chinese five-spice powder 84; in chutneys 32; fine spices 83; garam masala *84*, 85; in green curry paste *84*, 85; in harissa *84*, 85; in red curry paste 85
spicy: basil sauce 83; beef sausages *96*, 97; black olives 14; chicken omelette 22, *23*; herb oil, *81*, 82; plum sauce *75*, 76; potpourri *78*, 79; pomanders *44*, 45; ratafia 153; tomato sauce *75*, 77
spinach omelette cake 24
squash 143, 144; lemon 146
stencilling: fabric 124; paper *110*, 123, *123*; teddy bear gift cards *158*
sterilising 29
Stollen 128
strawberries: chocolate 168; in eau-de-vie 140; in summer berries in rum 140
strawberry: and lemon jam 39; liqueur 141, 153; syrup 146
sugar 4; in chutneys 32; in jams 29; in jellies 31; in marmalades 30; in pickles 33; vanilla 4, 24
sultana grape jam 40
sultanas, in Kashmir chutney 57
summer: berries in rum 140; fruits in a pot 141; pudding 135
sun-dried tomatoes in oil 52, *53*
sweet corn and celery relish 60
sweet and sour cherries 63
sweet tomato chutney 61
syrup 143, 144; fruit in, *139*, *139*, 170. *See also* fruit syrup drinks

table decorations: almond brittle centrepiece 156; bonbons 157; Easter nest 106, *107*
tahina paste 16
tamarillos in strawberry liqueur 141
tamarind chutney 62
tapénade 14, *14*
tarragon vinegar 80
tart: cheese 86; onion 87, *88*
tea: beef 25; billy 148; blackcurrant 34; borage 148; chamomile 148; dill seed 148; fennel 148; lemon grass 148, mint 148; peppery 149;

rosemary 149; sage 149; thyme 149
terrines: jellied chicken 95; jellied ham 95; jellied veal loaf 95; lamb meat loaf 94; pork and veal 91; potted beef 94
Thanksgiving food and decorations: pumpkin pie 133; roast turkey 98, *99*; salt-dough decorations 113
thyme: tea 149; vinegar 80
toasted chickpeas 16
toffee 156; almond brittle centrepiece 156; honeycomb 160; honeyed toffee apples 160; nut clusters 160; peanut brittle 163
tomato: chutney, sweet 61; jam, green 40; juice 148; and mango chutney 58; pickle, green 71; sauce, spicy *75*, 77
tomatoes: dried 52; sun-dried 52; sun-dried, in oil 52, *53*
torshi (mixed pickles) 72
Turkish delight 170
turkey, roast 98, *99*

vanilla: and pear jam 38; sugar 4, 24
veal: and ham pie *89*, 90; loaf, jellied 95; in pâté de campagne 92, 93; and pork terrine 91
vegetable and fruit pickle 71
vinegar 4, 73; blueberry 77, *78*; carnation 77, fruit 77, garlic 79; herb 79; in chutneys 32; in pickles 33; orange mint 79; raspberry 79; red rose 78, *78*; salad 80; shallots in 69; spiced 80; tarragon 80; thyme 80
vodka, peaches in 140

walnut: and banana bread 107; bars 163; biscuits 116; and garlic sauce 77; pie 133; truffles *164*, 167
walnuts, caramel 157
wassail bowl 154
watermelon: chow chow 73; conserve 50; jam 40
whisky, and orange marmalade 43
whole-wheat bread 108
wine, mulled 154
wine broth 27
wrapping. *See* packaging

yeast cake 121
yoghurt: and honey bread 108; drinks 143